How To Build A
Cheap Hot Rod

Dennis W. Parks

MOTORBOOKS

DEDICATION

To the memory of Steve Hendrickson. Thanks for all of the writing and photography advice you passed along and, most of all, for all of the opportunities to be published that you gave me over the years. Those of us who had the privilege of knowing you, still miss you. Those who didn't know you, simply don't know just how great a guy you were.

First published in 2007 by Motorbooks, an imprint of MBI Publishing Company, Galtier Plaza, Suite 200, 380 Jackson Street, St. Paul, MN 55101 USA

Motorbooks titles are also available at discounts in bulk quantity for industrial or sales-promotional use. For details write to Special Sales Manager at MBI Publishing Company, Galtier Plaza, Suite 200, 380 Jackson Street, St. Paul, MN 55101 USA.

To find out more about our books, join us online at www.motorbooks.com.

Library of Congress Cataloging-in-Publication Data

Parks, Dennis, 1959-
  How to build a cheap hot rod / Dennis W. Parks.
    p. cm.
  Includes index.
  ISBN-13: 978-0-7603-2348-9 (softbound)
  1. Hot rods—Design and construction—Amateurs' manuals. 2. Hot rods—Design and construction—Cost control—Amateurs' manuals. I. Title.

TL236.3.P368 2007
629.28'786--dc22

2007024441

On the cover: The Track T in progress, just about ready to put the body on.

On the frontispiece: Low-mounted headlights, painted steelies with hubcaps and trim rings, along with wide whitewalls, give this red roadster a real nostalgic look.

On the title pages: This cute budget-built hot rod in progress is a '28 or '29 Ford Model A Tudor sedan. Although they are on the small side, Model A's are easy to build, and almost everything is available in reproduction form.

On the back cover: These seats were made from an upholstery kit—no sewing required!

About the author

Dennis W. Parks is a professional technical writer and the author of several how-to books for MBI, including *How To Build a Hot Rod, How To Build a Hot Rod Model A Ford, How To Restore and Customize Auto Upholstery and Interiors*, and *How To Paint Your Car*. He lives near St. Louis, Missouri.

Editor: Jennifer Bennett
Designer: Chris Fayers

Printed in China

CONTENTS

FOREWORD

I was pleased to see this new book from Dennis Parks. It goes to the core of what is sadly overlooked in today's publications. That being, can the average home builder still do a car that is affordable and drivable, and will the builder be proud of the end result?

Follow along as Dennis shops for parts, explains various sources, and encounters typical problems that all of us have faced. This book above all should demonstrate how the average guy or gal can build a neat car in a home garage.

The author plans the car, gets the parts, overcomes the inevitable problems, and completes the project. Anyone, after reading this book, should come away with the confidence to say, "Hey! I can do this."

—Tom Prufer

Legendary hot rodder, Tom Prufer, has built rods gracing the covers of many magazines and books. Perhaps best known for his 1934 Ford Cop Shop Coupe, he has produced hot rods of many styles, from a basic Track T to chopped and channeled coupes and Model A roadsters. None of Tom's hot rods would typically be considered "cheap," as they have all had work performed by other legendary rodders such as Pete Eastwood, Ron Covell, and Rod Powell. Still Tom Prufer knows what it takes to build a hot rod, cheap or otherwise.

ACKNOWLEDGMENTS

Many thanks go to Geri Braziel and Dave Hanson at Speedway Motors, Rich Fox at Affordable Street Rods, R. J. at RJay's Performance Center, and Don and Nan Cain at K. C. Street Rod Parts for helping me get the right parts for this project. Special thanks go to Donnie and Jack Karg at Karg's Hot Rod Service, who did the welding on the rear suspension components, created the motor mounts, and welded on various other brackets. Of course, I can't forget Keith Moritz at Morfab Customs, who welded up the gas tank and has also shared lots of practical rod building experience over the years.

I also must say "thank you" to John Kimbrough, who has become my extra set of eyes. John has cheerfully reviewed my last few manuscripts, scouring them for glaring errors before I sent them to the publisher.

Starting with at least part of a vehicle would have been easier, but with the help of these great people, starting with nothing but an idea resulted in a great project and a downright fun car. I also want to thank everyone at High Ridge Auto Parts for their patience and understanding, as I had to ask them on more than one occasion how some of these parts were supposed to go together. Last, but certainly not least, thanks to Roger Ward for all of his advice on painting, working with fiberglass, and color selection.

—Dennis W. Parks

INTRODUCTION

Cheap hot rod . . . hmm, at first thought, those words seem to be mutually exclusive. Many rods in contention for accolades, such as the coveted Ridler Award and America's Most Beautiful Roadster, cost hundreds of thousands of dollars to build, while a more "average" hot rod is commonly priced at $50,000–$75,000. So cheap just doesn't seem to fit in here, anywhere. Truth is... *all* hot rods are built within a budget; some budgets are just exponentially larger than others.

I'm not going to say anything bad about those who can afford to spend big money for their hot rods, as their money ultimately raises the pedigree of our hobby or business. However, you don't have to have a six-figure budget to build a fun hot rod. In fact, for as little as $15,000, you can build a hot rod (a modest one with a high fun-to-dollars-spent ratio) of your very own. The point of this book is to show you how.

I know some of you are thinking that 15 grand is still a lot of money for a hot rod. Several people have built great hot rods for less money. A friend of mine built a real cool two-seat roadster for less than $3,000. Sam was able to do this by rescuing salvage yard sheet metal, having a network of friends who know how to find good deals, and being able to do most of the work himself. But not everybody has that kind of time, those connections, or that ability. Therefore, this is a cheap hot rod project for the average enthusiast.

Yet, this hot rod is also my hot rod. So there are times when I'll choose a more expensive option over a cheaper one, or vice versa, based upon what I ultimately want to do with the car. In these instances, though, I will explain how I could have saved money and why I chose to go the route that I did. Anytime you are dealing with a budget, you have to make choices and set priorities, and it was no different with the car being built in this book.

The Track T whose buildup is documented in these pages may not win any awards and most likely won't win any races, but I won't be ashamed to be seen in or around it either. It truly will be a fun hot rod, for which only a minimum outlay of cash was needed because I did some shopping around before buying.

I have been writing hot rod–related magazine articles for more than 20 years now, and this is the seventh book that I have written. For most of that time, though, someone else was actually doing the work, while I was behind the camera or at the computer documenting the process. This hot rod will mostly be built in my modestly equipped home garage, by me. So, if I can do it, you probably can, too. Some work will be farmed out simply because I don't have the experience or equipment required. For the most part, however, this will only be done when it is a safety factor.

Unlike some magazine articles that have documented "budget" buildups, this book uses no parts that just magically appear. I do have a 9-inch Ford rear end and a set of front tires (previously earmarked for another project) that may be used in this buildup, but their prices will be included in the total cost. Yes, under budget or over, the total expenses will be listed in the back of this book. Everything from lug nuts to license plate bolts will be documented.

One more thing . . . writing a book is different from building a hot rod. Most authors start with an outline that groups similar items together and transitions from one phase or scene to another. Construction of a hot rod begins this way, but what you don't always see on the cable TV shows or in the magazine articles is that the entire vehicle gets put together and taken apart several times during construction. Because of this, some photos of the construction process may seem out of order at first glance. But, as long as you pay attention to the captions, it should all make sense when all is said and done.

I hope you enjoy this book and thanks for buying a copy. You can do this. Believe, and read on.

CHAPTER 1
BUILD IT IN YOUR MIND

Whether you've wanted one for decades, or this is a new idea—a parent-child project, or a joint work for you and your spouse or with your buddies—one thing is clear: you don't already have a cheap hot rod. As with any other goal, building one starts in your mind, where you form a vision of what you want to create. There are many directions you can go, not just with the car itself, but with every major component and accessory that makes it whole. Before we dive for the wrenches or the checkbook, let's take a broader view of what this project will entail. It's going to cost you some money and it's going to take some time. Going in with a plan is the best way to come out with a hot rod. (We'll cover these subjects in greater detail as we proceed with our buildup.)

WHAT YOU WANT VERSUS WHAT YOU CAN AFFORD

Throughout life, we are all faced with decisions—decisions that often result in some sort of trade-off or compromise. In the case of purchasing big-ticket items, these decisions are based upon what we want (and sometimes need) compared to what we can actually afford. Of course, hot rods fall into this category. The kind of car you end up with is directly tied to the amount of money you can pull together for the project.

My ideal hot rod would be a highboy 1933 Ford three-window coupe with enough power to fry the tires at a touch of the throttle. It would have traditional suspension, flawless paint in a deep maroon color, and a leather interior. However, I know that a radical coupe like that just isn't in my budget at this time. (Perhaps if enough of you buy this book . . .)

More realistic, and equally challenging and satisfying to build, is a relatively low-dollar Track T that would be lots of fun and won't gouge a big hole in the checking account. Since it won't have air conditioning or heat, reclining seats with extensive legroom, or a mega-watt stereo system, the Track T won't be comfortable for cross-country jaunts. On the other hand, it could still have a good enough suspension system and adequate seats to make the ride comfortable—and a little fresh air never hurt anybody. Besides, hot rods began as stripped-down vehicles built for performance, not luxury. If not a race winner, this will at least be a vehicle with that original hot rod spirit.

TYPE OF VEHICLE

Before you purchase any potential project or parts, you really need to determine what you want from your hot rod when it is completed. Providing accurate answers to the following questions will help you build what you really want the first time around, which will save you money in the long run. This doesn't mean that your wants and desires won't change later on, but for the hot rod that you are about to build now, you should answer the questions as they apply now. Take a tablet or a clean page on the word processor and jot down your notes to each question. Whatever you build, it needs to suit your needs. You will also likely acquire parts piecemeal as they and the cash become available. Knowing all the basics up front will ensure that it all fits together.

Do you want an open car or closed car? Two doors or four? Are you looking to build something that will most likely be driven cross-country to distant rod runs, or will it mostly be driven around town on Friday or Saturday night? Will there need to be room for the entire family, or is it just for you? Comfort and reliability should be of prime concern if you plan to haul the family very far, but of course, safety should always be the main concern with any hot rod. Will it be driven by several people, or will you be the only person behind the wheel? If you plan to share driver seat time, an automatic transmission will be the most versatile. On the other hand, if you're looking for a vehicle that's yours alone, a stick shift will automatically cut down the list of potential drivers. If you are the only driver, you can lower the vehicle's stance a bit more, but other drivers may not get the hang of driving a lowered vehicle until after they have scraped a few speed bumps or driveway entrances. Is gas mileage and reliability more of a concern than having some exotic engine? Do you feel the need to build a rod from genuine vintage tin, or is a reproduction body more to your liking? Do you have the skills (or are you determined to learn) to fabricate or modify parts to make them fit your application, or does everything need to be a bolt-on component for you to be able to install it? Answering these overall questions should prompt you to ask yourself even more questions about your idea of a hot rod.

As you brainstorm a wish list for your perfect hot rod, remember that you're building on a budget. Money you throw in one place leaves less available elsewhere. Do you want/need air conditioning, stereo, and luggage space, or will a bare bones rod serve your purposes? Whatever you

Building a hot rod the way you wanted it in the first place, being content with the way it is, and not following trends that come and go over the lifetime of the vehicle will ultimately save you considerable amounts of money. Curtis Tanner bought this Ford pickup when he was a sophomore in high school, back in the early 1960s. Even with the rebuilt flathead engine, Curtis probably doesn't have $20,000 in the truck, unless there is a hidden safe. That's less than $500 a year, and I doubt if anyone has as much fun in a hot rod as Curtis.

do, don't try to build a hot rod with the sole purpose of impressing some judge at a local car show or to get a photo in a magazine. Car show trophies get dusty and magazines are old in 30 days, but that hot rod will probably still be in your driveway or garage for a few years or even generations.

What You Already Have

Although most antique cars have long since passed out of regular use, they still sit in barns and garages across the country. Maybe you already have a line on something, or even own a car of proper vintage. If the body and chassis are solid, obviously using this car could save you some money. But should you use it?

The great family of car enthusiasts has branches favoring both pristine, stock condition vehicles and hot rods. These camps don't always get along. You've bought this book, so obviously you like hot rods. Whether to take an antique car you own or could readily acquire and "rod" it depends on several variables. First off, how much is the car worth in its current condition? In the history of rodding and customizing, someone somewhere has probably hacked up an Auburn, Cord, Duesenberg, Delage, Bugatti, or Rolls Royce and turned it into a hot rod. On the very off-chance the car you inherited is rare and valuable, find out what its value is before you go near a wrench or a torch.

Roger Ward's tan (actually Nissan pickup taupe) Deuce roadster is no stranger to rodding events throughout the Midwest. Notice the lack of nonsense on this car. The timeless roadster even won a top 25 award in Pigeon Forge, Tennessee, to which it was driven while most of the other winners were trailered. I can vouch for that first hand as I rode shotgun on the return leg of the journey. Plus, I know that Roger would never trailer this car.

More often the car on hand is not a precious collectible, but a car that was common in its day and is rare now only because of its age. If Grandpa Joe willed you a stock 1936 Chevrolet coupe that's complete and in running, non-rusty condition, what's it worth? If it's a basic car and not pristine, chances are, not that much. A publication like Old Car Price Guide will give you a good idea. You can also search the internet for similar vehicles and see what sellers want. Breaking up a car like this is a choice a lot of rodders face. Here are two questions to consider: what have you done with it, or would do with it, if you left it stock? The logic that there's no reason to break up a perfectly good, working car makes sense only if someone wants it as it is. Can you sell it or trade it for something you'd rather make into a hot rod? The second important question is: can you turn this vehicle into a hot rod you'll use and enjoy? If no one's going to use the stock vehicle, and you can picture it as a very cool hot rod, then, as long as it's not worth more in stock form, why not transform it? On the other hand, if it's not quite what you want, and your neighbor, son, daughter, or work colleague would like to get hold of it, make a deal and hunt for your dream vehicle.

Assuming you have a vehicle you'd like to convert to your cheap hot rod, you are already ahead of the game. As long as the frame is straight and square and not weakened by rust, it can be used as is or with a minimum amount of modifications, depending on just what you plan to build. Same goes for the body. If it hasn't been wrecked, and doesn't have rust rot beyond fixing, you can make it look presentable with some plastic filler and epoxy primer. Sure, you may not win any top 25 awards, but if you are having fun with your hot rod, who else cares?

Dream Vehicle

Maybe you've come to this book with a longstanding dream to build a particular type of hot rod—and you need to do it cheap. By planning, using reliable parts, and resisting the urge to follow the latest trend, you can make an affordable hot rod. If you plan right, you can build a perfectly functional and enjoyable rod now to get that dream in motion, and continue to make changes and upgrades for as long as you own the car.

A good example of spreading the cost of ownership out over several years is Roger Ward's taupe 1932 Ford roadster. He has been painting hot rods for more than 50 years, so he has seen a fad or two come and go. When Roger built his roadster, he built what he wanted and didn't care about pleasing anyone else or winning any trophies. The car gets driven hard on a regular basis, but it still looks as good now as it did when it was first built. Except for replacing the painted steelies with American Torq-Thrusts, Roger hasn't changed anything, much less added any fad-oriented expenses. Although I don't know the exact dollar amount that he has spent on the car, or the number of miles he has logged behind the wheel, it would be safe to say that the cost of building it has averaged down to less than $2,000 per year over the car's lifetime.

MAJOR COMPONENTS

Now that you have determined what your hot rod project is going to be, you need to decide what is required to make it a reality. Hot rod basics consist of a chassis, a body, and a drivetrain. Somewhat more refined, the list includes the suspension, wheels and tires, brake system, fuel system, and cooling system. Of course, there are many subassemblies in each of these categories. As you are putting your hot rod

Except for Model Ts, Model As are about as low priced as anything in the hot rod world. Ford produced a very large number of these cars, so they are still relatively easy to find. The builder of this coupe saved some bucks by not using fenders. The unsightly Model A frame would be visible without fenders, which is why many rodders mount their Model As on the better looking, but more expensive, Deuce frames. Rather than spend money on a 1932 Ford chassis, this rodder channeled the body down over the frame to save some money. Epoxy primer and painted steelies without hubcaps and trim rings are a lot less expensive than paint and billet wheels..

together on paper and salivating over the volumes of catalogs currently available, it is a good idea to group similar items together. This will help you to decide which parts to purchase first when you finally start gathering components for your project.

There is no denying that the hot rod industry caters to those with Ford vehicles originally manufactured prior to 1948 and to the various generations of small-block Chevrolet engines. In no way does this dictate that you must build an old Ford car with a Chevy engine in it to have a hot rod. Suppose you were to find a 1934 Plymouth coupe that catches your eye. To you, the body lines look as good as anything else and the purchase price of the vehicle seems fair. Should you buy or pass? There are several things to consider before doing either one. First, you should ask yourself: How complete is this vehicle? Are all of the fenders

there, and if so, are they usable? Small dents can be repaired, but if a fender, hood, or other sheet metal component requires replacement, those parts for a less popular vehicle may not be available from the aftermarket. That leaves you hunting bone yards for some pretty old panels.

Before you shop for a potential hot rod project, become familiar with what the automotive aftermarket has to offer. The easiest way to do that is to head on down to your local magazine store and buy a bunch of hot rod publications. Flip through them, read the ads, look at the projects folks are building. Get hold of some parts catalogs—order them, borrow them, or go to a hot rod show and pick up a few. What's out there that looks good to you and suits your budget? If you're considering an unusual brand vehicle, can readily available parts, like suspension and brake components, be made to fit it?

Okay, this hot rod may not fall into the cheap category, but its inclusion is to make a point. Pretend for a moment that it isn't painted and doesn't have billet wheels. The 1932 Ford chassis would be about the largest single expense, but that could even be broken down into smaller, less expensive subassemblies. You would not have to buy the truck bed and hood to put the roadster pickup (RPU) on the road. Finding a gennie steel RPU body may be difficult, but they are available in repop form. You could put this on the road without a bed, hood, fancy interior, or top without spending a lot of money and you would still have a fun rod.

The hot rod aftermarket grows based on demand. The hot rod companies provide the parts for which they receive the most requests. Then, as builders start building different vehicles, the aftermarket follows the trend. When a reproduction company provides a chassis and body package for a vehicle that was never as popular, some rodders step up to buy this "new" offering in order to have something different. As these reproductions become popular, more original tin in this configuration emerges from barns and desert wrecking yards, creating a need for patch panels and other items. When I first began writing about hot rods, you could get just about any model of 1937 Ford almost for free, as no one wanted them. A few years later, one of the fiberglass reproduction companies started making a few different models of the 1937 Ford. Now there are more companies making them, and reproductions may outnumber the originals.

Chassis

Buying or building a chassis is a pretty major step, so you better be committed to the project before getting to this point. For pre-1948 hot rods (when cars had real frames), any particular frame is designed for a somewhat finite group of bodies. For instance, a 1932 Ford frame will fit any of the 1932 Ford body styles, whether it is a roadster, coupe, or sedan—fendered or unfendered. Those same frames can also be modified (narrowed at the cowl) to fit the earlier Model A and even Model T Fords. However, you cannot easily put a 1933 or newer Ford body on a 1932 frame. General Motors and Mopar frames share the same characteristics, as most bodies from their respective make and model will fit, but they will not be interchangeable across many years.

So, if you know that you want to build a 1932 Ford but are not sure what body style, you can go ahead and get started on the chassis and suspension, then decide on a particular body later. If, on the other hand, you know that you are going to build a hot rod out of your grandpa's 1940 DeSoto, you better research the differences in frames and suspension components for DeSotos a few years on either side of the 1940 model year. Even if that chassis is good, you'll likely want to change the suspension some, either for a different look or better performance.

Since many hot rod candidates have a small engine that you'll replace with something bigger and heavier, you may wonder about an original chassis' suitability for big-time buildups. While some may require boxing plates for added strength, most original chassis can be modernized for hot rod use. They must be dimensionally square, however, even if this means having some frame straightening work done at a collision repair facility. Any tears or cuts in the metal should be repaired and all rust must be removed. If rust removal by media blasting or electrochemical dipping reveals weak spots, replacement sections will need to be spliced into place.

For mainstream hot rods (Ford, some Chevrolets, and some Willys), chassis components are readily available in a variety of formats. You can start with a pair of bare frame rails, a bare perimeter frame, or a fully welded chassis; it just depends on how much you want to spend. If you already have one of these vehicles, you may just need to weld in some boxing plates, replace damaged crossmembers, or simply replace the engine and tranny mounts to accept a later model drivetrain.

If you possess superior welding skills and have the ability to clamp the frame in a jig while welding to maintain a square shape, you can start with a pair of bare frame rails. This will save you money, as the frame rails are the most complex pieces of the frame. Crossmembers can be purchased as prefabricated pieces or welded up from various shapes of steel found at your local steel supplier. This is also

Speedway Motor's Track T chassis is literally the foundation of this project. It doesn't necessarily look like an original Ford Model T chassis, but it doesn't claim to either. Unless you are under the car, you won't see any of this chassis when the car is completed anyway. The front kickup will be covered by the street rodder nose, the frame rails by a fiberglass body apron, and the rear by the body and a rolled pan.

the practical way to go if you are planning much in the way of a "custom" chassis.

For those of us who have not yet melted enough welding rod to feel safe welding a chassis together, perimeter frames are available for a growing number of vehicles. With all of the welding done in a jig, the chassis should be dimensionally square, with the suspension being a bolt-on process that almost any hot rodder could handle. Reputable chassis manufacturers build very nice products that are competitively priced, so shop with caution if someone tries to make you a "great" deal on a chassis that you haven't heard of. See what the chassis and its welds look like in raw steel, before they have been covered over with body filler, primer, or paint.

These same manufacturers will gladly build you a chassis and assemble all of the suspension for you as well. Purchasing the entire chassis from one dealer at one time is usually somewhat less expensive than purchasing all of the parts separately, but it still ends up being a hefty total. However, if a complete chassis fits into your budget, you will undoubtedly be farther along into the project in less time. (See Chapter 3, the Rolling Chassis, for additional considerations.)

Body

The body of your hot rod is what most accurately identifies it: "Hey, have you seen Jim's new coupe?" or, "Did you see that roadster cruisin' the strip earlier?" Who the rod belongs to, what color, or what year it is just pinpoints the specific vehicle, but the body style is what provides the basic identity.

Some basic hot rod jargon may be appropriate for those who may be new to hot rods, whether you are 17 or 70. A "T" refers to a Ford Model T, built from 1909 to 1927. In terms of hot rods, these are usually built as a Track T or as a T-bucket. Track Ts date back to the early days of hot rodding and were simply stripped down Model Ts that were used for racing, hence the name "Track T." A common characteristic of a Track T is that the engine is enclosed, as opposed to a T-bucket, which usually has an exposed engine. Although a T-bucket could be made from an authentic Model T, the term didn't really catch on until the early 1960s when the bodies were usually made of fiberglass. An "A" refers to Ford's Model A, which were built between 1928 and 1931. Most other hot rods are simply referred to by their year of manufacture and the body style. When speaking of hot rods, "Deuce" refers to anything (usually Fords) built in the 1932 model year.

Other body style terms are roadster, cabriolet, coupe (three-window or five-window), sedan (two-door or four-door), phaeton, and sedan or panel delivery. These can be used for most any make or model. There are variations on all of these between manufacturers and years, so the basics are presented as follows. A roadster seats two people and has a folding top. A cabriolet is the same, except it has roll-up side glass (door windows), while a roadster doesn't. A coupe seats two people, has a solid top (which may include a cloth insert visible from the outside), and has roll-up windows. Not counting the windshield, coupes generally have either three or five windows. For a three-window coupe, each door window counts as one, plus a back window makes three. A five-window coupe has smaller quarter windows behind the doorpost for a total of five.

Roadsters, cabriolets, and coupes can all have a rumble seat, to allow more seating room, or a trunk for storage. Sedans typically seat four or more people, have a solid top like a coupe, and have either two or four doors. A phaeton (a.k.a. touring car or tub) is a roadster that seats four or more and can have two or four doors. A delivery can be based on a passenger car chassis or a commercial truck chassis. If based on a passenger car chassis, it is called a sedan delivery and looks much like a two-door sedan with the rear quarter windows filled in and a delivery door on the back. A panel delivery is basically the same thing, but is built on a commercial truck chassis and with two rear doors.

Some hot rod terms worthy of mention are highboy, chopped, channeled, and fat fender. A highboy is a vehicle whose the fenders have been removed. This is typically done only on vehicles originally built prior to 1935, but is becoming popular on rat rods. Any vehicle that has had its body height altered by removing material from the door jambs, door posts, and glass areas has been chopped or has had a top chop. A channeled vehicle has had the floor altered so that a lower vehicle profile can be obtained by dropping the body down over the frame. Fat fendered vehicles have detachable fenders that are an integral part of the body (typically any vehicle originally manufactured in 1935 or later). The book, *How to Build a Hot Rod*, by yours truly (Motorbooks 2003), provides more information on these topics.

The body also greatly influences the number of passengers who can ride comfortably and the amount of luggage you can transport to the rod run. A fat-fendered four-door sedan will obviously transport more people or stuff than an early roadster.

You may be able to find the body that you want along with its original chassis. Both of these may be in unrestored condition, partially restored, or perhaps even in fully restored antique guise.

If you find some original vintage tin out in the desert or in someone's barn, it may be that the chassis has been damaged beyond reasonable repair or the body may be completely rusted away. Depending on the vehicle in

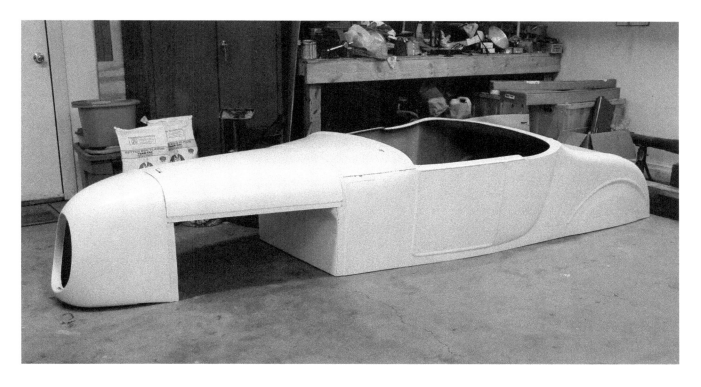

The Speedway Track T body, hood, nose, and grille sit quietly in the back of the garage until it is time to mount them onto the chassis. Aluminum hood sides are stashed away somewhere else in the garage. In all actuality, the body will be on and off the chassis several times during the vehicle's construction. Fortunately, the body is very lightweight.

question, it may still be cheap enough to make it a worthwhile purchase. You can buy this vehicle at a price that is suitable for what you will get out of it, knowing that you will still need to spend more money for another chassis or body. Sometimes it takes several vehicles to make one running hot rod.

Another familiar story is finding a collection of hot rod components for sale because the owner lost interest or got in over his head. Such an opportunity may be a good deal because you can get a cheaper price than if you source everything separately. You must realize, however, that you may have to redo some of the work that has been done by this once-ambitious person. Also, make sure you're happy with the major components the seller has assembled. Getting all the basics at one time isn't as good of a deal if you'd rather have a different engine and transmission in your car. Maybe you could resell what you don't want, if you have the space and time to deal with that. Otherwise, a deal is only good if what's on offer is what you want.

One way to obtain a decent body on the cheap is to purchase a fully restored antique. Now don't be looking for a fully restored Deuce three-window or a 1940 Ford Deluxe coupe this way. Oh, you may find one or two being advertised, but the asking price on these rarities is beyond the

scope of this book. On the other hand, thousands of people were restoring Model T and Model A Fords in the 1970s and 1980s. Many of these vehicles were subject to some pretty fierce judging, so the bodies have been restored to better-than-new condition. Now, many of these restorers are getting up there in years now and are willing to part with their prized possessions. Letting go of their labor of love might bring a tear to their eye, but if they must sell it, it might as well be to you, right? One word of caution, however: You might not want to mention that you plan to install a blown big block in it as soon as you chop the top on their 100-point restoration. Discretion in announcing your plans can often make or break a deal. (See Chapter 4, Body, for details on materials and approaches to building your body style of choice.)

Drivetrain

Although the body and frame for a hot rod pretty much have to have been originally built prior to 1948 (or be reproductions of that period), the basis for the drivetrain is as wide open as your imagination and your wallet will allow. A vast majority of today's hot rods are powered by one generation or another of small-block Chevrolet, yet many, many other options exist.

15

Some are mild while others are wild, but just about every engine has been shoehorned between the rails of a hot rod. Ford's flathead and overhead valve engines are obvious alternatives to Chevrolet, but what about Buick and Oldsmobile engines from the 1960s? The aluminum 215 V-8 from these manufacturers—made from 1961 to 1963 and carried on by Rover with displacement increases for many years—offers a lightweight option with good power. You can't forget the Chrysler Hemis, which have been built in a variety of displacements over the years, and while you are talking Hemi, don't forget Toyota. Of course, Maserati, Nissan, and Cadillac engines have also been used in hot rods.

As you wander the wrecking yards, thumb through magazines, and mull over your options, keep a few things in mind. First, size matters. Many people equate hot rods to honking V-8s. Yet a cast-iron big-block V-8 can weigh over 600 pounds. Will fitting this engine, cooling it, and finding suitable exhaust manifolds, or headers, and an adequate suspension blow your design parameters out of the water? Engines differ in weight and dimensions, and some will suit your project better than others. Cast iron versus aluminum makes a big difference in weight. Inline engines are longer but narrower than those in vee configuration. You can often run a straight steering shaft with an inline engine, but a V-6 or V-8 may require two joints on the column to go around the wider lump. Likewise, an inline engine offers more room to get exhaust out and down, though if you like symmetry, they emit exhaust from only one side.

A rare engine can make your rod a nice conversation piece, but if you need a head gasket, distributor, carburetor, pistons, or valves, are they available? Are they prohibitively expensive? In addition to searching out what's available in terms of engines, learn the same for parts for any engine you are considering. A cheap, running oddity needing a rebuild with hard-to-find parts that fetch top dollar may be a bad deal disguised as a good one.

Another thing to remember while selecting an engine is the transmission. Readily available engines like the 350 Chevy and 5-liter Ford V-8 are no sweat to fit with an automatic or stick shift gearbox to meet your needs. But oddball engines are a different story. Obviously the transmission originally paired with it fits, but how well does that suit your needs? A lot of adapters have been made over the years to combine a wide variety of engines and transmissions. If an unusual engine strikes your fancy, make sure you can match it to a good transmission, either bolt-up or with an adapter or aftermarket bell housing, before you buy. (See Chapter 5, Drivetrain, for additional considerations when buying, rebuilding, and fitting the drivetrain of your choice.)

OTHER COMPONENTS

Now that you have decided what you plan to build in regard to make, model, and body style, you must now formulate a plan for putting it all together and making it operable. This includes all of the various components that are never listed on the vehicle's registration. Choosing the right combination of these parts is what makes a hot rod a standout.

Suspension

The suspension, as a whole, consists of three basic components. The first are the components that attach, or connect, the wheels and tires to the chassis and maintain the location of the wheels in relation to the chassis. The other two components are springs to smooth the ride on all but a perfect surface, and springs to allow for some method of shock absorption (or damping) to prevent the springs from continuing to oscillate, or bounce, after they absorb a bump.

Unless a vehicle has independent suspension, the wheels are bolted onto the axle, which is attached to the chassis by way of a radius rod. One end of the radius rod is connected near to the end of the axle, while the opposite end of the radius rod connects to the chassis. Wishbone, ladder bar, and four-link (a.k.a. four-bar) are all variations of a radius rod type suspension. A wishbone (used in front or in back) was the stock style of suspension on many old vehicles, and had each radius rod angling to a common point near the middle of the vehicle. To allow for newer, larger engines and transmissions, the front wishbones are usually split and the end of each radius rod is attached to the frame rails. Wishbones are not commercially available in reproduction form, so their use is usually limited to vehicles with a nostalgic flavor.

Ladder bars are a direct descendent from rear wishbones, however, the 'bones are usually attached to a crossmember in the front and are about a foot apart, rather than all the way out at the frame rails. Ladder bars are common on rods that see some action on the drag strip, as their design lends itself to a stiffened chassis, which improves traction.

A four-link can be used in the front or the rear and generally provides a smoother ride than ladder bars. Prices for aftermarket suspension kits of the various designs are comparable, so the type of suspension is determined by the style of hot rod you are building. In a street driven hot rod, any of these types of suspension will perform sufficiently.

Springs for hot rods include everything from leaf springs and coil springs, to coil-overs and now air bags. Leaf springs may be transverse, running from one side to the other; parallel, mounted on each end and fore and aft of an axle; or quarter elliptic, usually similar to the parallel leaf springs except that only a portion of each leaf is used. Transverse leaf springs are common on hot rods with a front axle and

I had located a used Chevy 305 V-8 and a Powerglide transmission for use with this project, however, the small-block Chevy simply would not fit between the frame rails of my Speedway Motors Track T chassis. Speedway Motors does have a chassis available for use with V-8 power, though. With that said, I purchased this complete Ford V-6 and C4 automatic transmission for less than 300 bucks.

lend a nostalgic look when used in the rear. Parallel leaf springs provide a smoother ride when used in the rear, but are not as good as a set of coil-overs (a shock absorber that is integrated with a coil spring). Coil springs can be found on hot rods due to their lower cost, but their use is nowhere near as popular as coil-overs.

Hot rod shock absorbers are typically a tube type, such as on a late model vehicle, or a lever type. Performance of either type is comparable, although tube type shocks are more common.

Independent suspensions (front or rear) have good and bad points. Independent front suspension offers no real performance advantage on vehicles originally manufactured prior to 1938 due to these vehicles' light weight, but does give a better ride for vehicles that are newer (and heavier). For aftermarket suspension kits, the independent front suspension is about the same price as the components required in a front axle and its suspension. Although several production vehicles have an independent suspension that can be adapted to a hot rod, in their stock form they tend to look too bulky. An aftermarket independent front suspension kit typically has tubular A-arms that are much more stylish than the stamped steel ones used in production vehicles. An independent rear suspension probably performs

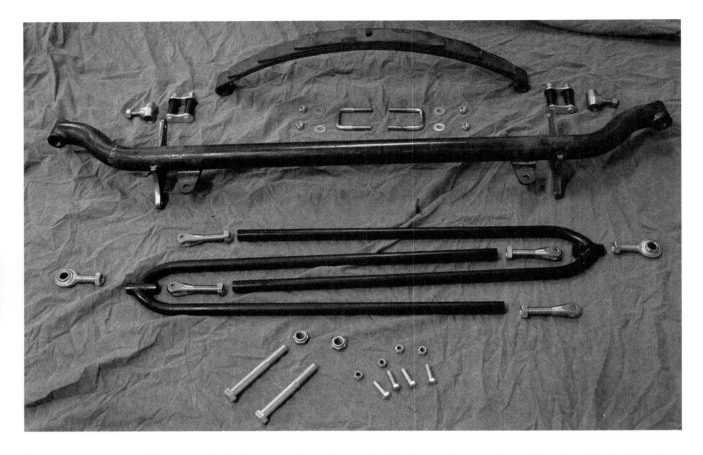

These components are the bulk, but not all, of the front suspension. The shocks are not included in the photo, nor are the drag link and tie rod (but these are not really suspension related). The heaviest part of the front suspension is the front tube axle, which already has brackets welded to it for the hairpin radius rods. A transverse leaf spring connects to the axle via shackles and spring perches. The spring is connected to the chassis with a pair of U-bolts. Hairpin radius rods connect to the chassis with Heim joints and to the front axle with clevises.

better than a solid rear axle on all hot rods, but its additional cost may not be justifiable, unless you are using your hot rod for autocross or some other driving competition.

An air ride suspension simply replaces the shocks and/or the springs (dependent upon specific application) with air bags. Air pressure in these bags can be increased to provide a stiffer ride, or reduced to provide a softer ride. An onboard air compressor allows the driver to quickly alter the ride and stance of the vehicle to meet the demand at the time.

With suspension components, you do have some latitude, depending on your ability to do some engineering. Many vehicle-specific suspension kits are available for Fords, some Chevrolets, and a smaller group for Mopar products. Although the limited requests for specific off-brand applications do not make it feasible for aftermarket companies to design, manufacture, and stock ready-made kits, the individual components are usually available as a "universal fit." Admittedly, these universal components usually require modification and therefore are not a "bolt it

in and go" situation, but they are at least a means to an end. Of course, you must take into account your personal level of mechanical experience, knowledge, and fabrication abilities (or resources) before you arbitrarily purchase some off-the-wall vehicle. Most any vehicle can be turned into a hot rod, but your personal ability to march to a different drummer (which often translates to all by yourself) has a great effect on whether your idea ever becomes a reality.

Shock absorption is commonly handled by tube shocks or coil-overs, however, lever shocks are still used for some nostalgic applications. You can use lever shocks almost anyplace where you can use tube shocks. It is really just a matter of taste and preference. The lever shocks immediately bring thoughts of nostalgia, but they can also be used on a high profile, state-of-the-art rod, as long as they are engineered into the design.

For locating the front and rear axles, original wishbones can be used and are usually split to make room for late-model drivetrains. For straight (or dropped) front axles, hairpin radius rod or parallel four-link systems are the primary choices. In the back, ladder bars, hairpin radius rods, parallel, or triangulated four-link systems are the most common.

For heavier vehicles, such as those originally manufactured in 1940 or later, independent suspensions on the front or rear work well. However, those same independent suspensions do little to improve the ride on lighter, earlier vehicles. Surprisingly, front independent suspensions are comparable in price to a typical four-link suspended dropped axle, while going independent in the rear adds a considerable amount to the price tag.

Air bags can be used with most suspension setups with the appropriate modifications. The air bags and suspension components may not be drastically more expensive than their non-air cushioned counterparts, but the additional cost of an air compressor, air lines, gauges, and air storage tank can quickly break the bank for a budget-built hot rod.

Wheels and Tires

Besides a flashy paint job, or the lack thereof, wheels and tires probably contribute the most to the overall appearance of a hot rod. This doesn't mean that bolting on a set of high-dollar wheels on an otherwise low-dollar hot rod is going to make it look better. In all reality, this combination might actually take away from the looks of any particular hot rod.

Since the wheel and tire combination is such a visual part of any vehicle, their quality, style, and expense need to be in line with the rest of the vehicle.

Wheels come in a seemingly endless variety of styles and finishes. Steel wheels are heavier but they cost the least. They can be painted, powder coated, or chrome plated, depending on your particular taste. Aluminum wheels (either cast or billet) weigh less than steel wheels, but cost more. Typically, aluminum wheels are polished, making them look like chrome, however, they can be painted or powder coated if you prefer color. Although the weight of the wheels is merely one component of the equation when fine tuning the suspension, the ride quality of most vehicles will benefit from less unsprung weight. (This term describes all of the components not supported by the vehicle's suspension—e.g., wheels, tires, hubs, brakes, plus a percentage of the suspension itself.)

I had purchased this 9-inch Ford rear axle housing, third member, and axles for use with another project, but this one came to fruition first. For installation of a set of gears and a set of drum brakes, I called upon Danny Miller's Rear Gears.

Hot rods always have the bigger tires on the back and the smaller tires on the front, but their sizes are merely in relation to each other, as tire sizes have changed considerably over the years. In the 1940s and 1950s, there were fewer choices in wheels and tires. The bias-ply tires were very similar in height and width, but even if the wheels were the same diameter, the back tires would be slightly wider than the fronts. In those days—or these days if you are building a hot rod of this style—a common set of tires was 5.00 or 5.50 (width in inches) in the front and 7.00 or 8.50 in the back, mounted on 15- or 16-inch diameter wheels. During the 1960s and 1970s, rodders began using wider, though not necessarily taller, tires. Since no suspension modifications were employed to allow for these wider tires, they usually stuck out from beneath the fenders, when present.

As the end of the century approached, sizes of front and rear tires on hot rod were probably at their farthest extremes. Front tires were commonly only 4 or 5 inches wide on 14- or 15-inch diameter wheels. Out back, tires that were 10 to 14 inches wide and mounted to 15- to 17-inch diameter wheels were common. These vast differences in tire and wheel size exaggerated the rubber rake (the stance of a vehicle based upon the difference in tire size) to the point where wheel alignment (namely caster) was adversely affected. For contemporary hot rods, larger diameter wheels (anything larger than 17 inches) and wider tires seem to be the current trend, but still the back tires are wider and taller than those on the front.

Since any particular make and model of hot rod is going to look basically the same, regardless of how it is built, the wheels and tires play a decisive role in defining the style of the finished hot rod. So, you should consider your choice of wheels and tires early on in the build process. True, you can change wheels and tires quite easily, so you are not locked into any particular style, but if you are trying to build a hot rod from a specific time period, be sure that you get the rolling stock correct.

If you have an inkling that you may choose to change your wheel and tire combination, it would be wise to select an electric speedometer that can easily be calibrated to compensate for the different tire size. Mechanical speedometers can be recalibrated, but they usually require sourcing the work to a speedometer shop, or at least installing a calibrated adaptor between the transmission and the speedo.

Brake System

A safe brake system is a high priority. Typically, disc brakes are more efficient than drum brakes, and four-wheel disc brakes are better than a disc/drum arrangement. Nevertheless, the disc/drum setup is often sufficient and is very

Rolling stock is made up of Vintique's Smoothies 15x5 (front) and 15x7 (rear) wheels, purchased from Coker Tire. Tires are Michelin 145/R15 XZX (front) and BFGoodrich P255/70R15 T/A Radials (rear). Although the exact color had not yet been determined at this time, the wheels will be the same color as the scallops on the body.

This is the brake master cylinder, bracket, and brake pedal arm in their stock configuration on the Track T. Note that the brake pedal arm must be modified to get the brake pedal pad in the correct location in the floor. After those modifications are completed, a sleeve will be welded onto the arm to which the pad can be attached.

common on both hot rods and production automobiles. Advances in braking systems by the original equipment manufacturer (OEM) ultimately make it easier and less expensive to have better braking systems on your hot rods. You must realize, however, that on occasion errant drivers cause panic situations that call for every bit of braking assistance that you can muster.

After deciding on the basic concept of which wheels and tires you plan to use, you can then decide on the brakes of your choice. I say basic concept, as you will most likely have at least an inch or two of latitude in both wheel width and diameter, regardless of your brake choices. Some of the large contemporary disc brakes kits (those that boast 13- and 14-inch diameter rotors) are designed for wheels that are 17 inches or taller. One of these brake kits simply will not fit if you are running a relatively small 14- or 15-inch wheel. Likewise, if your hot rod has 9- or 10-inch rotors, you should upgrade your brakes prior to bolting on a set of large diameter wheels. This is only one of the areas that requires you to spend lots of *time* planning, so that you don't waste lots of *money* on incompatible components.

Fuel System

The fuel system, comprising a storage tank, a supply line, a vent, and sometimes a return line, is really quite simple. As long as it doesn't leak it is safe, and malfunctions are therefore an inconvenience more than anything. In Model A Fords, the fuel tank was mounted higher than the engine, making it a gravity feed system that didn't require a fuel pump. That is no longer practical or desirable. Fuel pumps can be mechanical or electrical, although the latter

is somewhat more difficult to troubleshoot when there is a problem. Tanks, fittings, and lines are very adaptable and can be customized for virtually any application, design, layout, or situation. True, a custom gas tank will cost more than something off the shelf, but generally hot rodders tend to pencil out the look, style, and dimensions they want in the vehicle first, and then get a gas tank to suit it, rather than buying a cheap tank and conforming the body or chassis.

Cooling System

Whatever engine you may have beneath the hood and between the frame rails, it is going to generate some heat and therefore must be kept cool. Most of this is done by liquid running through a radiator, but the radiator alone cannot cool the liquid enough to keep the engine from overheating. Airflow, whether induced by a fan or from natural aerodynamics, also helps keep the engine cool, and some well-placed louvers in the hood and hood sides can help to minimize overheating problems. Remember, the engine you're jamming into the engine bay is almost always bigger and generates more heat, than what the engine bay initially held. A big motor in a tight space needs good airflow.

Heat is also a major cause of automatic transmission failures, so a separate transmission cooler is a good idea. Although late-model production vehicles usually have coolant lines running from the radiator to the transmission, this setup still aggregates the heat from both systems, even though their liquids, coolant, and transmission fluid are never combined. A separate cooler allows the transmission to run at a lower temperature, which is preferable.

Everything Else

Of course there are many more components and subassemblies that make up a hot rod. These include steering; electrical; heating, ventilating, and air conditioning (HVAC); and lighting systems just to name a few. Additionally, there is paint, upholstery, and glass to deal with. How simple or complex you want your hot rod to be plays a big role in what you purchase.

BUDGETING MONEY

As you come up with the list of what parts you want for your hot rod, keep your budget in mind. It's always easier (and less expensive) if you have established this early on. If you haven't, you could run out of cash for your dream hot rod and have to sell it. There's nothing worse than seeing your pet project trailered or being driven down the road by someone else.

You also probably want to discuss the project's cost with your family. Construction of a hot rod takes a fair amount of both time and money, so its cost needs to be factored in with your family life. Young children need your time and college students need your money, while teens need your time and your money. A hot rod can be a necessity too, but everything needs to be balanced out. Any voyage will be smoother if everyone is paddling in the same direction.

Lump Sum Available

Okay, you've discussed it as a family and everyone is excited about the new hot rod project. How are you going to pay for it? Many hot rods are built with a lump sum of cash. Whether that money is in the form of an inheritance, a loan from the bank (or a real good friend), savings, or the sale of another vehicle, what you have in hand is what you have to spend.

In the savings category, money can come from not only stashing your pennies away for years, but also from your discretionary income. Maybe the kids are out of college now and your house is paid for, so you can spend money on your hot rod. Another option is to use some money from your retirement fund. This should only be done after giving it serious thought.

Pay as You Go

If you don't have the luxury of a hot rod sized surplus in your checking account, paying as you go is probably the best way to go. The process may take longer, but building a hot rod is supposed to be fun, so why rush the process? The Model A that was featured in my first book, *How to Build a Hot Rod Model A Ford*, took me close to 13 years to build from start to finish, but I still got a great car in the end. By the way, discuss timeframe with your family as well as dollars. Most car enthusiasts understand that building or restoring a car can take several years, but not all spouses appreciate this fact. Start with the same expectations and the process will go more smoothly.

To make the pay-as-you-go method work, you really need to plan well. Sit down with pencil and paper, determine what parts you need for the complete hot rod, and write them down, including their approximate prices. Now rewrite the list (or type it in a computer spreadsheet) in the approximate order in which you will need the parts. There is some play here, obviously, but momentum is important to finishing an extensive project. If you have a sensible progression of build steps, you can incorporate each piece as you acquire it, which will keep you enthusiastically moving forward to each new step. Purchasing parts before you really need them minimizes the available funds for the parts that you do need at present. Good planning fosters and rewards anticipation; bad planning thwarts it. The pay-as-you-go method should be crafted around your regular income and expenses, but you can also spend additional sums that come your way—dividends from stock sales, a sales commission, overtime pay, a performance bonus, or, in my case, a book advance and royalties. Regardless of where the money comes from, be fair to your family's needs and your other financial obligations so you don't get in over your head. Go one step at a time, one day at a time, and you'll get there within your means.

Let's consider the suspension, for example. Although a reproduction hot rod chassis with suspension costs several thousands of dollars, you can purchase those suspension components separately. Excluding the perimeter frame, most individual suspension components you'll need—like a front axle, front four-bar suspension, or shocks and springs—retail for $500 or less. It may take several partial paychecks to get everything, but you should be able to make steady progress if you plan your purchases with some forethought.

BUDGETING TIME

Other than your finances, you may need to budget your time when building a hot rod. Whether you build hot rods as part of your occupation or as a hobby, completing a vehicle takes a significant amount of time. To be fair to your family, you'll need to budget hours as well as dollars.

If at all possible, make your rod building experience a family project. The entire family may not want to join in on your fun, but don't discourage it if they do want to help out in the garage. After all, a hot rod project is not just greasy car work, and it isn't all garage work, either. The best hot rods, even cheap ones, embody a lot of art and creativity. Your spouse or children's hobby interest in textiles, furniture, embroidery, electronics, stereo equipment, drawing, painting, etc., might contribute toward helping design or prepare any number of your project's necessities or accessories—carpets, seats, upholstery, paint scheme, sound system, lights, wiring.

Depending on the age of your helpers, you may not get much accomplished in some of your work sessions, but it can still be a great experience. Take this opportunity to pass on some of your knowledge to your sons and daughters. And don't forget to teach them safety in the garage while you are at it.

Do It Yourself

Okay, this book is about how you can build a cheap hot rod, not paying someone else to build one. Still, you may not be able to perform every task required. That's all right, you don't have to do everything yourself. There are welders, fabricators, and machinists capable of doing everything your project requires. Of course, doing everything you can do on your own will save you money and will also make your project a learning experience upon which you can build in future projects, repairs, and restorations—wherever the car hobby takes you.

If you are building a hot rod as a therapeutic project and time spent is not an issue, build it all yourself—as much as you can—and enjoy the process. Any labor that you don't have to farm out will save you money and will make you the authority on every nut and bolt on your hot rod. While you may be best served by having something like an engine

rebuild performed by a pro, you can handle the vast majority of the project's other tasks.

You will also be well served throughout this project if you buy quality manuals on the engine, transmission, and underlying body for your car. They can be invaluable in showing how even simple things, like door handles and latches, come apart and go together. They will also give you the confidence to rebuild many components on your own, things like the fuel pump, carburetor, and alternator. If you're unsure—particularly on safety items like the braking, steering, and fuel systems—you can always consult a professional.

Trading Work

Getting help with building your hot rod is often just a phone call away. For instance, you might be a pretty decent fabricator and welder and therefore can build your own chassis, but might not know squat about building an engine. Do you know someone who is good with engines? Is that person looking for someone to do some chassis work? The same principles work for bodywork, painting, upholstery, or whatever else you may need.

Even if you don't have hot rod building skills that are of trading quality, what do you do for a living? If you have some sort of skill, whether it is as a concrete finisher, a carpenter, an accountant, a business consultant, or whatever, you may be able to find someone who builds hot rods who needs someone with your abilities. Keep track of what you do and have done, so that your bartering stays fair and, in fact, saves you money.

The interior of this repop T roadster is very practical with its aluminum paneling and bomber style seats. Although it would still be less expensive than traditional upholstery materials, this kind of interior could be expensive if you have to pay someone to do it for you. If you or a friend has access to a bead roller and a shear, you could whip this up yourself pretty easily and for not much money. Even if you have to farm out the seat cushions, their cost should be minimal.

I couldn't find the owner to verify that this is a Speedway Motors kit, but I suspect that it is. From the firewall back, it is essentially the same as the Track T being built in the following pages. The grille shell is 1932 Ford and, with a straight windshield, this vehicle looks more like a traditional highboy roadster than my project. Low mounted headlights, painted steelies with hubcaps and trim rings, along with wide whitewalls, give this red roadster a real nostalgic look. Some might say that the all-tin interior and nostalgic styling are in conflict with each other, but it still looks like a fun car.

Jevan Morse's 1933 Ford pickup might look rough and may be confused with a rat rod by many people, but, unlike many rat rods, this truck is well built and could be safely driven cross-country if desired. Just because it has some rust does not mean it should be confused with junk. By rescuing some vintage tin from the back forty, spending a few dollars wisely on safety related parts like suspension and brakes, Morse built a fun ride that didn't cost a fortune. You usually don't have to look far to find a small-block Chevy engine to use for motor-vation. Add some rebuilt carburetors, rebuilt drum brakes, and new tires, and this truck is well on its way to a few thousand carefree miles on the odometer in its first summer of rod runs.

So what if the seats don't match the steering wheel? A tilt-out windshield instead of air conditioning provides ventilation, and if you are not going to be traveling far, you can get by without a mega-watt stereo that adds expense to the project.

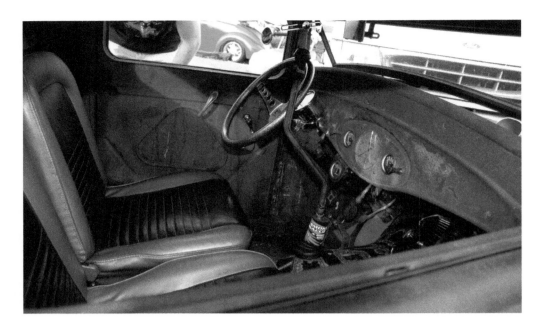

The second of this trio of Kentucky farm trucks belongs to Richard Sanders. The cab started life as a Model AA stakebed truck, but now has been channeled down over an original 1933 Ford frame. Richard claims to have less than $11,000 in his truck and more than 4,000 fun filled miles on the odometer. He and his buddies traded work amongst each other to keep the costs to a minimum. The largest expenses for any of the three trucks were for suspension, brakes, and other safety related items.

26

A stock 265-ci small-block Chevy with a generator and straight pipes is simple and a pretty cost effective way to power any hot rod. These three trucks run down the highway with the best of 'em and for a whole lot less money. For a weekend out with the guys, you don't need a plush interior. This steering wheel probably didn't cost $20, the tach looks to be from a salvage yard, and the new blanket seat cover could have been found just about anywhere pretty cheap.

Kirby Stafford must be the buck's up guy of the three. After all, he has a surfboard mounted on the roof of his 1936 Ford pickup. He also has a detailed flathead Ford engine between the frame rails, and what looks to be an original Ford greyhound atop the 1933 Ford grille shell. Like his two compadres, he kept the costs low by trading work and wisely spending his money on items contributing to the safety and reliability of his truck. Did you notice the un-split wishbones used to support the surfboard? All three trucks have several things in common that saved the owners money: no hoods, no fenders, no paint, and no upholstery. All are items that quickly add up by the time they are purchased, fitted, prepped, and finally installed on the vehicle.

The owner of this Ford T-modified saved a fair amount of money simply by not painting the car. It appears to be wearing a smooth coat of black epoxy primer highlighted by a minimal amount of red scallops, which may just be tinted primer as well. Although epoxy primer isn't cheap, it is still less expensive than final paint. I would suspect that many of the components in this car were swap meet purchases for pennies on the dollar, compared to buying new parts at retail prices. These bomber seats are similar in function to the ones seen earlier in the red T roadster, but are probably less expensive. These appear to have been cut out of flat stock and then rolled (perhaps over a welding tank), but lack the stiffening ribs or the cooling holes in the backs. Obviously, it has less padding as well.

29

Above: This super-smooth orange coupe provides an example of a fat-fendered car and a five-window coupe. Although the fenders can be removed during construction or repair, they are an integral part of the body's design, making it unlikely that this body style would ever be built as a highboy.

Top left: This cute budget-built hot rod in progress is a '28 or '29 Ford Model A Tudor sedan. Although it is on the small side, Model A's are easy to build and almost everything is available in reproduction form. Two adults can ride comfortably, but back seat passengers need to be pretty agile.

Bottom left: Perhaps the most recognizable grille among hot rods is that of the 1932 Ford. This roadster is a very nice example of the popular highboy style, that is, no fenders.

CHAPTER 2
WHERE TO FIND PARTS

Over the years while working on various hot rod projects, acquaintances and co-workers have inquired as to where I find parts for whatever particular project on which I might be working. For those of us who are actively involved in hot rods, it is difficult to imagine that anyone is not aware of the flourishing automotive aftermarket with which we are currently blessed. In any sizeable bookstore or newspaper stand, we can find a cornucopia of enthusiast magazines promoting our hobby. Between the covers of those publications are literally thousands of advertisements from companies, small and large, that have just what we need for our latest hot rod project. For products from most of those companies, a valid credit card, a ship-to address, and a few minutes on the telephone will have your parts on their way to you in a very timely manner. Quite often, those parts are easier and faster to obtain than a part for your late-model daily driver.

Although reproduction parts are very common in many street rods, not all parts that make up a hot rod are brand new. Even for those who choose new old stock (NOS) or even

If you are looking for vintage engine accessories, you may be able to find them at a swap meet. Every swap meet that I have ever attended has had plenty of intake manifolds available, with some rather exotic setups at the larger meets. This particular vendor had a variety of intakes complete with carburetors, along with some hefty price tags. If you are looking for something that is hard to find, being well informed on going prices, availability, and operational requirements, as well as being in the right place at the right time, can save you some money.

rare, no-longer–in-production parts, many businesses are out there locating and rounding up these items, so you don't have to. Whether the parts are new or old, the convenience of one-stop shopping usually comes with a hefty price.

SWAP MEET

If you are truly budget minded, a swap meet is often the best place for finding parts and potentially entire project vehicles. Most car shows and rod runs have at least some swap meet spaces at their events. There are also major swap meets that are regionally and nationally advertised. If you are merely looking for a replacement four-barrel carburetor for your small block, a swap meet will usually have what you are looking for. On the other hand, if you are looking for a vintage Hilborn fuel injection system for a flathead Ford, you may need to spend some time at one of the larger events.

Some people say that prices are typically higher at larger, nationally known swap meets, but they no doubt have more to choose from as well. There is no guarantee that you are going to find just what you are looking for, much less at the price you want, especially with rarer items. Like many things in life, success is a matter of being at the right place at the right time and having the coin of the realm at that precise time. The important resources not to overlook at swap meets are the people on hand. The hot rod community is pretty congenial; if you don't see what you need, a vendor or another attendee may know of a place to source it. It pays to be friendly and ask around.

Visual and Hands-On Inspection

Another benefit of shopping at the swap meet is that you can visually inspect your potential purchase to your heart's content. You can inspect for hidden rust in sheet metal pieces (such as fenders and doors), check for oblong or egg-shaped cylinders in engine blocks, or verify critical features or connections on many other parts. You can also check for broken mounting tabs on otherwise usable parts, or hairline fractures in pieces that are useless if cracked, like a distributor cap. Your sense of touch is also important here. Sometimes, as with a panel, it's easier to feel whether it's straight than to see it. Experienced body workers and painters are also adept at finding body filler by feel. Just because something is a little warped or filled doesn't mean you can't use it, but you don't want to pay top dollar for it if it needs work.

Good information, like from a factory manual, will come in handy at any swap meet. Different versions of the same part, like a transmission, can look very similar. To get exactly what you want, show up with all of the critical

This pair of solid doors for a 1940–1941 Ford truck is probably worth the asking price of $750 if you needed it. Being able to find the pair at a swap meet, inspect for rust or other damage, and not have to pay for shipping is sure to be less expensive in the end than finding them in a classified ad or on the internet.

details for the parts you're seeking. Bring along the manual, photos, drawings, or a written list of identifying features. The big drawback with a swap meet is that it isn't a brick and mortar store where you can return a part. If you don't realize you bought the wrong thing right away, you may not be able to return or exchange it, or you may face expensive shipping charges once the vendor has moved on.

Measure

Shopping in person also allows you to measure items such as wheels, axles, and any other items that involve specific dimensions. Do yourself a favor and take a tape measure whenever you are going to a swap meet. Not that anyone would intentionally lie to you, but you want to be able to check dimensions before you buy. Get the specs you need before you leave your house, or if you're searching for another example of a small part you already own (like a door handle), you can bring the one you have for comparison. For something like the bolt pattern on your hubs, you can make a template out of heavy paper or cardboard.

Wheels are a common staple of the swap meet. Be sure to know the bolt pattern of your vehicle and what size (width and diameter) you can use. Knowing the minimums and maximums, along with having a tape measure and knowing how to measure bolt patterns, can save you some money. The wheels may need some elbow grease to get them looking like brand-new, but most anything that you buy at a swap meet is going to be less expensive than buying brand-new.

Immediate Availability

Hot diggity, you scrounged through that big pile of parts and found the diamond in the rough that will be the crown jewel of your hot rod project. If you and the seller can agree on a price and you have enough greenbacks in your pocket, it's a done deal. The part is yours to carry or drag around for the rest of your time at the swap meet.

It is no surprise that you see lots of kid's wagons, two-wheel dollies, and backpacks in use at swap meets. Most swap meet vendors will gladly set a purchased part aside for you if they know you are going to come back, or if you have already paid for it. Common courtesy suggests that you ask the seller how long he or she plans to be there if you are not going to be back sooner than about five minutes.

Bargain Prices

Swap meets are generally the bargain basement of hot rod parts. If I take something to a swap meet, it means that I don't plan on ever using it and I am willing to let it go for almost any reasonable offer. If I think I may use it on another project or need more than a swap meet price, I simply don't bother loading it on the truck.

Keep in mind that most anything is for sale if the price is right, even items that say "display only." If you absolutely have to have it—it's the only one you've seen and it's what you need—it never hurts to ask politely about buying it. Even vehicles in a field or open barn, with no sign to be seen, might be for sale. In the latter situation, however, you need to exercise some caution and courtesy. Could be a recent widow would love to turn that vehicle into cash. Could also be that you're the 30th person to stop and maybe not the first to meet some mean dogs or some unkind words about trespassing.

Also put the word out at work and among your friends and neighbors that you're going to build a hot rod and are looking for parts. It's not at all uncommon for people to learn that someone they've talked to or worked with for years has a line on a cool old car that isn't technically for sale, but might be freed up with a kind word and some folding money.

Cash Is King

If you find that part or project vehicle that you have been looking for, but the asking price is more than what you care to spend, don't be afraid to pull the (spendable) cash out of your pocket and let the potential seller know that you are serious about buying. Like they say, money talks. At a swap meet, if you are anywhere close to being in the ballpark where price is concerned, letting the seller see a little green can go a long way toward closing the sale. Just remember not to pull out more than you're willing to spend, or more than you've told the seller you have on hand.

INTERNET

The internet has definitely played an important part in the recent history of hot rod building and finding the parts. To some people it has been a fantastic tool, but to others, it has become a hindrance to finding those same parts. Online auctions have driven the costs of some parts way beyond their reasonable value in the eyes of some rodders.

Sight Unseen

Unlike at a swap meet where you can inspect pieces and parts at will, items advertised on the internet (whether a classified ad or an online auction) are not available for your immediate evaluation of their suitability and adaptability to your current (or future) project. You are at the mercy of the potential seller and his or her conscience. We all want to

If you were looking for a 1934 Ford Fordor sedan project, this one was still at the NSRA nationals on Sunday morning. The sign on the firewall read "solid, rust free California car, boxed frame, Mustang II front suspension, $9,900." The body looked fairly straight and the fenders certainly were not the worst we've seen.

Not far away was this 1940 Ford convertible that was also a solid, rust-free car. Asking price was $10,900, which isn't much more than a fiberglass repop. Update the original suspension, add a drivetrain, and I think you could be driving this one for less than $20,000. Depending on a buyer's negotiating skills, it may have been sold for less, since this car was still available on Sunday morning.

I don't recall for sure, but I think the owner was asking $1,500 for this 1928–1929 Ford Tudor. The good thing about Model As is that plenty of patch panels are available. A trip to the stripper, a coat of epoxy primer, and a repop chassis of your choice, and you could have this on the road, albeit not finished, for around $10,000.

believe that people placing the advertisements are perfectly accurate and honest in their description of what they are trying to sell. Sometimes, they are not.

We also have ourselves as readers of classified ads to blame on occasion. When we find that rare ad for just what we are looking for, we sometimes fail to register all of the description, even though it is all the same sized print. Subtle descriptions, such as "not running," "no title," or "wrecked, left side," sometimes makes a difference, sometimes it doesn't.

Photos at Best

Unlike conventional classified ads, internet ads usually allow for more than one photo, albeit at an additional cost to the advertiser. This allows the seller to provide some different angles, so you can usually determine the stance of a particular vehicle, but unless you are searching for a complete car, this probably doesn't matter. Overall, photos usually don't give you a great feel for how straight the sheet metal is or if rust is a factor. And, let's not forget about the ability of many people to manipulate digital photos, be it through angle or design programs.

On the other hand, most internet ads give the seller's telephone number or e-mail address so you can contact him or her for more information. If you are sincere with the seller, he or she will usually provide you with more photos and information upon request. Just don't be expecting 8x10 color glossies to add to your personal collection of hot rod photos.

Questionable Description

Before you call the seller, who may be several states away, about your potential dream car project, you need to know something about that particular make and model in the first place. The person on the other end of the line may mention that this vehicle has rust in the cab corners. If you are familiar with old pickup trucks, you will have assumed that was the case already and have already checked the price for a set of cab corner patch panels for this particular make and model of truck. If you aren't familiar with this particular model, however, the seller's description of a common and easily repaired defect may steer you away from an otherwise good purchase.

During your search for hot rod parts, you will have to develop the ability to ask the right questions and read between the lines of the answers given. If after the seller describes some negative aspect of the vehicle, ask, "Is it repairable?" The answer may well be, "Well, heck yeah," which may really translate to, "It is if you junk this piece of crap and buy something else."

Not 100 Percent Accurate Condition

"It's in great shape!" That may sound great, but when you are talking about a vehicle that was originally manufactured 60 or more years ago, that description loses some credibility. You have to realize that vehicles with features like original paint or upholstery can vary a lot, depending on the conditions and environment in which they were stored. What is there may not be obvious, either. A bleached out, faded vehicle from the Arizona or California desert may have solid metal nonetheless, while a garage-kept vehicle from a damp, snowy state, where salt has been used for decades on the roads, may be hiding advanced rust on its frame or inner panels.

Often times, older vehicles that are for sale are offered by relatives of the deceased owner and these relatives may have no real technical knowledge of the vehicle. They just know that it was the owner's pride and joy, and therefore must be worth a large sum of money because that person spent lots of time working on it. Whether all that work improved or decreased the car's value depends on the owner's mechanical skills, not just the time spent.

May Not Be What It Is Thought to Be

Some owners of vehicles simply do not know what they have and don't know the difference between it and what someone else thinks it is. For example, someone may have inherited a vehicle from their long lost uncle's estate. This person has no interest in old cars and has no idea what it is, so they ask around. Someone mentions that it looks like the 1932 coupe that the parents had years ago. Of course, this person who is "in the know" was only four years old at the time and the coupe he or she is referring to is actually a sedan. The next thing you know, the car for sale is advertised as a 1932 Ford coupe. In all actuality, the car inherited from the estate is a 1925 Hupmobile. It might become a cool hot rod, but you'll have trouble finding parts. This example may be an exaggeration, but it is a good idea to know what models look like before you actually set out to find them.

Shipping Expense

Perhaps the worst part of shopping via the internet (whether you are looking for a project vehicle or just parts) is the cost to get the item to you after you make the deal or become the winning bidder. Unless the seller is offering to pay for the shipping, you really need to have an estimate of the shipping costs so you can factor that into your offer. It would be senseless to make a long-distance purchase just to have the shipping costs delete the savings. Of course, you might not be able to find what you are looking for any closer to you.

Whether you have the time to drive across the county, or the country, to pick up a new project or rare parts is for you to decide. Although the cost of having a vehicle shipped halfway across the country may be comparable to the cost of the vehicle itself, it may still be cheaper than you going to get it if you have to take off of work. And towing a vehicle won't help your gas mileage, either. A thousand-mile roundtrip at $2.50 a gallon with average economy of 10 miles per gallon will run you $250 in gas alone. Renting a car trailer, if you don't have and can't borrow one, can run two to three times that amount for a good one. A shipper will also be insured—ask and make sure—whereas you may not automatically be. If the vehicle is a rare find, check with your insurer or the trailer rental company about covering your purchase en route.

Additional Methods of Payment

Shopping the internet does have its advantages over swap meets, as there are more payment options available to the consumer. Not everyone who sells over the internet can or will accept all of the following payment options, but different options provide some shopping ease.

Check Although someone who is selling items on the internet might insist on making sure that your personal check clears the bank prior to shipping the item, it is a convenient option. Almost everyone has a checking account, so even if it takes a little longer for your new purchase to ship, the transaction is still relatively painless. You can pretty much forget about paying by check at a swap meet, though.

PayPal For people who make many transactions over the internet on sites such as eBay, PayPal works great. A quick overview is that your PayPal account is tied to one of your existing credit card accounts or bank accounts, allowing you to shop now, pay later. For those who do online transactions on a regular basis, PayPal also offers shipment tracking capabilities, allowing individuals the ability to conduct trade like real businesses.

Credit Cards Although credit cards are typically accepted only by established businesses, those that do accept credit cards make it very easy to shop online. Elaborate websites complete with product descriptions, photos, application data, shipping weights, and prices usually allow the retailer to ship your order within 24 hours if you provide a valid credit card number.

Certified Check This is a very common form of payment, especially when purchasing a complete vehicle or any collection of parts that adds up to a large sum of money. It's safer for the seller, as the buyer has already paid the financial institution, and therefore there is no worry of the check bouncing.

CLASSIFIED ADS

Classified ads have the same advantages and disadvantages as ones on the internet. Other than *Hemmings Motor News* and a few other publications that are available worldwide, classified ads are typically placed by local sellers. This fact alone usually makes it easier to drive to where the advertised item is located and see it firsthand, *before* you commit to making a purchase.

Poor Quality Photos

Photos in classified advertisements are a constant source of amusement for me, as quite often the photos are of poor quality, do little to give an accurate description of the vehicle, or sometimes aren't even of the vehicle being advertised. On several occasions, I have seen advertising photos that show a vehicle directly from the front. If a photo that shows you only the grille, headlights, and front fenders tells you anything about the vehicle, you probably already know what it looks like anyway. I also have to laugh at the ad photos that have a woman standing in front of a door that looks like maybe it is part of a 1940 Ford coupe. I have to ask what they are really trying to sell.

Questionable Description

For various reasons, the person writing the description may not be 100 percent accurate. Whether he or she doesn't know or doesn't care is immaterial. If the item remotely sounds like what you are looking for and is within reasonable driving distance, a road trip might be in order. It may

Club newsletters or magazines provide a wide variety of classified ads from other car folks, making them somewhat more reliable in description than ordinary classifieds in the local newspaper.

not yield what you really want, but that, my friend, is all part of hot rodding.

Limited Methods of Payment

Classified ads are usually placed by private parties, which typically minimizes your payment options. Unless the seller also has his or her own retail-oriented business, the seller most likely will not accept credit cards. Cash will always work, but the seller's acceptance of a personal check will vary from transaction to transaction. For larger purchases, both parties may be more comfortable (and feel safer) with a cashier's check.

LOCAL HOT ROD SHOP OR AUTO PARTS STORE

Your local hot rod building emporium will prove to be an asset when you are building a hot rod. Almost all hot rod shops do at least some amount of retail sales. Since they already purchase many parts from other vendors for the hot rods that they build, it only makes sense to sell additional items to other customers as well.

Can Offer Expertise

Since rod builders make their living building hot rods, they develop a working knowledge of how parts are installed and which ones work best. Quite often, they can show you the hot rod part in question on one of their projects, enabling you to gain a better grasp of the product than what any catalog can provide.

Building a good rapport with the person behind the counter at your local auto parts store will also help you with your rod building project. Most of these guys and gals are

Perusing a collection of catalogs can help you determine just what is available for your particular application, as well as the prices. Just like the internet, you can shop from the comfort of your own home if you choose. Of course, there's nothing quite like walking into a fully stocked rod shop, where you can actually see the parts and ask for assistance from experienced hot rodders.

knowledgeable on application, installation, and troubleshooting of parts designed as OEM replacements. Although you may think of your project as being 100 percent hot rod, it will have some parts that are straight from the ordinary auto parts store.

New Parts, More Expensive

Both hot rod and auto parts shops will usually have the parts you are looking for, although they may have to order them for you, depending on how much inventory they keep on hand. The new parts will most always be more expensive than swap meet parts, but they will also be new, rather than used.

CATALOG

If you are building a hot rod, but there aren't any rod shops in your general area, your best way to purchase parts may be through a catalog. Your favorite rod magazines have plenty of advertisements for companies that specialize in hot rod parts, and most of them have some sort of catalog. While some companies charge for their catalogs, some don't. Most rod parts companies will gladly send you a catalog if you request one by telephone or in writing. Delivery, however, may be slower than you would like. Some catalogs offer more parts to peruse than others, while some also provide useful technical information.

New Parts, More Expensive

Just like when buying parts from your local shop, the parts you buy from a catalog are brand-new and therefore have a brand-new price tag. Although the price might be more initially, it may be money well spent, depending on the part in question and its availability.

Wide Selection of Parts and Manufacturers

Manufacturers and vendors of hot rod parts are, for the most part, one big happy family. Like in all industries, there is competition for the almighty dollar. However, most rod shops will gladly sell you a particular piece from one of their competitors if they don't manufacture a similar component themselves. Building a hot rod is supposed to be fun, and from personal experience, I can tell you that if you have developed a rapport with any particular rod shop, it will do whatever it can to help you get your hot rod on the road. Whether you purchase the part directly from the competitor or through your main source is up to you, but you should remember to be loyal to those who help you out.

Shipping Expense

One thing to keep in mind when you whip out your fantastic plastic and begin ordering parts is to remember the additional shipping expense. These days, when you can order almost any part you need and have it delivered directly to your door, this convenience comes with a price. The voice on the other end of the telephone will usually always ask, "How would you like this shipped?" What that really translates to is, "How much do you want to pay us to get it there?" Of course, this shipping expense will depend on the size and weight of the parts being shipped, but do you *really* need them to be shipped overnight? It would be nice, but that extra money spent on rush delivery charges could be better spent on actual parts.

CHAPTER 3
THE ROLLING CHASSIS

Okay, the plan has been made and it is finally time to start making some real progress on building a hot rod. Not that *all* of the planning is completed, but there is a point at which you have to start bolting at least some parts together before deciding what to do next. Building a hot rod is very much like sailing across the ocean; you chart your course in the beginning, you set sail, and then you constantly adjust your directions to maintain your overall course.

After weighing the pros and cons of several different vehicles—parts availability and their prices, suitability, personal tastes and desire to build—and approaches toward completing them, I decided to go with a Track T kit from Speedway Motors in Lincoln, Nebraska. Going with this kit approach will allow me to mix and match parts as I choose, yet still have at least a body and chassis that are designed to go together at a fraction of the cost of a reproduction hot rod chassis and body. We are trying to keep this under a predetermined budget, you know. Having open access to a well stocked salvage yard might have presented other options, however, salvage yards are not what they used to be. Even finding a salvage yard is getting more difficult in some areas, and when you do, you can pretty much forget about finding anything originally built prior to 1970—at least with good parts on it.

FRAME

The Track T frame from Speedway Motors is all new material, yet it is not a reproduction of an authentic Ford Model T frame. Most hot rod chassis are reproductions of original frames, albeit boxed and often times fitted with more elaborate crossmembers. They allow you to use a reproduction hot rod frame under an original stock body with minimal fitment issues and, depending on the judges, can be used for a restoration (back to original) project. You can't do that easily with the Track T frame, as it simply does not look anything like an original frame.

Although the Track T frame doesn't look like a stock Model T chassis, it doesn't really matter, as it will all be hidden from view when the car is completed. It is constructed from new material, is jig welded (so it should be square), and, once again, is less expensive than a reproduction frame.

Original

Depending on what type of vehicle you are building, an original frame might be usable. This really depends on what you are able to find, what condition it is in, and what kind of drivetrain you plan to put in it. For example, a Ford Model A frame is pretty simple; it has a simple profile and is straight on each side, except for one angle located at the

An original sketch by Steve Gilmore, who interned for Mattel at one time. One of his projects was the Track T Hot Wheels car, which served as inspiration for my project.

back of the front door. You could probably install a mild late-model four cylinder in one without boxing the frame rails, but I would be hesitant even at that, as I prefer to box the frame rails the full length. By the time that you do this yourself or pay to have it done, you would have been better off purchasing a reproduction (or repop) chassis, saving you time and/or money. A repop chassis will also most likely have some other subtle modifications done that will allow you to run some bigger tires, sit lower, etc., without any additional cost, while each of those modifications will require more time or money when using an original frame.

On the other hand, a frame from a 1932 or newer Ford is substantially stronger in its original configuration, simply due to contour (bigger and heavier material was used) and stock crossmembers. As long as boxing plates are added to the engine mounting area, a healthy big block can be installed in one of these stock frames. Whatever type of frame you use, it must be straight and square. This does not mean that the frame rails must be parallel (straight) or that the crossmembers must be as long as the frame rails (square). Straight and square, in this case, are geometric terms meaning that the frame must not be bent, twisted, displaced, or otherwise damaged.

The frame does not have to be perfect to begin with. Any vehicle that is old enough to be considered a hot rod is nearing 60 years in age, so pristine condition is pretty much out of the question when discussing original frames. Minor frame damage can be repaired by an auto body shop that has frame straightening equipment. Before purchasing the frame you will just need to determine if the cost of straightening it is feasible. Sometimes it is, while other times it isn't.

It depends a lot on how well the reproduction aftermarket supports the particular frame in question.

After the frame is straight and square, it will most likely need reinforcing, such as with boxing plates in the engine mounting area (minimal reinforcement) or preferably the full length of the frame rails. It should be obvious that a blown big-block engine will require more reinforcing than a relatively stock four banger. The more torque the engine develops, the more twisting forces the frame must withstand. For this reason, a more substantial transmission crossmember (one that mounts in more than one place on each frame rail) will help to eliminate torque-related chassis flex. Even a fully boxed, reproduction Model A Ford frame can be twisted by two grown men if there is no transmission crossmember in place.

Reproduction
Unless you are an accomplished chassis quality welder, a reproduction frame might be money well spent even on a cheap hot rod project. The frame is literally the foundation of your hot rod, so you should not skimp here. If you have to cut something out of the budget, let it be on paint, upholstery, or wheels, but not on the frame and suspension components.

Custom
If you are an accomplished welder, have good fabrication skills, and have a way to maintain a square chassis during construction, you can design and build a purely custom chassis to meet your needs. The simple way to do this is to start with a set of bare frame rails and then add your own or prefabricated crossmembers. If you are building an early

This Speedway Motors chassis for its Track T kit is a combination of custom and reproduction chassis. It is custom in the fact that it is not OEM stock nor is it a repop thereof, though some might consider it a repop since it is reproduced on a small scale, rather than built from scrap tubing by some private individual in his or her garage. The main frame rails are contoured to fit the lower edge of the body, although they will be covered by fiberglass panels. A square tubing K-member ties the frame rails together in the middle and adds considerable strength. The vertical support will mount to the rear shocks and will also tie the back half of the frame rails together. The chassis being "kicked up" in the front allows the car to sit lower.

1930s Ford, this is a common practice, but for other hot rods, you might have to fabricate your own frame rails. Having an original frame that is at least good enough to use as a pattern will make this task much easier. Take lots of measurements, and then create a pattern that can be transferred to flat plate steel. After laying out the pattern on the flat plate, it can be cut out with a plasma arc cutter, cutting torch, or band saw.

The method that you use will have some bearing on how much additional work is required to make both frame rails match. If using a plasma arc cutter, a template can be followed, making duplication fairly easy as the plasma arc cutter makes a very precise cut. You can follow the same procedure with a cutting torch, but the metal will need some grinding or filing to smooth the relatively rough edge left by the cutting torch. A band saw will suffice, but the operator will have to follow a line that is marked on the flat stock, leaving it more susceptible to minor variations.

Repair

Chassis repair can vary from relatively minor to quite extensive, to perhaps the point of asking yourself why you even brought the frame home in the first place. Minor or extensive, many of the necessary repairs to a frame can be done by welding.

A common situation with almost any frame is that there are existing holes that you don't need. If the holes are small enough, you can simply fill them with weld, and then grind the welds flush with the surrounding frame. Holes larger than about a quarter inch in diameter should be filled by welding in a filler piece. This can be done by cutting off a slice of round bar stock that is reasonably close to the diameter of the hole. Cut the slice the same thickness as the frame where it will be welded. Clamp it in place and then finish welding it to the frame. After welding around the entire circumference, grind the weld flush.

Another common problem is a crack or tear in the frame. A tear is simply a crack that was never repaired. A crack can be repaired by filling it with weld if it is small, while a tear can be repaired by welding in a small piece of flat stock that has been shaped to fit the void.

It should be pointed out that extra holes or cracks and tears should probably be repaired after more serious collision damage is repaired. Not that it will really matter, but if for whatever reason you are unable to get the frame straight and square, all of the welding practice you gained filling holes will be just that . . . practice.

Collision Damage

To check your frame for collision damage, you need a flat floor, three jack stands, a tape measure, a level, and someone to hold the other end of the tape measure. Set one jack stand under each of the front frame horns and the third under the center of the rear crossmember. Yes, if you want to, you can put the two jack stands under the rear frame horns and the third under the center of the front crossmember. Either way, you should position the frame so that whichever end is on two jack stands is level side to side. (More about this in a minute.)

Now measure diagonally from a known point (such as a mounting hole or rivet) on the front of one rail to a known point on the back of the opposite frame rail. Record the measurement and then measure diagonally between the opposite sides from similar known points. If the measurements are the same, the frame is square and, conversely, if not the frame is not square. It is also a good idea to measure across smaller spans in a similar fashion to check for less obvious damage. That is, measure from the same points in the front to known points near the middle of the opposite frame rail. Then measure from the same known points in the back to known points near the middle. If after measuring in several places you find that the pairs of measurements match, you can be assured that the frame is straight and square.

Before removing the frame from the jack stands and with the frame level as mentioned previously, measure from the floor to similar points on the bottom of each frame rail. Different measurements between similar points and the floor indicate that the frame is twisted. If after using these methods of measuring you find that your frame is bent or twisted, you should enlist the help of an auto body shop that has frame straightening equipment to bring the frame back to specs.

One thing to keep in mind when measuring for twist is that the frame rail flange might be bent and is slightly higher or lower than the metal around it. Typically, the flanges of the frame rail will be at approximately 90 degrees from the frame rail web. If this is the case at one measuring point, but not at the same point on the opposite frame rail, it should be obvious that the damage is localized. If this is truly a localized situation, it can be corrected with judicious use of a Ford hammer (also know as a BFH—a "big Ford hammer," at least when the kids ask).

Rust Repair

Even if the frame for your hot rod is straight, if is covered in rust, it needs to be cleaned up before you can be sure that it is worthy for use under your hot rod. Unlike body sheet metal, most frames are made from substantially thicker metal, so rust through is not as common. That does not mean that it is non-existent, however. If the rust seems to be little more than surface rust, it can be cleaned off with an electric or pneumatic sander or grinder that has been fitted with a sanding disc. An 80-grit sanding disc should take off any surface rust without grinding into the frame and causing damage.

If it appears to be more than just surface rust, the frame should either be sandblasted or stripped with a chemical paint stripper. Sandblasting or media blasting works well on heavy-duty items such as frames, as they are typically thicker than easily damaged body sheet metal. Another benefit of a vehicle frame is that it usually does not trap the blasting media. Blasting media can easily be trapped between inner and outer panels of body sheet metal, often times causing problems later on.

If you choose to use a chemical stripper on your frame, you should do this before the frame is boxed. This is not so much of a problem if you are stripping the frame by hand, but if you have the frame dipped by a commercial stripper, the inside of the frame rails will be stripped also. Since you will not have any way to spray primer, much less paint on the inside of the boxed frame rails, they could begin rusting from the inside.

After cleaning the frame to the point of bare, or at least clean, metal, you can make an accurate assessment of the frame's condition. If there are portions of rust through, patch panels can be fabricated and welded in place. You must make sure, however, that the frame patch panels are similar in thickness to the frame.

After cleaning the frame and making any necessary repairs, the frame should be coated with epoxy primer to keep it from rusting again. Additional coats of epoxy primer, primer/surfacer, and sealer may need to be applied prior to painting, but a good coat of epoxy primer now will keep the frame from rusting in your garage during construction.

Modifications

Common modifications to the frame include kicking up (or "Z"-ing), narrowing, adding a more substantial transmission crossmember, or adding bolt-on running board brackets. A kickup or "Z" in the frame rails allows the front and/or back of the vehicle to sit lower. You can easily envision this if you consider the frame rails above the front or rear axle as the top horizontal portion of the "Z." The lower horizontal portion of the "Z" is the frame under the middle portion of the vehicle. The depth of the "Z" is frame material that must be added and can be whatever depth you choose, but must be the same from side to side. However, the amount of kickup does not have to be the same on the front as on the back, or vice-versa. Kicking the front up slightly more will give the vehicle more rake, thus a more aggressive stance.

Narrowing the frame is commonly done on pro-street vehicles to make room for extremely wide tires in the back. Just how much you narrow the rear frame rails is dependent upon what size tires you are planning to run. Even if you are only running a 7- or 8-inch-wide rear wheel, you may choose to narrow the rear portion of the frame in order to keep the larger than stock tires beneath the fenders.

Many transmission crossmembers are simply a tube that connects to each frame rail and passes beneath the transmission, serving as a mounting point. Typically, each end of the crossmember bolts to, or is welded at, the frame rail and has a removable center section to allow for transmission removal. To help minimize twisting of the frame due to high torque engines, the transmission crossmember can be designed to attach to the frame rails in as many points as possible. Fords manufactured in 1932, and later, utilized an X-member that greatly strengthened these frames.

A simple, but effective way to increase the strength of a basic transmission crossmember is to add a straight tube from side to side above the lower tranny mount tube, and tie both tubes together with a short tube running vertically between the two on each side of the transmission. The next step is to run a longer tube from the junction of the vertical tube and the upper tube to a point rearward at the frame rail (or to a point on another tube that connects both frame rails) on each side. Then run a long tube from the junction of the short vertical tube and the lower transmission mount tube to a point near the end of the previous bar that runs rearward on each side. This can easily be done with a tubing notcher, a welder, and some lengths of straight tubing. Just be sure to leave enough room to route the exhaust and driveshaft rearward beneath the vehicle.

Most American built cars featuring running boards utilized running board brackets that were riveted to the frame. In a perfect world, this would be okay. As we all know, however, we do not live in a perfect world. We may choose to remove the running board brackets while detailing the chassis, remove the running boards completely, or on occasion we may need to repair a running board or bracket due to a minor collision.

The metal that makes up the frame most likely isn't going to be thick enough to drill and tap in order to install a bolt-on bracket. If the frame has not yet been boxed, a backing plate made from 1/4- to 3/8-inch-thick steel plate can easily be welded to the inside of the frame rail. First, you must remove the rivets securing the running board brackets, either with a hammer and chisel or by drilling them out. Determine the necessary size and number of backing plates and cut them out from steel plate. Position each backing plate on the inside of the frame rail behind where the brackets were originally riveted on. Clamp and then tack weld them in place. Be sure to alternate side to side when welding to avoid building up excessive heat in any one spot. The backing plates do not require a weld bead around their entire circumference, but they should be more than tack welded when you are finished.

When all of the welding is completed, drill mounting holes through the original frame and the backing plate, using the rivet holes as a template. Now tap the holes for the particular bolts you are going to use for mounting the running boards. This modification may not do much to turn your project into a hot rod, but if you ever decide to remove the running boards and their brackets for any particular reason, this will make it much easier. This procedure is very useful if you are using saddle-mount fuel tanks that mount behind the splash aprons of a Model A Ford.

SUSPENSION

Hot rod suspensions could be the main subject for an entire book. The aftermarket covers this area very well, however, and catalogs and magazines will show you all the various options. For our purposes, I'll give an overview of the suspension that will be used in the Track T. The front suspension will be typical, in theory, of what is found on many contemporary hot rods, but with slightly different components used as a cost savings measure.

Most hot rods that use a dropped axle do not have anything welded to the axle. The brackets that secure the radius rods to the axle are usually held in place by the spring perch. This makes the front suspension a completely bolt-together assembly that requires no welding, thus user friendly to the weekend hot rodder. The Speedway Motors Track T kit uses a tube axle that comes with tabs welded onto it already for mounting the hairpin radius rods. This is easy enough for installation assembly, however, should the vehicle ever be involved in a front-end collision or any other event that might damage these mounting tabs, repair might be difficult.

Without passing further judgment, the front suspension consists of a tube axle that is located by hairpin radius rods and a transverse front spring. The spring perches for the latter are mounted to tabs welded to the axle, but are in a horizontal orientation rather than the common vertical positioning. This should eliminate the need for a Panhard rod, which is typically used to minimize the frame's lateral movement in relation to the axle through the use of a transverse leaf spring.

Conventional tube shocks will cushion the bumps. Spindles will be reproductions of 1949–1954 Chevrolet passenger car spindles. These will fit with an adaptor to use Ford Pinto rotors and disc brake calipers.

Mounting onto a 9-inch Ford rear axle housing longitudinally will be a set of quarter elliptic springs and essentially the upper half of a rear four-bar setup. The flat portion of the spring will be captured between a flat bracket that is already welded to the Track T chassis and two pieces of bar stock that are bolted to the flat bracket. The opposite end of the springs will be mounted to the axle housing with bolts. These bolts will be passed through brackets, which will need to be welded to the lower side of the axle housing. A bar with an adjustable Heim joint on each end will be bolted to the chassis ahead of the rear axle and to a tab that will be welded to the top of the axle. Conventional tube shocks will locate the rear axle vertically. Locating the rear axle housing laterally will be a Panhard rod that will mount to the frame on the driver side and the axle housing on the passenger side.

Assembling the Front Suspension

Whether you are telling a story or building a hot rod, the best place to start is usually at the beginning, so actual construction of the Track T will begin with the front suspension. The Speedway Motors assembly manual begins there as well. Assembly of the front suspension is fairly straightforward if you follow the assembly manual, however, being at least somewhat familiar with the components involved will make the process much simpler.

Rear Axle Housing

For a lightweight and modestly powered vehicle like this Track T, almost any rear-wheel-drive automotive rear axle would be sufficient. The important considerations are the correct axle width and suitable gear ratio.

Correct axle width is dependent largely upon the particular vehicle being built, and will also vary depending on whether you fit fenders, as well as on the rear offset on the wheels. For fendered vehicles, you must pay particular attention to the wheel and tire size, and provide sufficient room for the wheel and tire assembly within the fenders. Unless you are re-creating a hot rod from the 1960s, good taste dictates that the tires should not protrude beyond the fenders. Looking back at hot rods from that turbulent decade, it appears that contemporary good taste was certainly in its infancy back then, as many rods featured tires that protruded from beneath the fenders.

To determine the proper axle width, it is best to have the body (with fenders, if applicable) secured to the frame and resting safely on a set of jack stands. Then roll the mounted wheels and tires that you plan to use into their respective positions inside of the fenders or outside of the body on a fenderless car. Simply measure between the mounting surface of both wheels and you will have your required rear axle width.

With the frame supported on four jack stands, it was finally time to start wrenching pieces together. Although you may be inclined to build the car at its actual ride height, do yourself a favor and lift the jack stands to their maximum safe working height. At this point, we are much too early in the build process to be bending over that much. According to the Speedway Motors assembly manual, the transverse leaf spring is installed first. It is held in place by two U-bolts and four lock nuts. A locating pin in the spring stack fits into the hole seen in the mounting plate, which is already welded to the chassis.

Shackles are then mounted onto each end of the spring stack. The shackle consists of two shafts attached to a link. The link on the opposite side is removable (held in place by two lock nuts) so that the shafts can be inserted through the eye of the leaf spring and the spring perch. Nylon or urethane bushings fit over the shafts and work as a bearing surface. If you are not going to be installing the engine soon, you can simulate ride height by removing all but the main leaf from the spring stack. I chose to go ahead and keep all of the leaves in place.

Left: With the shackle already inserted through the end of the leaf spring, you need to insert the remaining bushings into the spring perch. The bushings are a slightly tighter fit in the perches than in the spring, so you may need to use a vise or a mallet to drive them into place. The perch on the left has the bushings at the start of installation, while the bushings are fully seated on the perch on right. **Right:** After installing the bushings, slide the remaining shaft of the shackle through the spring perch. Install the remaining link over the threaded portion of the two shafts of the shackle and then secure it with two lock nuts.

Well, it's almost that easy. You should allow at least 1 inch between the inner lip of a fender and the outer edge of the tire while the vehicle is at rest. You should also allow this amount or more clearance on the inside of the tire and any sheet metal. This may require installing wheel tubs or at least some metal massaging, depending on the size of the tires you are using. With fenderless vehicles, although you do not have to worry about fenders rubbing the outside of the tire, you must still provide at least 1 inch of clearance on the inside of the tire. Esthetically, you do not want a lot of space between the side of the body and the sidewall of the tire. Depending on how the rear suspension attaches to

The spring perch is what connects the spring to the front axle. On this particular axle, the spring perch attaches to a bracket in a horizontal orientation. This bracket is already welded to the axle and also serves as a mounting point for the hairpin radius rods via clevises and bolts. On many hot rods, nothing is welded to the axle, but a batwing is used to mount the hairpin radius rods or four-link. In this situation, a spring perch with a longer shaft passes through the upper batwing mount, through the axle boss, and then through the lower batwing mount.

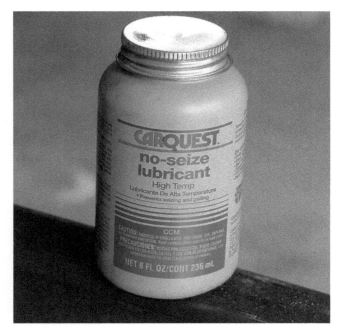

To help minimize galling or seizing of threaded fasteners, dab a bit of anti-seize lubricant onto the treaded portion of the fastener prior to assembly.

A Heim joint with jam nut is threaded into the closed end of the hairpin radius rod. The hairpin radius rods with the clevises and Heim joint need to be the same overall length on each side of the vehicle. They will be adjusted later for front end alignment, but do yourself a favor and make sure that they start out even. Rather than counting exposed threads of the clevises, verify that they are the same length by laying the hairpins (or four bars on a four-link setup) on top of each other and inserting a bolt through the corresponding holes for each side. With a bolt through both Heim joints, one through both upper clevises, and another through both lower clevises, rest assured that the hairpins are the same length.

Left: *This is the bracket that mounts the front spring to the front axle (controlling lateral movement) and mounts the hairpin radius rods to the axle (controlling longitudinal movement). For initial assembly, I threaded the upper and lower clevises into the hairpins slightly more than halfway. Threading the clevis inwards will shorten the hairpin, while threading it outwards will lengthen it. Adjustment of these clevises will affect caster. Shortening the upper or lengthening the lower will increase caster in the positive direction, which will cause the vertical axis of the kingpin to roll back at the top. This is essential to providing better straight-ahead steering and is what causes the wheels to naturally return to straight ahead after a turn.* **Right:** *This is the Heim joint connecting the back end of the (front) hairpin radius rod to the frame. Adjusting this Heim joint in or out will affect wheelbase, but will have no other bearing on front end alignment. However, if wheelbase is different from side to side, thrust angle alignment will be off, making the vehicle appear to be dog-tracking.*

These are the reproduction 1949–1954 Chevrolet spindles from Speedway Motors and their related hardware. Below the spindles are the kingpins that pass through both the upper and lower bosses of the spindle, with the axle in between the two. A kingpin also passes through a thrust bearing that is installed between the bottom of the axle and the top of the lower spindle boss. Also in the photo are bushings, which go into the upper and lower spindle bosses, and caps and retaining snap rings that keep the assembly together.

47

 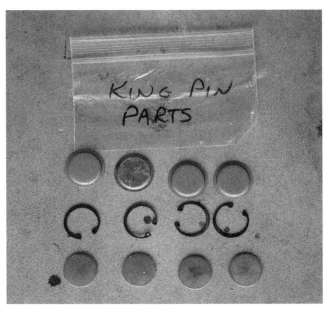

Left: This photo shows how the retaining snap ring secures the bushing in place. Special pliers are designed for easily installing or removing these snap rings. Difficult to see in the photo are the little round holes in the ends of the snap ring. Prongs in the snap ring pliers fit into these holes and easily open or close the rings.

Right: During preliminary assembly, I opted to leave out the caps and retaining springs. I promise you, however, that they were installed before the vehicle moved under its own power. In the meantime, these parts were stored in a plastic storage bag identified with a permanent marker. Obviously, the bag was clear so I should have been able to tell what was inside of it, but by the time I needed these parts, I might not have remembered where they belonged.

The next step is to install the spindle, thrust bearing, and kingpins. Install the upper and lower bushings in the spindle. Remember to position the thrust bearing under the axle boss. You will need to align all of the openings in these parts before installing the kingpin. Refrain from using a hammer to move the thrust bearing. Secure the spindle and thrust bearing to the axle by driving the kingpin in from the top after applying a thin film of grease. Do not hammer the kingpin directly, and instead use a brass drift between the hammer and kingpin. If you have used or worn parts, you may need to use shims to eliminate vertical play. On all new repop parts, you will most likely be wishing that you had a little bit of slop before getting both kingpins installed.

the rear axle, this may necessitate a wider rear axle simply to have room to mount the radius rods to the axle between the backing plate and the body.

A suitable gear ratio is dependent upon the engine's normal operating rpm, the rear tire's outer diameter, and your style of driving. Assuming a 1:1 final drive gear ratio, the following formulas can be used to determine engine rpm, miles per hour (mph), rear end gear ratio, or tire diameter. As long as you know any three of these four variables, you can determine the fourth by using the appropriate formula.

Left: The Vega steering box mounts to a gusset on the left side frame rail with three bolts. Insert the three bolts through the gusset, and then slide a spacer over each bolt on the inside of the gusset. *Right:* The ears of the Vega steering box (in this case a reproduction unit from Flaming River) are threaded. Hold the steering box in place and tighten the three mounting bolts.

The pitman arm is what connects the steering box to the drag link. The end with large spline hole connects to the steering box and is tapered so it only fits one way. However, both the steering box output shaft and the spline of the pitman arm contain four indexing marks so that the two components can be aligned properly.

rpm = (mph x rear end gear ratio x 336) divided by tire diameter

mph = (rpm x tire diameter) divided by (rear end gear ratio x 336)

Rear end gear ratio = (rpm x tire diameter) divided by (mph x 336)

Tire diameter = (mph x rear end gear ratio x 336) divided by rpm

Used

Knowing the ideal rear end width and armed with a tape measure, you should be able to find a usable rear axle housing during a trip to your favorite salvage yard. If you find a rear axle housing that is the appropriate width, you should give it a thorough inspection for obvious damage (dents, gaping holes, leaking fluid, or obvious bent axles). Minor dents in the housing can be repaired with some body filler, if they are indeed minor. Gaping holes or other significant damage, such as an obviously bent housing, that may have occurred in a collision should be a warning to pass on that one. If fluid is leaking, you will need to find its source. If it is coming from the ends of the axles, it likely needs new bearings and seals. If the fluid is coming from around the third member, the cause of the leak may be more substantial than what you care to undertake, depending on your budget or mechanical expertise.

Check the rear end fluid to make sure that it doesn't appear to be burnt and is not full of metal shavings. You will replace the fluid anyway, but burnt fluid or metal shavings may indicate a problem that is best avoided, especially when you are working with a limited budget.

Most likely, some or all of the existing suspension brackets will need to be removed for use on your hot rod. Some work with a cutting torch or grinder should take care of this. You will also need to check the wheel bolt pattern. If it matches the wheels that you plan to use, you are in luck. Otherwise a competent machinist can re-drill the axles and install new wheel studs if necessary.

If the newfound rear axle housing passes your inspection criteria, your next step will be to determine its gear ratio. You won't want to install a rear end with real low gears (numerically higher) if you are planning on long drives, or one with real high (numerically lower) gears if most of your driving is going to be around town. Depending on your particular situation, you can have different gears installed or, if it is too good of a deal to pass up, change the rear tire size to dial in the performance of the rear end. Refer to the equations given previously to determine more suitable gear ratios or tire diameters.

You may be able to determine the gear ratio from vehicle info found on the door tag or glove box sticker, but not always. If all else fails, you can open up the differential and count the teeth on the pinion gear and the ring gear. How you gain access to the gears will differ depending on the housing, but should be easy enough to figure out after close examination. On a General Motors or Mopar rear end, you can usually remove the rear cover to gain adequate access for inspecting the gears by removing a number of nuts from the bolts or studs that secure the rear plate to the housing. On a Ford rear end, you must pull the axles out of the axle housing before you can remove a number of bolts and pull the third member out the front of the rear axle housing.

After you have gained observation access to both the pinion and the ring gears, place a spot of paint or other distinguishing mark on one tooth of each gear, and then count the number of teeth. The ring gear (the gear that rotates on the same plane as the rear tires) will have between 30 and 50 teeth, while the pinion (the gear that rotates on the same plane as the driveshaft) will have between 8 and 16 teeth. Since the gears are used in matched sets, the number of teeth will vary from one set to another. Divide the number of ring gear teeth by the number of pinion gear teeth and you will have the gear ratio. For example, 37 ring gear teeth and 10 pinion gear teeth results in a gear ratio of 3.70:1.

Depending on what you are looking for and the supply in your locale, you can probably locate an acceptable rear end housing for $200 to $300 or less. A number of years ago, I purchased a complete Ford 8-inch rear end, which was the correct width for the Model A Ford that I was building, for the paltry sum of $75. Although less desirable than the larger and stronger 9-inch Ford housing, the 8-inch Ford housing is now getting scarce and therefore more expensive.

For this Track T, I used a 9-inch Ford housing, even though it was overkill. I had purchased the housing, third member, and axles (no gears) for $100, earmarking the 9-inch housing for use in another project. The Track T project presented itself and the 9-inch was available, so it became part of this project. For a new set of gears and drum brakes, I took the collection of parts to Danny Miller's Rear Gears. Danny and his crew also verified the housing was straight and installed new bearings and wheels studs while it was there.

New

You can purchase a new or reconditioned axle housing as easily as making a telephone call. A number of companies, including Danny Miller's Rear Gears, can build a rear axle assembly to meet your specs. Before you order, you will need to know exactly what width, what gears, and what brakes you plan to use. Rear ends involve a lengthy list of other specs that may or may not matter to you. Although you will be able to have exactly what you want, having a rear axle housing, gears, axle, and brakes custom-built to your specifications can be expensive.

WHEELS AND TIRES

You already have a good idea of the look you want from your wheels and tires. You may already have lined them up. If not, you can buy new items in many sizes and styles from the aftermarket. In addition, wheels and tires are widely available used, from wrecking yards, individual sellers and at big gatherings like swap meets.

Most swap meets have many vendors selling wheels. Often the wheels will have decent tires on them already. It has always been my practice to spend a little extra money when it comes to safety related items, such as tires and brakes, and scrimp if necessary on items such as wheels. If you find a set of wheels that you like with the correct size (diameter, width, backspacing, and bolt pattern), make your deal as if you are buying only the wheels and spend accordingly. If good tires are included as part of the bargain, that is a bonus.

Buying used tires (without wheels) simply doesn't make much sense to me, as you have no clue what condition the tires are really in or how many miles they have on them. I did purchase tires once from someone who decided they weren't what he really wanted. Although there was no warranty, those tires still had new tire stickers on them, it was evident that they had never been mounted on a wheel,

and the price was right for a set of tires that had gone out of production.

Unless you are looking for a specific type of vintage tire—such as grooved dirt track tires or cheater slicks—new tires (with a warranty) are as close as the corner tire store. And now, even vintage styles of tires are available from Coker Tire and other companies that cater to restoration buffs.

For this cheap hot rod project, I chose to run a set of steelies. A number of factors played a role in this decision. First, steelies are typically less expensive than comparable size aluminum wheels. This allowed me to purchase new wheels without breaking the bank, rather than spending a lot of time searching for a complete set of wheels (in the appropriate size) at the salvage yard or at swap meets. Secondly, no aluminum wheels on the market seemed appropriate for the nostalgic styling of a Track T, except perhaps a set of Kelsey-Hayes wires or a set of vintage Halibrands. A quick-change rear end, along with a set of Sprints from Halibrand, would be very appropriate for the car, but beyond the budget. Keep in mind that wheels are a comparatively easy change to make. If you get yourself on the road with a cost effective wheel to start, you can always upgrade it later.

Priming and Painting Wheels

Although I am a firm believer that components on a hot rod project should not be painted until after all parts have been assembled and their proper fit and operation have

These wheels that were used on the Track T are coated in gray primer just as they came from Coker Tire. They are 15x5 Smoothies for the front, and 15x7 Smoothies for the back. Before painting, the wheels need to be scuffed with 400-grit wet or dry sandpaper, and then cleaned with wax and grease remover.

been verified, wheels are the exception. Using anything other than the actual wheels and tires that you plan to use when the vehicle is completed during the critical fitment stages is merely asking for troubles later. This is not to say that you cannot use old wheels and tires to make the project mobile during construction, but substitutes should be avoided when you are determining how everything is supposed to fit together.

For all of the above reasons, I chose to go ahead and paint the wheels for this project so that the tires could be mounted and balanced. I could have mounted the tires before painting the wheels, but that would require dismounting the tires later to paint, and then remounting them. If this were a simple task that could be easily accomplished with ordinary hand tools, it wouldn't be a concern. However, I don't have a tire changer . . . and chances are that you don't either. The going rate in my area for having tires mounted or dismounted is about $10 a tire, so I chose to pay only once. After all, less money spent for tasks such as this leaves more for actual parts.

The wheels of my choosing for this project are steel Vintique Smoothies, purchased through Coker Tire. They are available in a primered finish for you to paint, or powder coated in your choice of colors for an additional charge. I chose the primered wheels as I intended to paint the wheels the same color as the scallops that would accent the body.

Since the wheels were already primered, there was no reason to prime them again, but the primer should be scuffed with 200-grit wet or dry sandpaper to provide good topcoat adhesion. If the wheels had not been primered, applying two or three coats of epoxy primer would be a prudent practice.

No doubt, most professional painters (if truthful) will tell you that painting wheels is a pain. If you hang the wheels to provide simultaneous access to the inside and outside, the wire used to hang the wheels will undoubtedly touch the wheel somewhere and leave a bare spot in the process. To avoid this, I sit the wheels flat when painting, but I do not put them directly on the floor. To keep from painting the wheels to the floor, I sit each wheel on a quart or gallon paint can, depending on the size of the wheel. I position the wheels far enough apart to provide access all the way around them and paint the backside first. This allows initial errors to be limited to the backside, rather than in plain view on the front.

With the primer scuffed, I clean the wheels once again with wax and grease remover, use an air nozzle to blow away loose dust, and then tack them off with a tack cloth. I then mix the paint, hardener, and reducer per the mixing instructions, using a calibrated mixing cup. To start, I mix

the components to provide a quart of sprayable material. For this project, it took about a quart and a half, total, to do all four wheels.

Using a high volume, low pressure (HVLP) spray gun, spray the inner lip first, then the inner face, and finally the inside portion of the wheel that will ultimately be covered by the tire. Spraying the edges first helps to prevent overspray from the face surfaces. After applying two coats to all four wheels (allowing proper flash time between coats), the wheels can be flipped over after waiting the proper drying time. Painting the wheels in this flat position takes additional time, but it's easier than hanging them. Using the same procedures as on the back, three coats of paint can be applied to the front of the wheels.

Although wheels can certainly be painted with a conventional siphon-feed spray gun, a gravity-feed spray gun (with the paint cup located on top) sure seems to be easier to maneuver around wheels. An alternative to a gravity-feed spray gun would be a detail or "jamb" gun, as the entire spray gun is smaller, thus easier to maneuver within the limited confines of a wheel. In an ideal world, you can use an HVLP spray gun for all of your painting. Overspray is greatly reduced, minimizing wasted paint. Another benefit is that without the cloud of overspray, it is easier to see what you are doing. A third benefit is that less atomized spray is in the air getting into your lungs and those of others.

After the paint has been sprayed and you are waiting for it to dry before applying clear, use your time wisely by thoroughly cleaning your spray gun. Disconnect the air hose from the spray gun and pour any unused paint into a container suitable for proper disposal (consult your local paint retailer for proper disposal recommendations). Pour some reducer (suitable for the paint being used) into the spray gun cup, swish it around, reconnect the air hose, and then spray all of the reducer through the nozzle. If any paint is still coming out of the nozzle, pour more reducer into the spray gun cup and repeat the process until nothing but reducer exits the spray gun nozzle, ensuring that all of the nozzle passages have been cleaned. Then disconnect the air hose and clean the inside and outside of the spray gun cup and any other surfaces with a cloth, or paper towel, moistened with reducer. (Wear rubber gloves when handling a rag with solvent on it.) Now reconnect the air hose and blow some air through the entire spray gun again to eliminate any reducer that may be lingering in the nozzle passages.

After you have reassembled your spray gun and paint has dried per the instructions, you can now apply clear if desired. Mix the clear and hardener per the mixing instructions, re-adjust the spray gun if necessary, and flip the wheels back over so that the inner sides are exposed.

To avoid the possibility of having a hanging wire causing a bare spot where it would touch the wheel, I chose to paint the wheels on the floor. To avoid being painted to the floor, they are sitting atop discarded paint cans. This way takes a little longer to paint, but eliminates the need for touchup.

To match the interior kit swatch from Speedway Motors, I chose PPG Ford Toreador Red under hood color (DCC29343). The exterior color by this name is very red, while the under hood color is a rich chocolate brown. The engine and scallops on the hood and hood sides will be this same color.

The under hood color was flat by design, but was followed up with Omni SV 4+1 urethane clear for durability. As I recall, I applied four coats of clear.

Today's paint products are safe to use, *if* you follow the safety precautions. I purchased a pair of machine washable painter coveralls and a head sock to go along with my half mask and safety glasses. At less than a hundred bucks, this safety equipment is certainly worth several times the price.

RATTLE CAN VERSUS AUTOMOTIVE PAINT VERSUS POWDER COATING

Most parts and components of a hot rod can be painted with an aerosol can or with a spray gun, while some components, such as wheels, can be powder coated to add color. Each method has its pros and cons, and just like most of life's decisions, budget plays a part in determining which to choose. Of course, if the body is fiberglass, the wheels aluminum, and the chassis constructed from some "rust-free" material, you may not have to paint anything.

To paint a set of wheels purely on the cheap, you can pick up some spray cans (a.k.a. rattle cans, spray bombs, spray paint) from your local hardware, discount, or even grocery store. For the widest selection of colors and the best price per can, you will have the best luck at your local discount department store such as Wal-Mart, K-Mart, or other such retailer. You should probably allow one and a half cans of paint for each wheel, so six cans should do it. If you paint the wheels before the tires are mounted and follow the same paint preparation steps given for using automotive paint, you can get pretty decent results. The main drawback to using a rattle can is that you may not be able to obtain an exact match to the paint that you are using on the rest of the vehicle, but steel wheels are not usually painted the same color as the car anyway. Another problem is the possibility of runs or excessive overspray, but you could easily have either using automotive paint. Depending on where you shop, you can probably paint a set of wheels with a rattle can for less than $20. The result may not be perfect, but if you keep the car moving down the road, who will be able to tell?

Perhaps a better, but certainly more expensive, choice is to use automotive paint and a spray gun to paint the wheels, as described previously. This method allows a far greater variety of colors (useful for complementing or matching other paint on the vehicle). Another benefit is that you can gain some practice prepping and painting before actually spraying the body of the car. Depending on your choice of color, the materials to paint and clear a set of wheels will most likely cost between $50 and $150.

Powder coating will give wheels a more durable finish than any kind of paint, but it comes with a price. Although powder coating is available in more colors than just a few short years ago, it is still not as varied as paint. Having your wheels prepped and powder coated will average between $40 and $75 per wheel, depending on where you have the work done. You can do powder coating at home, but the equipment necessary to do it makes it impractical, unless you plan to get into it professionally or at least as a sideline. If you cannot do the work yourself, you also have to factor in the time involved to have this done. This may or may not make a difference to you, but for a truly budget hot rod, the $160 to $300 spent for powder coating could go quite a ways toward parts. Of course, that is a decision for you to make.

If you have never sprayed clear before, you will quickly find that it is different from spraying paint because it's harder to see where you have or haven't sprayed. Make sure you have good light before you start. Allowing the proper flash time between coats (as per the clear's instructions), apply three or four coats of clear to the backside of the wheels. After proper drying time, flip the wheels over and then apply four coats of clear as before.

While you are waiting for the clear to dry, clean your spray gun again, and then wait the appropriate sanding time before wet sanding the clear using 400-grit wet or dry sandpaper. Pour a small amount of dishwashing liquid into a bucket of water and let the sandpaper soak for about 15 minutes before you begin sanding. Keeping the sandpaper wet at all times, use light pressure and move the sandpaper in a circular motion to bring the clear to a smooth finish. If you would like to make the wheels look better, you can use 800-grit and then 1200-grit sandpaper to wet-sand the clear. Just make sure that you keep the sandpaper wet, use a light touch, and don't sand into the color coat.

MOUNTING AND BALANCING TIRES

A benefit I enjoyed at my former job as a technical writer for Hunter Engineering was that I could mount and balance wheels and tires, as well as align vehicles at will in the name of gaining product knowledge. I no longer have that option so, to mount my new tires on my freshly painted wheels, I contacted Scott Bullock at Showcase Custom Automotive. Showcase sells and installs lowering kits for sport trucks, lift kits for off-road vehicles, and custom wheels for everything. If its employees can mount high dollar, large diameter, low profile tires, they can certainly handle my steel wheels and highly flexible sidewall tires.

55

After mounting each tire and wheel, Scott balanced each assembly, using the static plane setting on the balancer so that all of the weights would be positioned on the inside of the wheel. This will be great for appearance sake, as clip-on weights are ugly. However, if this balancing does not prove to be suitable when the vehicle is on the road, you can have a dynamic balance performed on it, even though it will cause some balance correcting weights to be placed on the outside of the wheel. On a vehicle this light (estimated to be around 1,800 pounds when completed), out of balance wheels will be more pronounced than on a larger, heavier vehicle. For this same reason, lighter wheels in general would provide a better ride, but for this project, aluminum wheels are out of the budget.

ASSEMBLING THE REAR SUSPENSION

Unlike the bolt-in front suspension I chose, the rear suspension requires some tabs to be welded to the rear axle housing. I personally don't possess the welding experience to feel comfortable doing chassis quality welding, so I arranged with Donnie Karg at Karg's Hot Rod Service to have this work done by a professional.

The Speedway Motors Track T kit is designed to use rear leaf springs from a Ford Pinto or similar vehicle. Realizing the rarity of those vehicles, I purchased a new set of replacement springs through Summit Racing. Whether new or used, for this suspension design, you will need to cut the springs and only use a portion of them. The unused portions can be discarded or used as a flyswatter.

Take the cut end of the spring and sandwich it in between a clamp, which is secured by four bolts to a plate already welded to the chassis. The eye of the spring will fit between two tabs that must be welded to the rear axle housing. The Speedway Motors Track T assembly manual provides the dimension to which you should cut the spring (22 inches from the center of the eye in this case). Before you cut any of them, though, verify the dimension by measuring between the spring's mounting plate on the chassis and the rear axle location. Remember to double-check all measurements before cutting anything. This is good advice

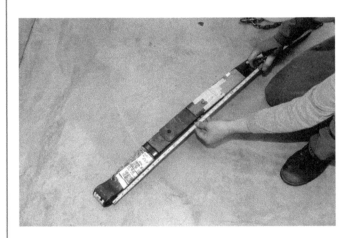

The rear springs must be cut essentially in half to create the quarter elliptic springs that will suspend the rear axle. Donnie Karg at Karg's Hot Rod Service measures the prescribed distance.

After measuring both springs and marking them, Donnie cuts them to length using this industrial duty band saw. Having the correct tools makes any job much easier and more fun, which is what hot rods are all about.

To eliminate any problems, the cut ends of the spring pack are sanded smooth on this belt sander.

For the springs to fit beneath the chassis bracket properly, you need to remove the centering pin and reinstall it from the opposite side. Before removing the nut from the bolt that holds the springs together, make sure that you clamp the springs together with a welding clamp.

for any building project, and is especially true when parts and components are from a wide variety of sources.

Before installing the rear springs, secure two rear axle mounting tabs to each spring by passing the appropriate bolt through one tab, the spring eye, and the other tab, and then secure it with a nut. Now, tighten the nut just enough to keep the tabs from spinning on the bolt.

If not done already, the chassis should be securely supported on jack stands and sitting level, both laterally and longitudinally. If necessary, use shims between the jack stands and the frame to obtain a level position. If the front end is supported by the front wheels and tires, the frame won't be level longitudinally, which is okay, but it must be level side to side.

SETTING THE PINION ANGLE

With the wheels and tires mounted, the rear axle housing can be rolled into position beneath the chassis and

With the springs securely clamped together, the nut securing the centering pin can be removed. It may be necessary to tap the centering pin a couple of times to remove it from the spring pack.

Remove the centering pin and reinstall it so that the pin portion is at the top of the spring arch. Then reinstall the nut before removing the welding clamp or other clamping mechanism.

Below: The rear axle mounting tabs are mounted to each spring with the hardware included in the spring mounting kit. The bolt and nut should be tightened just enough to keep the mounting tabs from spinning.

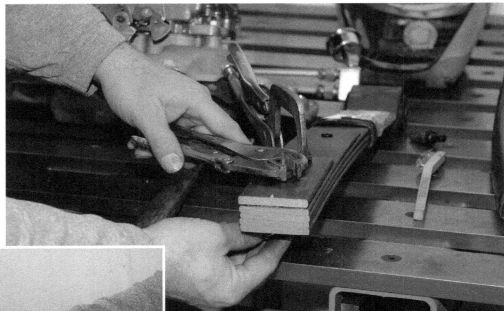

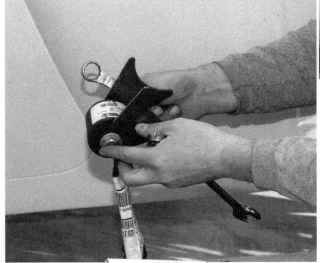

centered side to side. Use a jack stand to support the pinion at the correct height to achieve the correct pinion angle with respect to the engine and transmission. If the engine and transmission are already mounted, the pinion of the rear axle housing must be at a specific angle to match the output shaft of the transmission. For example, if the tranny output shaft is pointing down 3 degrees (from level), the rear axle pinion would need to be pointing up 3 degrees (again from level), making the output shaft and pinion parallel. Note that 2 to 4 degrees from level is common for

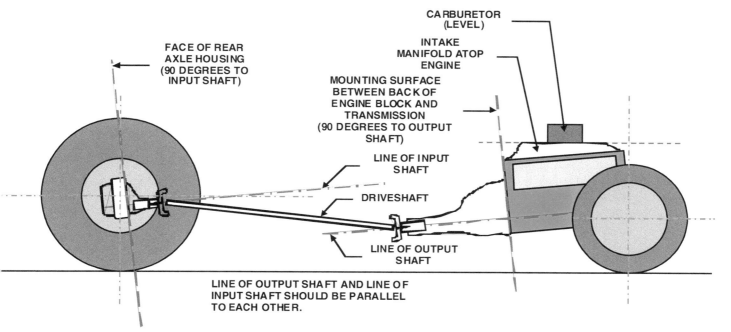

FACE OF REAR
AXLE HOUSING
(90 DEGREES TO
INPUT SHAFT)

CARBURETOR
(LEVEL)

INTAKE
MANIFOLD ATOP
ENGINE

MOUNTING SURFACE
BETWEEN BACK OF
ENGINE BLOCK AND
TRANSMISSION
(90 DEGREES TO OUTPUT
SHAFT)

LINE OF INPUT
SHAFT

DRIVESHAFT

LINE OF OUTPUT
SHAFT

LINE OF OUTPUT SHAFT AND LINE OF
INPUT SHAFT SHOULD BE PARALLEL
TO EACH OTHER.

Above: *It should be obvious that this sketch is not to scale and is quite exaggerated, simply to make the concept easier to grasp. Note that the pinion "input" shaft and transmission "output" are parallel. Also note that the front universal joint on the driveshaft may be higher or lower than the universal joint at the back.*

Left: *The square end of the spring is positioned beneath the spring plate so that the centering pin slips into a hole in the middle of the mounting plate.*

street driven vehicles, while a larger angle is necessary for some vehicles and a smaller angle is required for others. Keep in mind that hot rods typically have larger tires in the back than in the front. This "rubber rake" (difference in front and rear tire diameters) also comes into play when setting the pinion angle.

Since the engine and transmission have not yet been installed in this project vehicle, it is necessary to reverse engineer the setting of the pinion angle. This is one of those situations where experience and common sense are both

important. It is not that difficult, but you must be thinking about what you are doing in order to get it right.

For proper fuel delivery and ultimate performance, the carburetor(s) should be sitting level while the vehicle is sitting on a level surface. Of course the engine keeps running while you are driving uphill or downhill, but when you are setting the motor mounts or the rear axle pinion angle, you should set the carburetor at level. By using an angle finder, you can determine the relationship between the mounting surface of the intake manifold (on which the carburetor mounts) and the output shaft of the transmission, if the latter is mounted to the engine. These will be roughly parallel, but should differ by less than 5 degrees. If the transmission is not mounted to the engine, you can determine the relationship of the aforementioned intake manifold and the surface of the rear of the engine to which the transmission attaches. These measurements will be roughly 90 degrees different, so make sure you add or subtract properly to determine what the output shaft angle is in relation to the intake manifold. Making a simple sketch may make it easier to double-check your accuracy in taking these measurements and recording them. The output shaft from the engine/transmission should be parallel to the pinion shaft (input) and to the rear axle housing.

By studying the diagram on page 59, you should be able to determine the proper pinion angle setting, even if the transmission or rear axle third member is not installed. From high school geometry, we know that if the output and input shafts are parallel, then the back of the engine block and the face of the rear axle housing must also be parallel. Therefore we can set the rear end as long as we know the engine's final position.

With the rear axle housing roughly in place and the pinion supported in the approximate location, bolt the shortened springs onto the mounting bracket that is part of the chassis. The length of the springs will determine the longitudinal location of the rear axle housing. Rotate the spring mounting tabs so that the axle rests in the concave portion of the tabs. An imaginary line through the center of the axle and the

center of the spring eye should be completely vertical. Measure from a point on the chassis to a point on the axle backing plate (or wheel rim if the wheels are mounted) and compare this measurement with others between the same points on the opposite side of the car. This will verify if the rear axle housing is centered side to side. Keep measuring and making slight adjustments until it is correct. It is also necessary to measure a known point on the chassis to both ends of the axle to verify that the rear axle housing is square with the chassis. When the rear axle housing is centered side to side and is square with the chassis, and the pinion angle is correct, you can tack weld the spring mounting tabs to the rear axle housing. Note that if the axle tubes are tapered, or stepped, the spring mounting tabs may need to be modified slightly to achieve a proper fit with the axle housing.

Now that the spring tabs are tacked in place on the rear axle housing, it would be a good time to set the body in place. This will verify that the rear axle housing (and therefore the wheels and tires) is centered in the wheelwell. It will also give you the opportunity to determine how much of the axle is available for mounting the rear radius rods.

To mount the rear radius rods to the chassis at their forward point, insert a long bolt through a Heim joint that has been threaded into the end of the radius rod. Pass the long bolt through a boss in the frame rail and then secure it with a locking nut. At the back, pass a bolt through a mounting tab from the inside, through a Heim joint that has been threaded into the radius rod, and then

Instead of trying to hold the spring and the clamp securing that spring to the mounting plate while installing the nuts and bolts, work smarter by clamping the spring to the mounting plate with a pair of locking pliers (e.g. Vise-Grips).

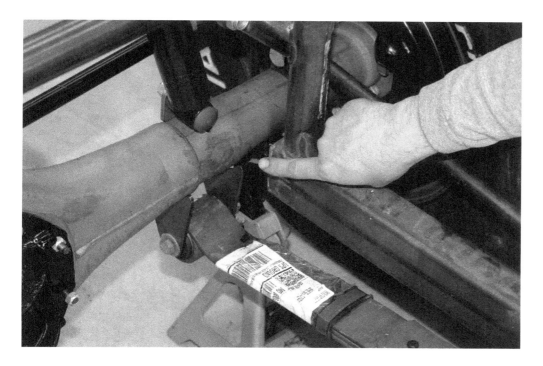

With each rear spring clamped into place, the rear axle housing can be moved into position. The springs will determine its location front to back, while it will still need to be centered side to side before any welding is done. Donnie points out that although the spring eye tabs are the same size, the axle actually necks down between the two tabs, resulting in a larger gap on the one tab. To achieve a proper fit, the tab that mounts to the larger portion of the rear axle housing must be ground down some.

Secure the spring to the mounting plate by passing down four bolts through the mounting plate beside the spring, and then through one of two tie plates (one sitting on the top of the frame rail and the other upon the spring in this photo).

secure it with a locking nut. Although it may seem natural that the radius rods should be parallel with the frame rails, on this particular vehicle, however, the body will not fit down over the axle unless the radius rods are mounted farther out on the axle housing. Be sure to mount the radius rods far enough away from the backing plate so that you can actually connect the brake line to the backing plate or caliper. You can mark the location for the radius rod mounting tabs on the axle, remove the body,

and then weld the mounting tabs in place, or you can weld the tabs in place while the body is in place. Most likely, it will be easier to remove the body rather than attempting to weld around it. For this same reason, it may be easier to support the chassis on jack stands and remove the rear wheels and tires, too, before final welding of the rear suspension. You can slightly adjust the pinion angle by threading the Heim joints in or out to change the length of the radius rods.

continued on page 64

Thread nuts onto each of the four bolts and then tighten them, securing the spring in place. Be sure to use some type of self-locking nuts for this application.

Be sure that the nuts are tightened evenly and securely. Another reason for using the locking pliers is that it allows the nuts to be tightened completely.

Before any welding can be done, the rear axle housing must be centered side to side. Most rodders know that the differential of a stock Ford housing is not centered (i.e., not in the middle of the overall width), however, it may be if the housing has been narrowed. In either case, the axle housing needs to be centered in the vehicle so that the left wheel is the same distance from the body as the right wheel. Remember to measure twice and weld once.

Careful measuring between a known point on the vehicle chassis and the brake backing plate and the corresponding locations on the opposite side is required to get the axle housing centered. Move the axle housing as needed until the measurements are the same on both sides. With the axle housing centered side to side, it also needs to be positioned so that the pinion angle is correct. To do this correctly, it is essential that the chassis is level side to side; otherwise, you will get bogus readings from your angle measuring device.

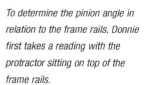

To determine the pinion angle in relation to the frame rails, Donnie first takes a reading with the protractor sitting on top of the frame rails.

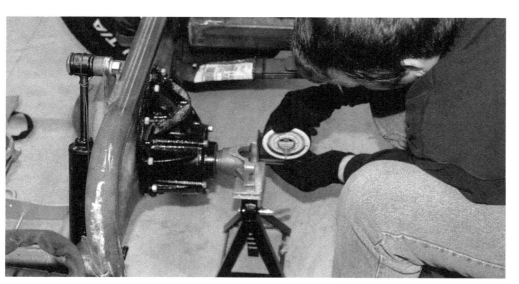

Donnie then measures the angle at the front of the pinion shaft. The difference in this measurement and the one taken previously provides the angle between the frame rails and the rear axle.

Left: Not very obvious in this photo is a tape measure. It is important to measure from a similar point on each side when locating the suspension brackets. Donnie uses the wheel rim as a standard reference point for locating the radius rods and the shocks. Right: It is also easier to locate the suspension brackets if the chassis is sitting level. In this case, a level spanning both sides of the chassis' horizontal hoop also serves as a reference point when measuring.

As Donnie says, "We build hot rods a quarter inch at a time." You have to determine how moving the location of one component will affect another component. Measure everything twice before welding it in place.

continued from page 61

Mounting tabs for the rear shocks are already welded in place on the rear vertical hoop on the chassis. You should secure the shocks to these mounting tabs with the supplied bolts and locking nuts. Then secure the shocks to the lower mounting tabs using similar hardware, and weld those tabs to the rear axle housing. The shocks should be mounted so that they expand and contract in a true vertical motion (perpendicular to the mounting studs) when viewed from the side, and should be between 30 and 45 degrees from vertical when viewed from the front or back. Note that some vehicles have shocks that are not mounted in a vertical position, but are mounted perpendicular to their shock mounts, as binding during shock travel will result in shock failure. The shocks should be mounted so that they are the same distance from each end (rather than the center) of the rear axle housing. This will not be an issue, unless you are using a non-centered Ford rear axle housing.

Donnie measures one more time, just to double check that the shock mount is in the right place.

The suspension brackets can now be welded in place. MIG welding is adequate, but Donnie is using TIG welding, which is better. No matter what type of welding is used, be sure the welder is competent.

Everyone knows to use a welding helmet or goggles when welding, but many don't wear long sleeve shirts. Be sure to wear the necessary protective clothing when working in the shop.

65

The rear shock brackets are almost welded in place. Be sure to skip around from the shock brackets, to the radius rod mounts, and from side to side to minimize any detrimental heat buildup.

The Panhard rod was too long for our application originally. After determining a suitable location for the axle mount for the Panhard rod, the necessary amount was cut from the rod, using a metal cutting band saw.

This shot of the rear suspension shows that there are several components situated in a fairly confined area. A radius rod mount, a rear spring mount, and a shock mount were welded to each side of the rear axle housing.

Okay, we admit we goofed, but that happens. A close look at this photo will reveal that the rear radius rod mount has been moved outward on the axle. This was done to clear the body—a point that wasn't considered when the radius rod was mounted originally. I'm just glad that I didn't have the rear axle housing narrowed.

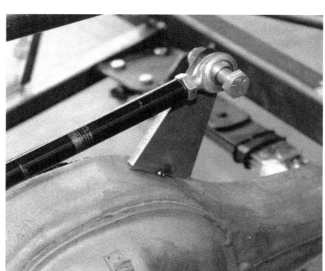

Left: With the Panhard rod shortened, the axle mounting bracket could be welded into place. *Right:* No matter how many hot rods you have built, it is always a good idea to simply tack weld components in place, then double check how their location affects anything else, before doing final welding. Tack welds are much easier to undo than final welds.

To secure the frame end of the rear Panhard rod to a mounting tab on the rear horizontal hoop of the chassis, pass a bolt through a Heim joint that is threaded into the Panhard rod. Also pass this bolt through the mounting tab, and then secure it with a locking nut. Mount the opposite end of the Panhard rod to a large tab in the same fashion. Then weld that tab to the rear axle housing. Adjusting the Panhard rod (by threading the Heim joints in or out) will move the chassis in relation to the rear axle housing.

Lengthening the Panhard rod will move the rear axle housing toward the passenger side, while shortening it will move the rear axle housing toward the driver side, assuming that the frame mount is on the driver side of the frame. I hope this is clear for my foreign hot rodder friends.

BRAKES

No doubt about it, good brakes are essential on a hot rod. Fortunately, brakes are fairly easy to install. If you are not

Above: Although it looks somewhat funky without the nose in position, the Track T has hit a significant milestone by just having the body in place. *Below:* This is what the rear suspension looks like in relation to the body. Certainly not lots of extra room. Eventually, the floor and a rear bulkhead will be 'glassed into position.

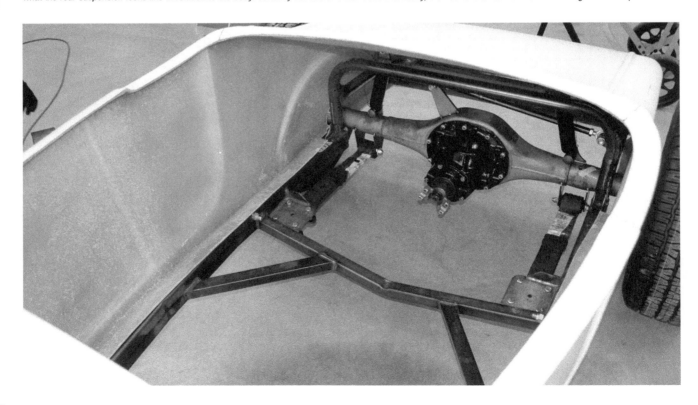

This is what the spindle, steering arm, and brake caliper assembly looks like from the front. The hole in the caliper mounting bracket adaptor is threaded, so the bolt that secures it to the spindle does not require a nut. This does require the bolt to be inserted through the spindle first and then into the bracket adaptor. The spindle is not threaded, so the bolt that secures it and the steering arm together does require a nut.

familiar with the particular brakes that you are installing, however, it would be worth your time and money to purchase a repair manual that describes their assembly and adjustment. You will find that the instructions included with replacement brake pads typically don't do much to inform you of how the calipers, rotors, and spindles all fit together.

Installing Front Brakes

Unless you are building a period perfect hot rod from the 1930s or 1940s, it only makes sense to run disc brakes on the front, rather than drum brakes. Since you are reading this book, it's safe to presume that you are building a hot rod to drive, not to polish and stare at, which is all the more reason to run disc brakes in the front. I personally prefer four-wheel disc brakes, but rear drums are a little less expensive.

With a little brake installment experience or a quality repair manual, installing disc brakes in front is fairly straightforward. The process will vary somewhat from one application to another, but for the Track T being discussed here, it went something like this. The spindles are for a 1949–1954 Chevy with a brake adapter kit that mounts Ford Mustang/Pinto rotors.

Attach the caliper bracket directly to the spindle at the bottom and secure it to the top by an adaptor. At the bottom, pass a bolt through the caliper bracket, the lower rear tab of the spindle, and the rear tab of the steering arm, and then secure it with a lock nut. Secure the adaptor to the lower front

Left: Another bolt secures the C-shaped caliper mounting bracket and the steering arm to the spindle. **Right:** After packing both the inner and outer wheel bearings with grease, you can install them in the rotor, fit the bearing seal on the inner bearing, and then install the rotor on the spindle. The bearings are what aligns the rotor on the spindle and allows it to spin. **Note:** If you do not grease the wheel bearings during preliminary assembly, *make sure* you grease them before final assembly.

Left: *Now install the outer bearing washer with the tab in the keyway. This is what holds the outer bearing in place.* **Right:** *The spindle nut can now be installed to secure the rotor on the spindle. Tighten the nut per the instructions included with the spindle/rotors. You will need to tighten it enough to seat the bearings, and then back off approximately one-half turn. Then insert a cotter pin through the slots in the spindle nut and the hole in original spindles. These spindles being reproductions, they do not yet have the cotter pin hole drilled, so a 1/8-inch hole will need to be drilled through the keyway in the spindle. Before I completed this step, I waited until final assembly to verify that I could position properly.*

These are Pinto/early Mustang brake calipers and rotors. Their assembly is quite different from GM calipers with which I am somewhat familiar. It was fairly obvious how the caliper fit between the upper and lower arms of the mounting bracket, but I had no clue what actually held the caliper in place. If you are not familiar with these calipers, don't have a good reference photo, and are missing a small but critical part, they will leave you scratching your head wondering what you are missing. For you other GM guys, these have no slider pins securing the caliper. After a phone call to Uncle Ed, I found that I was missing a very critical piece. A small piece of metal and a miniature leaf spring fit between the lower arm of the mounting bracket and the caliper. After they are driven into place, they are secured with a short shoulder bolt that threads into the caliper mounting bracket.

tab of the spindle by passing a bolt through the front tab of the steering arm, the spindle, the adaptor, and then secure it with a lock nut. Thus far, the mounting bolts run parallel with the spindle. At the top of the adaptor, pass a long Allen screw through the adaptor and thread it into the caliper mounting bracket, so that it runs perpendicular to the spindle.

The rotor along with inner and outer bearings and seal should be installed next. If you are merely in the mockup stage, you may choose to not pack the wheel bearings at this time. However, be sure that you pack the bearings with grease before you drive the vehicle. Anyone who has ever had to remove a frozen bearing will tell you that packing the bearings is much easier than removing one that has failed—not to mention the high possibility that you'll have to replace the spindle.

Slide the rotor with the bearings installed over the spindle, then install the spindle washer on the spindle. The spindle washer will have a tab on the inside that slides into a keyway in the spindle. Thread a castellated nut into the spindle, making sure that it is not cross threaded. Using a wrench, tighten the nut completely to seal the outer bearing, and then loosen the nut between a quarter and a half turn. Align the castellated nut so that you can install a cotter pin through the small hole near the end of the spindle. Use a pair of pliers or a small hammer to bend the end of the cotter pin so that it does not back out. Note that if a cotter pin is not installed, there is nothing to keep the castellated nut from backing off the spindle and allowing the rotor to part company from the rest of the vehicle. For similar reasons, cotter pins also should be used on all drag links and tie rods ends.

Before mounting the caliper, install the inner and outer brake pads. Whether the pads slide on the caliper housing or on pins depends on the type of caliper, but they must slide freely. Most auto parts stores sell a type of lubricant that is supposed to make the pads slide easier. It has been my experience, however, that the lubricant just attracts dust, dirt, and other grime that causes the pads to stick and then end up wearing unevenly.

These calipers are for a Ford and feature a notch at the top and the bottom where they slide into the caliper mounting bracket. A small wedge (a specific Ford piece) slides between the caliper and the mounting bracket and is secured in place by a short threaded shaft with a large head (about the size of a dime). Without the wedge, the caliper can easily fall out of its mounting bracket.

Installing Rear Brakes

How the rear brakes are installed depends on a few different factors, but it is usually an easy procedure regardless. There may be several stock disc brake configurations available, as well as aftermarket upgrades, depending on the rear axle housing being used. Drum brakes have been available on most, if not every, rear axle housing ever made, so a stock rebuild kit should be available at your favorite auto parts store. Installation varies, however, depending on whether you are using disc or drum brakes and on the manufacturer, so having a repair manual for the vehicle that is the source of your rear brakes is best.

For the Track T constructed in these pages, new backing plates, brake shoes, and brake drums were purchased from Danny Miller's Rear Gears when new gears were installed in the rear end. To install, simply bolt each assembled brake backing plate (one on each end) onto the Ford axle housing with four T-bolts and nuts. Install a bearing on the axle, and then insert the axle into the axle housing (make sure that the axle engages properly with the third member gears). Then secure the axle to the housing with four bolts and nuts. Repeat these instructions for the opposite side axle. After sliding the brake drum over the wheel studs, you can mount the rear wheels and tires.

Installing the Master Cylinder

Master cylinders are typically located in one of two distinct locations: hanging on the firewall or beneath the floor. On most, if not all, current production vehicles, the master cylinder and its optional power brake booster are mounted on the firewall and can be accessed from under the hood. From a serviceability and practicality standpoint, this setup makes perfectly good sense. The only downside is that the brake booster is sometimes very big and usually not very attractive. Alternatively, many hot rods have the master cylinder located beneath the floor. This is usually done because of a lack of available room beneath the hood, but it comes with drawbacks. With the master cylinder located beneath the floor, it is usually more difficult to check the brake fluid level. To prevent having to actually put the vehicle on a rack to check or add brake fluid, an access panel needs to be installed in the floor. If you have a plush interior and accidentally spill, this setup can make an aggravating mess.

Several different aftermarket brackets are available for mounting the master cylinder and power brake booster on the firewall or under the floor. You simply have to decide which location will work best for your particular application. Mounting brackets are also available for bolt-on or weld-on installation. No matter which location or type of mounting bracket you choose, the master cylinder must be mounted solidly and not be allowed to move in relation to the rest of the vehicle. Regardless of how the mounting bracket is attached to the vehicle, you must bolt the master cylinder and optional power booster in place. Two important things to remember are that if the master cylinder has a drain plug in the bottom, you must verify that it is in place and tight, and that the power brake booster has a vacuum line (such as from the carburetor) connected to it.

Since some vehicles simply don't have room for a master cylinder mounted to the firewall, and having the reservoir beneath the floor is inconvenient, a cure is to use a remote-fill master cylinder. This setup requires the master cylinder to have outlet ports on both sides, one side for the plumbing from the remote reservoir, and the other to run to the brakes. The remote reservoir can be mounted wherever it is convenient and can be plumbed into the master cylinder.

There are a couple of important things to remember about a master cylinder. First of all, you should always use a dual reservoir master cylinder (and therefore dual reservoir remote units if used) on a vehicle that will be driven on the street. This is purely a safety feature, as a dual system will provide either front or rear brakes should you develop a leak in either system.

Secondly, the master cylinder is typically mounted in the opposite orientation if located under the floor with an upright pedal than when mounted on a firewall and with a hanging pedal. When connecting brake lines, an easy way to remember or determine which way the master cylinder may have been mounted in its original application that the largest reservoir should be connected to the brakes that do most of the stopping—the front brakes. If the reservoirs are the same size, then it doesn't matter.

Routing, Bending, and Installing Brake Lines

Now that the master cylinder (and power brake booster, if used) is mounted, you can begin running the brake lines. If the master cylinder is mounted lower than the brake cylinders (as in a below-the-floor installation), you must use residual check valves to prevent the brake fluid from running away from the brakes. If the master cylinder or remote reservoir is mounted higher than the brakes, then residual check valves are not necessary. Residual check valves are available in 2-pound and 10-pound ratings. For disc brakes (front or rear) a 2-pound valve should be used, while a 10-pound valve should be used with drum brakes (front or rear).

The first decision now is determining the best route for the brake line. A diagram shown elsewhere in this chapter provides a typical layout for routing and the components used in plumbing the brakes. Due partially to cramped spaces and partially to a non-standard chassis configuration, the brake line routing for the Track T differs from the typical, but only in its basic routing. The main rule of thumb for routing is to choose a path where the brake line can be held firmly out of the way. You never want brake line exposed to being snagged by something you might need to straddle in the road, or broken if the car bottoms out, or mashed if the vehicle is placed on a service rack. Secure it

so that structural members (e.g., frame rails) shelter the lines and protect it from damage. Likewise, don't run the line so close to the exhaust system that it will boil the brake fluid and compromise your stopping power.

If using residual check valves, they should be installed within 12 inches of the master cylinder. For this reason, I started with a 12-inch-long piece of 3/16-inch brake line. A brake line in this length is available in most auto parts stores, so with the factory flare on both ends, that is two less chances for leaks. Not being certain of the best possible brake line routing toward the front, I opted to start running brake lines to the rear end first. After installing the correct adaptor fitting into the master cylinder, so that 3/16-inch brake line could be installed, I bent the 12-inch-long piece of brake line to clear the master cylinder. Then I ran it back to the driver side frame rail and bent it rearward to run along the frame rail. At this end of the brake line, I installed a 10-pound residual valve, since drum brakes were being used on the rear. The residual check valve has markings to indicate which end should be toward the master cylinder and which end toward the brakes. Make sure that it is installed correctly.

The adjustable proportioning valve should be installed in the rear brake circuit. Since it can be installed almost anywhere in that circuit, you should be installed in a location that is convenient for you. To place it in a convenient spot, I cut a piece of brake line to the appropriate length, installed a fitting, and then double flared the cut end with a double flaring tool. I then bent the brake line to conform to the inside of the frame rail and the location of the inlet fitting in the adjustable proportioning valve. I threaded the brake line into the "inlet" side of the adjustable proportioning valve. The hard brake line was continued to a point just past the rear edge of the floor, close to the rear axle housing. Next, I double flared the end of the line so it would be compatible with a flexible stock Ford brake hose. The opposite end of this hose has a fitting that is designed to be held in place by the rear axle housing vent tube and to allow for brake lines to be installed from opposite sides. From here, I cut, bent, and flared a length of 3/16-inch brake line to connect it to the rear passenger side backing plate. With a shorter piece of 3/16-inch brake line, I cut, bent, and flared it to connect to the rear driver side backing plate. Other than actually securing the brake line to the frame rail (which was done after the chassis was painted), the rear brakes were finished.

Whether it is between the wheel cylinders and the chassis, or the rear axle housing and a rear crossmember, a length of flexible line must be used somewhere to allow for adequate suspension travel. Obviously, there must be enough play in this line to accommodate the rear axle's full range of vertical movement.

Just like in the back, brake lines in the front must allow for suspension travel, but must also allow for the directional turning of the wheel. Because of this last consideration, the flexible hose must be run between the front brake assembly and the chassis. Determining a suitable location for this chassis mount and how to avoid a very crowded situation near the Vega steering gear are two decisions that make brake line routing on the Track T a head scratching experience. Conventional wisdom says to route the brake line forward from the master cylinder into a tee for a flex line to the left front wheel, then to continue forward and across a crossmember to the right side frame rail, and ultimately into a flex line that runs to the right front brake assembly. To make life and the routing of the front brake lines easier, one method is to have the front brake line exit the master cylinder, and run across the transmission crossmember. Then turn it forward, run it to a tee at the right front wheel, and continue forward and across the front crossmember, and finally run it back toward the left front wheel. This will use slightly more brake line (crossing the vehicle twice rather than once), but will avoid passing a brake line through a non-existent space between the steering box and the chassis.

Before you can begin running brake lines to the master cylinder, you will most likely need to purchase an adapter fitting to make the connection. To make things easy on yourself, unbolt the master cylinder and take it with you to the parts store. Almost any reputable parts store will have exactly what you need, but with the master cylinder with you, you can get it all in one trip. Depending on the distance to the parts store, cutting down on unnecessary trips may indirectly buy you some more parts.

With a good tubing bender, some rubber coated brake line clamps, and self-tapping sheet metal screws, running your own brake lines is not difficult. The red fitting seen near the transmission crossmember is a residual valve, used to keep brake fluid from backing away from the drum brakes. The purple box with a knob is an adjustable proportioning valve, used to adjust the balance between the front and rear brakes.

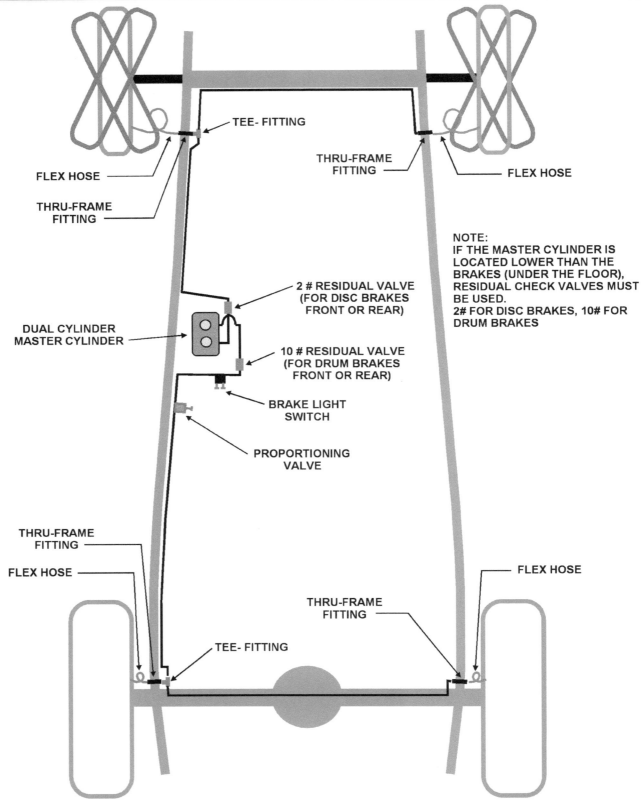

TEE- FITTING

THRU-FRAME
FITTING

FLEX HOSE

FLEX HOSE

THRU-FRAME
FITTING

NOTE:
IF THE MASTER CYLINDER IS
LOCATED LOWER THAN THE
BRAKES (UNDER THE FLOOR),
RESIDUAL CHECK VALVES MUST
BE USED.
2# FOR DISC BRAKES, 10# FOR
DRUM BRAKES

2 # RESIDUAL VALVE
(FOR DISC BRAKES
FRONT OR REAR)

DUAL CYLINDER
MASTER CYLINDER

10 # RESIDUAL VALVE
(FOR DRUM BRAKES
FRONT OR REAR)

BRAKE LIGHT
SWITCH

PROPORTIONING
VALVE

THRU-FRAME
FITTING

FLEX HOSE

FLEX HOSE

THRU-FRAME
FITTING

TEE- FITTING

Brake line routing can be done several ways. This illustration shows a very typical routing and the components involved. My Track T project had the front brake line circuit running across the transmission crossmember, forward on the passenger side, and then around the front and back to the driver side, due to lack of clearance around the steering box. Additionally, a flex hose was not used at each rear wheel (as shown), but one flex hose was connected to the rear axle (to allow for suspension travel) and then hard lined to each rear wheel.

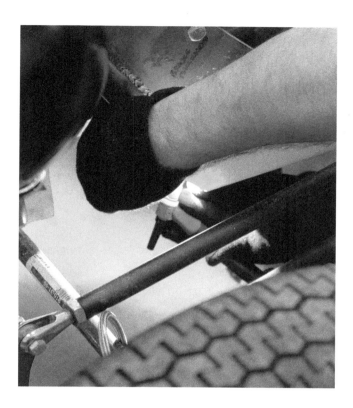

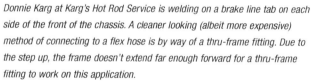

Donnie Karg at Karg's Hot Rod Service is welding on a brake line tab on each side of the front of the chassis. A cleaner looking (albeit more expensive) method of connecting to a flex hose is by way of a thru-frame fitting. Due to the step up, the frame doesn't extend far enough forward for a thru-frame fitting to work on this application.

With the brake line tab securely welded to the chassis, you can clamp a bulkhead fitting in place with a spring clip on the backside. A flex hose threads into the front of the bulkhead fitting. An ordinary brake line fitting will thread into the bulkhead fitting from behind, making this an inexpensive alternative to the typical front brake line setup.

BARE STEEL VERSUS CHROME VERSUS STAINLESS STEEL

Okay, which of these three materials is least expensive when used for hot rod products? If you look in any variety of hot rod parts catalogs for similar products—such as radius rods, tie rods, drag links, and many others—these pieces can usually be purchased in bare steel or chrome plated. Some pieces are even constructed from stainless steel, which for even more money are usually available in a polished finish. As you might imagine, the bare steel is always priced at the lower end, with polished stainless being at the higher end of the price list.

Does that make bare steel the cheapest material to use when building a budget hot rod? Not necessarily. If you don't at least apply some epoxy primer or other rust inhibitor to bare steel, it will quickly rust in all but the driest climates. So, in addition to the original piece, you need to determine how it will be finished and what the related expenses will be.

For bare steel parts, you will need to include the cost of primer, paint, and labor. If you are doing the work, the labor doesn't cost you anything but time. If you are paying someone else to prime and paint the pieces, their time equals your money. Stainless steel is more expensive than bare steel, but it won't rust, so you don't have to paint it unless you want to. Depending on the shape and size of the part, a stainless steel part may be less expensive than the overall cost of a bare steel piece. Chrome plated or polished stainless pieces are pretty much "bolt it on and go" with no additional expense.

It may be that you prefer primer or painted look to sparkle, and that is fine, but it doesn't necessarily mean that it is less expensive. A tasteful combination of the two is probably best, as chrome everything is obnoxious, whether it is the cheap way out or the most expensive (at least in this author's opinion).

CHAPTER 4
BODY

You've chosen your chassis to suit the body style you planned in the early chapters of the book. Now you're ready to make that body a reality and affix it to your rolling chassis. Maybe you got a usable body with your chassis; if so, consider yourself lucky. Otherwise, there are several ways to create the body for your hot rod.

Hot rod bodies are typically steel or fiberglass. While carbon fiber is also used to make some automotive bodies and components, this material is more popular with the tuner car and sport truck markets than hot rods.

STEEL

Since all of the vehicles that hot rods were originally built from were steel, this material remains a popular choice. The price for quality steel bodies ranges from outrageous for a

relatively pristine piece, to next to nothing at the local trash heap. Obviously, there is a difference in the quality of those two extremes, although sometimes it may be a perception established by the seller's selling ability.

Vintage tin—that is, sheet metal from a vehicle that was originally manufactured prior to 1948—is between 60 years and a century old. If you're lucky enough to find something original, solid, and within your price range, you really can't go wrong; everyone respects good, original tin. And if you get the whole car in the bargain, you will pick up many useful parts, even though the engine, transmission, and suspension will likely have to go.

Other pieces of vintage tin seem to become available everyday on eBay and various other sources. Oftentimes, the ad will claim that the parts being sold are great for a rat

This radical pickup truck is typical of many of the rat rods being built today: a collection of vintage tin parts that may not have come from the same vehicle. Often built without fenders or hood, rat rods also often have no sheet metal connecting dissimilar components that don't line up when connected. In its weathered patina, this truck is neat but too rough for some.

On the other hand, this truck is basically the same, yet has a much more finished appearance due to the painted chassis and primered body components.

rod. That is a pretty good clue that the parts in question are pretty rough. Either the part is reasonably straight but half eaten away with rust, or solid but bent considerably. That is not to say that you can't combine a bunch of parts and create a pretty cool hot rod though.

Perhaps what is for sale is a rat rod for a cheap price. Many rat rods are not painted because the metal surfaces are too rust pitted (resembling a golf ball), or because the welding done to patch a bunch of pieces together simply wasn't done with appearances in mind. Although this weathered material may never be finished on par with a top 25 winner at a national event, a little plastic filler and some primer will go along way toward improving the image of some of these creative hot rods.

Of course, you needn't purchase a rat rod to get a finished car made from many body pieces. With an affordable MIG welder, a little skill, and a collection of OEM parts, you can create your own one-of-a-kind hot rod body. Although this isn't the same as using an English wheel and creating a complete body from a few pieces of sheet stock, you can become a custom coachbuilder by combining sections of pre-shaped sheet metal.

It's no wonder that many rat rods become pickup trucks, as there is less body to contend with and a new bed is easy enough to bend up out of sheet stock. With a little imagination, a sense of proportion, a tape measure, a plasma arc cutter (or some other metal cutting device), and a welder, you are well on your way to building a truly one-off hot rod that may catch lots of attention, depending on how well you finish it. Just take a section of roof and position it so that it has a nice profile. Add a couple of cab corners at the bottom, along with a cowl up front, and you are almost there. Now just start cutting pieces of sheet metal to the right shape to begin connecting the dots, so to speak, and you are on your way. Sit this atop a rectangular box tubing chassis that is equipped with proven suspension and brake components, and you can quickly be in an affordable hot rod.

FIBERGLASS

If you don't have steel to work with, there is always fiberglass. Hot rodders seem to have two thoughts about fiberglass: they either swear by it or swear at it. On the good side, fiberglass won't rust. Even a new, reproduction steel body will rust if not protected from the elements. Although fiberglass is

77

susceptible to impact damage, it is typically easier and therefore less costly to repair than a similar repair to a steel bodied vehicle.

On the bad side, not all fiberglass are created equal and there have been several examples of poor quality fiberglass on the market over the years. Anyone who has ever dealt with one of these poor quality bodies most likely won't have anything good to say about fiberglass. This material can be full of pinholes that may not be readily apparent when you first look at a body, but will be after you have paid your money and are doing paint prep work. Therefore it is a good idea to ask around and find out whose glass bodies are recommended and whose aren't. Along these same lines, fiberglass molds suffer a certain amount of wear each time they are used. For this reason, the quality within any one particular company may differ from one body style to another. Plus, there is always the possibility that the original used to make the mold is not absolutely perfect.

Something else to beware of when shopping for a fiberglass body (especially a used one) is that many fiberglass bodies are available in "street weight" or "race quality." Even though a street body will flex quite a bit, it is fairly rigid when compared to a lighter weight race body. This is not to say that you cannot use a race body on the street, but the efforts necessary to beef up the body for street use may negate any savings on the original purchase.

One way to stiffen a glass body is to 'glass-reinforce some beads (similar in function to rolling a bead in a piece of sheet metal) to the inside of the body. You can do this by stretching a piece of rubber hose across the panel after coating it with release agent. If you purchase your fiberglass materials from a knowledgeable source, such as an auto body paint and supply jobber, it will know what a release agent, or a mold release, is, which is available under several trade names. Then fiberglass a covering over the hose and to the back of the fiberglass panel on all but the end. After the fiberglass has kicked (set up), simply pull out the hose.

With this wonderful, space-age product known as fiberglass, and some time and effort, a person could make a purely one-off body completely out of fiberglass if so desired. Customizers George Barris, Ed Roth, and numerous others were doing this a long time go, creating some very memorable vehicles that never existed in production form.

There are multiple ways to create a fiberglass body. When attempting to recreate a particular body, fender, or any other part, a mold needs to be made from an original. Without going into great detail, a mold is made by coating the original with a release agent, and then coating the original with layers of fiberglass. After the fiberglass cures, this new fiberglass can be separated from the original and used

as a mold. Depending on the size and shape of the part being copied, molds may need to be made of each side, along with a method of clamping them together when the new pieces are laid up. The number of layers of fiberglass to use to make the mold will depend on whether it will be for a one time use or will be used for a number of copies.

For custom creations, a framework can be made by applying several layers of fiberglass matte, resin, and cloth. Usually the chassis is built and a wire frame of electrical conduit, rebar, or some other material is welded together to establish the character lines of the body. This method is probably most desirable for a body design where the wire frame can remain inside and part of the body. Another method that is often used begins with wooden bucks or stations being assembled on a chassis. You can visualize this method easily by picturing what a cross section would look like if taken at several intervals through the body. With these wooden bucks assembled and substantially supported, layers of fiberglass matte and cloth are draped across them, resulting in an outer skin. As each section is solid, there would be no room for passengers or an engine, so the new fiberglass panels must be removed from the bucks and ultimately supported by some other type of framework or be rigid enough to be self-supporting.

For the Track T used as the project of this book, the body (from Speedway Motors) was a fiberglass reproduction of a 1927 Ford roadster. It was a fairly decent replica and was comparable in price to other similar bodies on the market. There were some significantly better 1927 Ford bodies on the market, however, their prices are significantly higher as well. Those higher priced bodies included considerable reinforcing and a floor that was already a part of the body. Other features included opening doors and deck lid, as well as the buyer's choice of a couple different types of dash.

To minimize expenses and construction time, I ordered the body without opening doors. I simply built the car low enough to hop over the side. I might regret this choice as I get older, but I won't have to worry about door latches that rattle or don't work properly this way. I also needed to build my own dash, as one was not included.

FITTING BODY APRONS

Since the frame of this Track T is a custom frame that in no way resembles an actual 1927 Ford frame, Speedway Motors includes a set of fiberglass body aprons that are designed to cover all but the inside of the frame rails. The upper flange of these body aprons fits between the bottom flange of the body and the frame rail, so its use requires some thought before the body is mounted to the frame rails.

*Left: Although difficult to see in the photo, an important mark is placed on the top of each frame rail where the firewall sits. You will need to refer to these marks later. **Right:** Another good place to make a reference mark on the body is where the rear radius rod attaches to the frame. While working with the body, the floor, and the body aprons, you will not be able to see all of your alignment marks, so having extras will be helpful.*

This shot shows that a portion of the body flange has been removed to clear the vertical hoop of the chassis.

The body must be situated on the frame rails so that it is centered side to side. Front to back, the body should be located so that the rear axle housing is centered in the wheelwell. For these particular bodies, the body slips down over the rear axle somewhat. This requires you to cut a notch in the sides of the body at the center of the wheelwell. You cut this notch just wide enough to clear the axle at this time. You will also need to trim the bottom flange of the body to provide adequate clearance for the body to fit around the vertical hoop of the chassis.

The Speedway Motors assembly manual provides a measurement distance from the front hairpin frame mount to the firewall, which should at least get you in the ballpark. Depending on how accurately you centered the notch for the rear axle and the adjustment of the rear radius rod, you may or may not get precisely this measurement, but the latter is not an absolute. You should sit the body in place with the tires fitted, and then stand back to see if it looks

With the body off the frame and upside down, the body aprons must be aligned to the body. Distinct angles in the body and the body aprons make it fairly easy to align them. The body aprons are long and will need to be trimmed eventually.

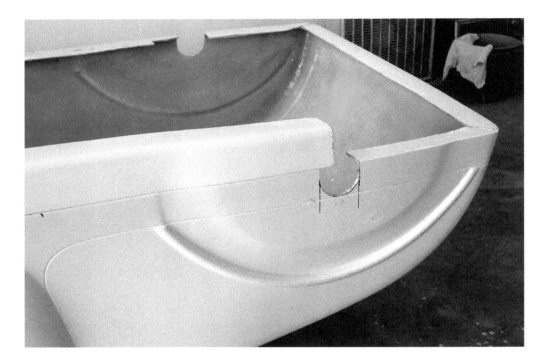

Matching the body apron to the body is probably most critical in the area around the rear wheelwell and just forward of that, as this is where the most predominant shape is located.

correct. When the vehicle is finished and sitting at a rod run, admirers will take notice of how well the wheels and tires are centered in the wheelwell, but quite honestly won't care how far away the firewall is from anything. In some instances, the measurement is critical, while on others, what looks right is what matters.

With the body in place, use a suitable marker (Sharpie, permanent markers are a favorite in many rod shops) to indicate reference points on both the body and the frame. I placed

marks on the chassis to indicate the firewall location and on the inside bottom flange of the body to indicate the location of the frame mount of the rear radius rod. As is often the case when mounting a body on any frame other than what it rolled out of Detroit on, the body does not always simply fall into place. You may need to push or pull on the body somewhat to get the same spacing from side to side. Often you will need to split the tolerances to achieve an acceptable fit.

When you have established the location for the body and

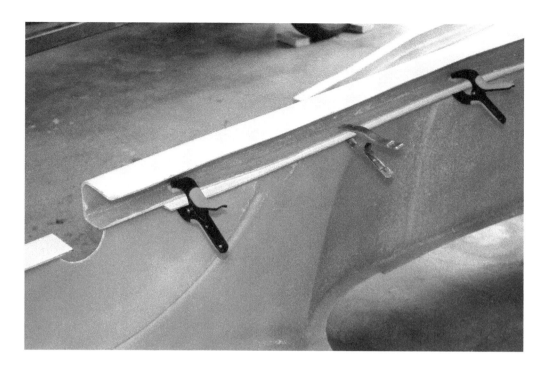

With the body apron and body aligned, clamp the two together with clamps. These spring-loaded clamps work great, but you can use bar clamps or C-clamps if spring clamps are not available.

The body apron encroaches into the notch cut in the body to clear the rear axle housing, so you will need to trim them. Using a straightedge and a marker, extend the line from the body onto the body apron.

marked all your reference points on the body and chassis, you can remove the body. Flip the body over and carefully set it on the floor. You may choose to set it on some sort of padding, but since no bodywork has been done yet, damage will be minimal if you gently place it on the floor. The body aprons are always longer than you need, so you will need to cut them the proper length. Begin by locating them on the bottom flange of the body, so that the contours of the body are aligned with those of the body aprons. Clamp the body

aprons in place with spring clamps or C-clamps.

The back end of the body apron extends slightly into the notch that is cut out for the rear axle clearance. You will need to trim this off the body apron as well. Use a marker and a straightedge to mark the line that needs to be cut. To minimize splintering the fiberglass, center a piece of masking tape over the line, and then cut the body apron with a saber saw. Fiberglass is very tough, so you will probably go through a couple of blades before all of the cutting

Before cutting, place a piece of masking tape over the area to be cut to minimize splintering the fiberglass.

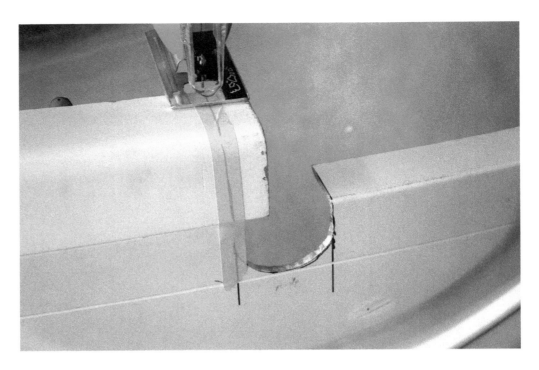

You will need to smooth the rough edges anywhere that fiberglass is cut, which can be done later, but before applying primer.

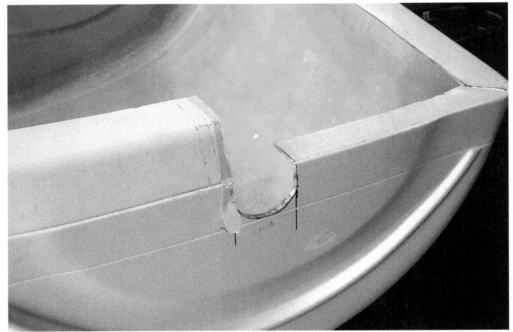

is done for mounting the body. After cutting both body aprons, align and clamp the rear rolled pan in place at the rear of the body. Mark the location where the excess needs to be cut off, and then trim the rolled pan as necessary to clear the rear axle.

The body aprons will need to be cut to length in the front as well, but you should hold off on that for now. Before removing the aprons from their positions on the body,

transfer locations of the firewall/frame rail and body/rear radius rod location. The body aprons closely follow the contours of the frame, but not exactly, so you will need to use reference marks to obtain the correct alignment.

Before the body aprons can be fully positioned over the frame rails, you need to drill holes in the apron for the rear radius rod mount and the front hairpin mount. Additionally, you will need to make clearance on the lower

The rolled rear pan needs to be trimmed where it encroaches onto the notch for the rear axle. It is aligned to the body, clamped in place, marked, taped, and then cut in the same manner.

BODY

Left: The body aprons needs to be drilled so that the mounting tubes for the rear radius rods and the front hairpin will fit through them, allowing the body apron to fit flush with the frame rails. *Right:* This mark on the top of the body aprons (representing where they align with the base of the firewall) is used to align them with the frame rails.

flange of the body apron for the spring mounting plate, and on the top flange in front for the gusset portion of the frame kickup.

With the chassis securely supported on jack stands, remove the frame mounting bolts of the front hairpins and the rear radius rods. At the mounting points for the front and rear suspension components, there is a round tube that protrudes through the frame rail. By positioning the body apron in place against the frame, and tapping the body apron with a rubber mallet against this tube, you will leave a slight indention on the inside of the body apron. You can then eyeball the center of this ring, use a center punch to mark that center, and drill a correct-sized hole for the tube to protrude. Repeat this step for the remaining mounting point on the first body apron, and then repeat it again on the remaining body apron. More than likely, you will need

83

Left: You will need to trim the lower flange of the body apron to clear the plate that mounts the rear spring. You can mark the lower flange directly, but will need to remove the apron to actually make the cut. Right: For the front of the body apron to fit flush, you must trim the top flange to fit around the gusset at the front of the chassis. I used a carpenter's square to lay out the cuts square to the body apron.

With the body aprons in place and the suspension components reinstalled, the body can now be reinstalled on the chassis.

to do at least a little bit of touch up with some plastic body filler in these four areas, but that will come later.

For the clearance of the spring mounting plate and the front gusset, you can mark the body aprons directly from the protrusions around which they need to be trimmed. After the body aprons have been drilled and trimmed as necessary, you can place them into position, covering the frame rails. Now re-secure the front hairpins and rear radius rods to the chassis with the hardware previously removed. You will need to either remove the tie rod and drag link, or trim the body aprons. I did a little bit of both, leaving the body aprons plenty long. The Speedway Motors assembly manual doesn't include any photos or text that gives a definitive answer for where the body aprons need to be terminated in front. My thoughts are that the aprons should be cut parallel with the front kickup, but that decision doesn't have to be made quite yet. Whenever you are in doubt about a particular aspect of building a hot rod, avoid cutting anything that might be difficult to stretch later. It's easier to cut more off than replace material.

With some help from a friend, your spouse, or a garage gnome (you know, those creatures that drink all of your beer, cola, or lemonade, as well as borrow all of your tools), sit the body back onto the chassis, sandwiching the upper flange of the body aprons between the body and the frame rails. This is where the body fitting process begins to get a little hairy. Unless my body and chassis combination is a complete anomaly, the body doesn't just automatically align itself with the body aprons that are now on the frame. Position the body as accurately on the frame as you can. Ideally,

the body aprons will fit flush with the outside of the frame, and the flange of the body will overlay the body apron and the top of the frame perfectly. Measure from known points—such as from the front hairpin frame mounting tubes to each side of the base of the firewall—to ensure that the body is square on the frame. When you are satisfied with the positioning, clamp the body in place using every bar clamp and C-clamp that you can find.

Before your clamps start losing their grip, drill approximately five pilot holes somewhat evenly spaced through the body flange, upper flange of the body apron, and the top of the frame rail on each side of the vehicle. These holes should be between 1/8 inch and 1/4 inch in diameter and be aligned as close as possible to the center of the top of the frame rail. Depending on how closely the body's lower flange and body apron line up with the frame rail, you may have to bias the pilot hole a bit to the left or right. When the holes are drilled, insert bolts of the same size down through the various layers of fiberglass and steel. You can now remove the clamps and then step back to check the alignment of the body and the body aprons once more. Now is the time to make any necessary adjustments. Some assistance from one or two of your buddies may be necessary to push or pull on the body slightly as you drill additional body mounting holes.

MOUNTING THE BODY ON THE CHASSIS

There are two basic schools of thought on how to mount and secure the body to the chassis. One is to drill body mounting holes through the body flange, the body apron

Before drilling the pilot holes for the body mounts, you have to position the body correctly on the chassis. This is when you may first realize that the body, body aprons, and frame rails don't line up as accurately as you might have hoped. Using all of the clamps you have, position the body aprons so that they are as close to the frame rails as possible, and then move them slightly to align with the contours of the body.

Now that the body is clamped down in the position that you determine is the best fit, attach the body to the chassis with approximately five self-tapping machine screws along each side. Position the screws as close to the center of the frame rail as possible, which may place the screws very close to the edge of the body flange. This will not be a problem, however, after the floor is fiberglassed into place.

With the body aprons and body in place, the Track T is looking much more like a complete car—but looks can be deceiving.

The body aprons are plenty long and will need to be trimmed in the front. At this point, I trimmed them just enough to clear the front axle, with more precise trimming performed later.

(top and bottom), and the frame rail (top and bottom). This method requires a long drill bit and even longer bolts to secure the body in place. Once the pilot holes, mentioned above, are drilled to the appropriate size, a bolt is passed through the lower flange of the body and all the way through the frame (top and bottom), and then secured with a nut. In addition to the difficult task of keeping the holes in the various layers properly aligned and plumbed, this approach leaves the nuts exposed beneath the car. This isn't an attractive alternative, plus it makes it awful easy to skin your noggin' anytime you may be doing service work beneath the car.

A cleaner method of securing the body to the frame is to weld nuts into the top flange of the frame rail. Donnie Karg at Karg's Hot Rod Service still needed to fabricate the motor mounts, so he welded the body mount nuts in the frame while the Track T was at his shop. Since pilot holes have already been drilled through the body, body aprons, and top of the frame rail, you can now remove the body from the chassis. Use 3/8-inch bolts to mount the body, so

the pilot holes are drilled out to the size required for a 3/8-inch nut to slip down into the frame rail, and so that the tops are flush.

Before inserting the nut into the frame rail, slightly chamfer the hole in the top flange to allow for full penetration of the weld. Obtain a bolt long enough to allow you to hang onto it while welding and thread it into a nut. Then position the nut in the hole, which may take a couple of hits with a hammer to seat the nut properly. Use a square or framing triangle to verify that the bolt (and therefore the nut) is square with the frame rail flange. Now tack weld the nut in place, making sure that the nut is flush with the top of the frame rail (or slightly below) and is still in square. Repeat these steps for each of the body mount holes, removing the bolts and final welding each nut. Skipping around from one side to the other minimizes heat buildup in any one location, a situation that might distort the frame slightly. After all of the nuts are welded in place and have cooled, run a tap through each hole to clean the threads.

87

Rather than simply using self-tapping machine screws to hold the body in place, a threaded nut was welded to the frame rail. When finished, a set of bolts and washers was all that will be needed to secure the body to the chassis. Donnie Karg at Karg's Hot Rod Service begins by enlarging the original pilot hole to a size suitable for a 3/8-inch nut to be welded inside of it.

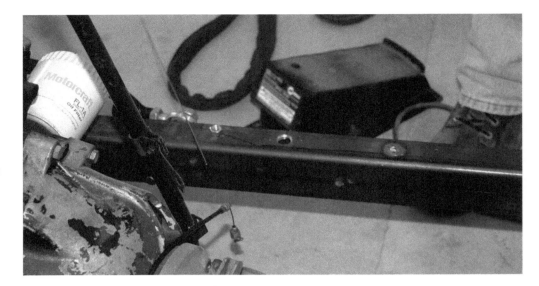

A long 3/8-inch bolt is threaded onto a nut, and then tapped into place.

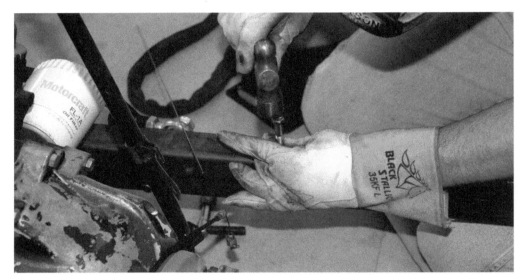

The nut is then tack welded to the frame rail. The top of the nut should be flush with, or slightly below, the top of the frame rail.

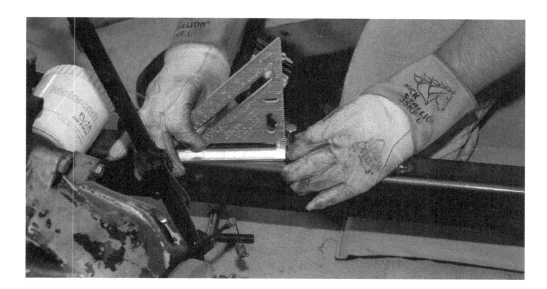

To avoid alignment problems later, Donnie verifies that the bolt is square with the top of the frame rail prior to doing any more welding.

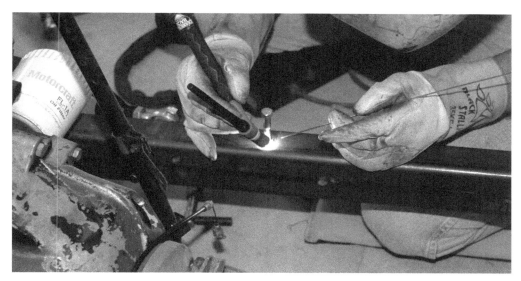

The nut is now welded in place around its entire perimeter. To avoid concentrating too much heat in any one location, you can skip around between several mounting holes that need to be welded at this stage of the buildup.

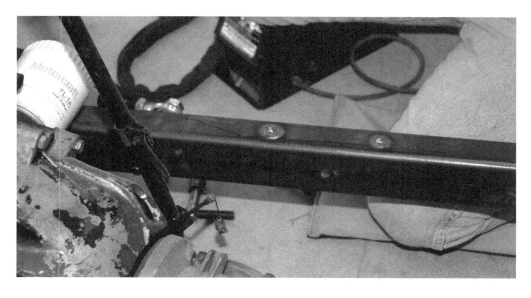

After the welding is completed and the welds have cooled, chase each body mount with a tap to clean the threads.

As evidenced by the shadow, there is no floor installed yet, but the body, engine, and transmission are now in place—a perfect time to push the project into the driveway and make vroom, vroom sounds. Photo by Sandy Parks

ATTACHING THE FLOOR TO THE BODY

One of the reasons this body is less expensive than others is because the floor is not attached to the body when it is purchased. Depending on what body you buy or construct, you may face the same situation, so this is how the body and the floor become one. Note that the floor could have been fiberglassed into the body before the body was secured to the frame. I chose to attach the body first. This gave me good visibility and access as I aligned the body shell and aprons, and measured for and installed the mounting hardware. Either method can work; do some planning, eyeballing, and test fitting to determine which approach works best for you.

To fit the floor in place, I had to remove the body from the chassis, slide the fiberglass floor panel into position, and then set the body back down onto the chassis. With the floor in place but not 'glassed in yet, a few areas of concern arose. The top of the master cylinder was sitting slightly above the top of the frame rail, keeping the floor from sitting flush with the body flange. The floor-mounted master cylinder needed an access panel anyway, so this wasn't a major problem. It just needed to be domed to allow clearance.

A larger area of concern, however, was the poor fit of the cowl support. Being made of tubular steel and angle iron, it could be remedied, but it seemed like something the factory should do rather than the hot rodder. I was not going to send it back, so I undertook the fix myself. The cowl support consisted of a vertical hoop in the front and another piece of tubing that angled back from the front hoop and then turned down toward the floor on each side. I welded a piece of angle iron in between each of the angled pieces to serve as a mount for the steering column. Then I tied each end of the front vertical hoop to the angled piece at the floor with a piece of flat plate. Nowhere did the flat plate align with the top of the chassis, when looking down from above, in the stock configuration from the factory.

When Donnie Karg was welding the body mount nuts in place, he modified the cowl support to match the taper of the frame rails. He also positioned two body mounts on each side, so that the cowl support was firmly secured to the chassis. However, when the floor was put into position, the transmission hump/toe board area of the floor encroached on the area where the cowl support needed to be. The offending area of the floor was cut out, using a die grinder,

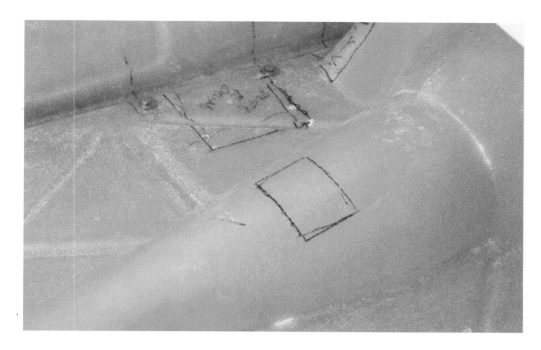

Obvious in the photo is the area that needs to be removed from the transmission tunnel to allow installation of the shifter. The lines in the area to the left (above in the photo) indicate where the floor needs to be trimmed to allow for master cylinder clearance. A die grinder with an abrasive disc makes easy work of these two cuts.

and was to be modified as necessary later on, after the floor had been 'glassed into place.

Before the floor can be 'glassed into place, holes for the body mounting bolts need to be drilled in the floor, and then the floor needs to be bolted down along with the body and the body aprons. You can go ahead and snug them down firm, but not so much as to crack the fiberglass.

For the fiberglass task ahead of me, I purchased fiberglass resin, fiberglass matte, and some all purpose lacquer thinner. I also purchased a couple of paint roller liners, a cheap 1-inch-wide paint brush, and a 50 pack of disposable gloves. Because fiberglass bits are not very pleasant to inhale, you should also use some sort of mask to keep them out of your nose and mouth. I already had a pair of scissors to use, but buy cheap ones if you don't—this is not the time to grab your wife's best sewing shears. Hindsight being 20/20, I would have also found some inexpensive cups in which to mix fiberglass resin, as this would have been an easier way to pour resin onto the second coat of fiberglass. Whenever you are buying anything to use for mixing or

This steel cowl support from Speedway Motors should provide support and rigidity to the body, as well as make a great mounting point for items such as the steering column and the wiring panel. Unfortnately, it does not fit around the transmission tunnel in the floor very well. Actually, it just plain doesn't fit.

To make the cowl support fit (it does have a purpose, so I want to use it), I needed to remove a portion of the floor in the toe board area from each side. This, of course, called for more fiberglass work to be done later to avoid having a gaping hole on each side of the floor.

These are the materials needed for working with fiberglass: fiberglass resin, fiberglass matte or cloth, lacquer thinner or acetone (for cleanup), scissors, cheap paint brush, disposable gloves, and a tray for mixing the resin with its hardener. Whenever you are purchasing supplies for use with fiberglass, think disposable rather than cleaning after use, as cleanup is very time consuming.

spreading fiberglass, think disposable and buy cheap. Resin, matte, and cloth are different, but for mixing and applying, you will have to throw everything it in the trash when you are finished.

Not knowing just how fast the resin would set (the temperature in my garage on this particular day was 98 degrees Fahrenheit), I wanted to be able to move quickly if necessary. Go ahead and put on a pair of disposable gloves if you haven't already. I cut the fiberglass matte into strips roughly 6 inches wide and about 18 inches long. I then centered these strips along the junction of the floor and the body. After cutting enough pieces out to make two layers on one side of the car, I mixed a batch of resin and hardener in one of the disposable paint roller liners. The label

I was not going to risk getting fiberglass resin on my camera gear, so you'll have to bear with me on this part. Prior to mixing any resin, I cut strips of fiberglass matte about 6 inches wide and 18 inches long. I cut out enough strips to put two layers around the entire perimeter of the floor. With the strips for the first layer, I positioned the center of each strip approximately at the seam of the body and floor, while I set the rest aside.

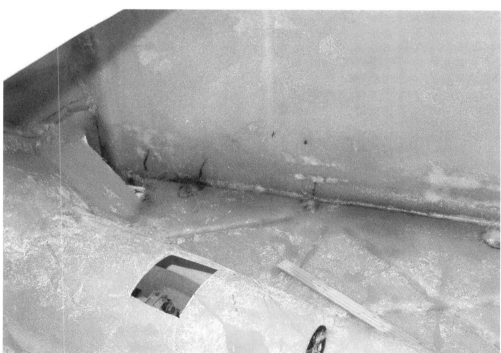

Resin was mixed with its hardener in the disposable paint roller tray and stirred slowly with a paint mixing stick. Each piece of fiberglass matte was dipped into the fiberglass resin and then repositioned around the floor/body seam. Each piece of this first layer of matte was dipped and put into position, and then any bubbles were worked out with a body filler spreader. After giving the first layer of matte some time to tack up, the matte for the second layer was pressed into position, with an overlap between pieces from each layer. Fiberglass resin was then brushed onto both layers with a cheap paint brush.

on the resin can usually gives approximate mixing ratios based upon the ambient temperature.

I dipped the first piece of matte into the resin. When it was thoroughly saturated, I put it into position and used a plastic spreader to squeegee out any air pockets. I continued this process until one layer was in place on one side of the car. All of the printed materials and word of mouth info that I have received says that the first layer of matte should be dipped into resin, while the second and successive layers can be placed onto the still wet first coat and then saturated by pouring or brushing the resin on. Armed with that advice, I positioned the second layers of matte so that none of the edges would precisely overlap each other—to avoid a pronounced ridge and provide the

REWORKING THE FLOOR

A problem with the floor of the Speedway Motors Track T kit that will come to light later on in the project is the transmission hump. It is no doubt made large enough to accept any transmission a buyer may try to install. While this is convenient from that perspective, the large hump leaves very little room for a steering column, a brake pedal, the driver's two feet, and a gas pedal. (A builder installing a manual transmission will be especially hard pressed to fit in a third pedal.) One solution to this is to bend the brake pedal arm to the left of the steering column, leaving braking duty to the left foot. To some, this might be a safety issue, especially for the driver who has only piloted automatics and has thus never used his or her left foot. You can imagine in a panic stop situation, this driver would reach for the brake with the right foot and be blocked by the column. Whether this arrangement is acceptable depends on a driver's confidence in braking with the left foot, but an alternative is to trim the transmission hump to provide more floor space. (Due to the very narrow floor space in the Track T, I used the left foot brake pedal *and* trimmed the tranny tunnel. I sure won't be wearing my cowboy boots while driving this car.)

Before cutting out any of the floor, put the car on jack stands to get a good look underneath. You need to verify that there is indeed room to trim and determine approximately how much to remove. Return the car to solid ground and mark a dotted line at the base of the transmission hump and driveshaft tunnel, indicating where to cut. Using an electric saber saw and several coarse blades, cut away the appropriate portion of the transmission hump.

With the excess removed and the hump resized to fit the transmission without taking extra footwell space, cut pieces of thin cardboard or poster board to serve as a mold for the new fiberglass. The cardboard will need to be stiff enough to maintain its shape, yet flexible enough to create smooth curves. Since the hump is not going to have a consistent shape where it meets the floor or the firewall, you can cut out strips for the edges, and then use larger pieces of cardboard to fill in the area after establishing the basic shape. Plastic strapping tape can be used to fasten the pieces together.

When the entire new hump has been skinned with cardboard, cover it with waxed paper, plastic wrapping material (Saran Wrap or other similar product), or a layer of plastic strapping tape to act as a release agent for the fiberglass. Cut several pieces of fiberglass matte into manageable sized pieces. Then mix fiberglass resin and hardener together in a disposable mixing cup. Lay the first piece of matte into position, pour the mixed resin onto it, and spread the resin out with a disposable paintbrush, gently working out any bubbles. Apply the adjacent piece of matte and saturate it with fiberglass resin as well. Continue this process until the entire transmission hump has been covered with one layer of fiberglass matte and resin, making sure that the new transmission hump is tied into the floor and firewall.

Before the resin has fully cured, add a second layer of matte, making sure to overlap any seams in the previous layer. Brush on more resin so that this layer is fully saturated. Smooth out any bubbles or wrinkles, but take care to avoid overworking the matte, as it will begin to ball up. Repeat this process with a third layer of matte. Now allow the fiberglass to fully cure in a well ventilated area. Afterward, any high spots can be ground down with a grinder and a 36-grit disc. If necessary, you can fill or smooth up low spots with a layer of plastic body filler. Finally, you can pull the cardboard away from the body from underneath.

extra strength of a lattice—and saturated them by brushing on the resin.

Allow the first side to dry and, if you're pleased with the results, do the opposite side in the same manner. Two bits of caution here: first, fiberglass resin cures by means of a chemical reaction; when the hardener reacts with the resin, it gets damn hot. So don't drop a blob of it onto your skin; if you do, wipe it off before it begins to cure. Secondly, the fumes of fiberglass resin are quite strong, so make sure that you are working in a well ventilated area. Even after you are finished, leave the area ventilated for as long as possible to clear out the offensive odor.

MOUNTING TAILLIGHTS (INCLUDING A THIRD BRAKE LIGHT)

Over the years, quite the variety of taillights have been used to illuminate the backside of many a hot rod—everything from 1939 Ford teardrops (first available on 1938 Fords) and 1937 Chevrolet bullets, to flush mount billet pieces and most everything in between. Some hot rodders emphasize their safety purpose and choose taillights that are big and bright. Other rodders see them as a necessary evil, and do whatever they can to conceal them to avoid interrupting the smooth lines of their ride.

 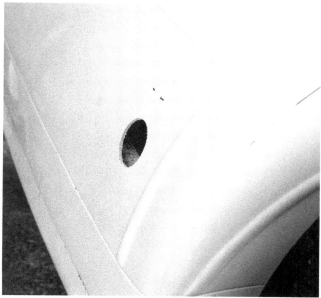

Left: Since the 1950 Pontiac taillights are round, their installation is very easy. Easy is good on occasion. After determining their intended location, punch out the center hole and drill a small pilot hole. Then use a 2 1/2-inch hole saw to cut the hole for the back part of the light housing that won't be seen. Right: Depending on how sharp your hole saw is, you may need to sand the edges of the hole to remove any splinters or burrs.

Taillights don't have to be big to be effective, and they shouldn't have to conflict with the lines of the vehicle either. Well designed taillights that are located properly on the hot rod will help keep you safe and will not be anywhere near as ugly as a smashed fender. Depending on the make, model, and year of vehicle that you are building, your choice in taillights and placement may be simple or overwhelming.

For the Track T, the choice in taillights seemed easy for a variety of reasons. First of all, it didn't have any fenders, so the lights obviously needed to be mounted on the body itself or below it. Mounting them in or below the rolled pan would be lower than what I felt would be prudent for safety. With the large expanse of sheet metal (well, okay, fiberglass in this case), something that can be surface mounted would be ideal. To make installation easy, something round will hide any slight variation in mounting angle between the two sides, although the line between them will still need to be parallel to the road. A contemporary favorite is the 1950 Pontiac taillight, which is a round, surface-mount light that also features lots of surface area, meaning that it is easy to see.

Once you have determined a location, installing these taillights is pretty easy. I wanted to install them on the back of the car, where the surface was as close to vertical as possible. However, the horizontal hoop of the chassis was situated very close to the inside of the body and these lights protruded into the body somewhat. As luck would have it, the ideal placement was right into the aforementioned hori-zontal hoop. I realized this potential concern before I drilled any holes, though.

Begin by determining the location of the center of the lights. Measure in from the bead positioned between the quarter panel and the deck lid. Then measure down from the line that indicates the lower side of the deck lid is the same distance on both sides. The intersection of the horizontal and vertical lines is the center of the lights. After using a 1/8-inch bit to drill a pilot hole at this intersection, use a 2 1/2-inch hole saw to cut a hole for the housing of the light to protrude through the body.

Now, two holes for mounting screws need to be drilled. Center the gasket, which already has two mounting screw holes in it, over the 2-1/2-inch hole and mark directly through those holes in the gasket. Remove the gasket and drill a 1/8-inch hole at the two locations just marked. Slide the gasket over the wires and two mounting studs of the light fixture, and then insert the light into the body. Secure it in place by threading the supplied nuts onto the mounting studs from the backside. Other than wiring, installation of the taillights is complete.

Under federal law, all new vehicles sold in the United States must have a third brake light. Whether the law in your state requires one for a kit car or hot rod is beyond the scope of this book. They do prevent accidents, however, so I went ahead and installed one, even though the big Pontiac lights provide a pretty good splash of red when anyone hits

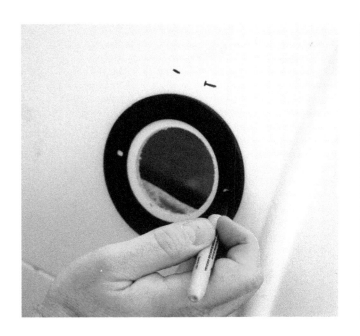 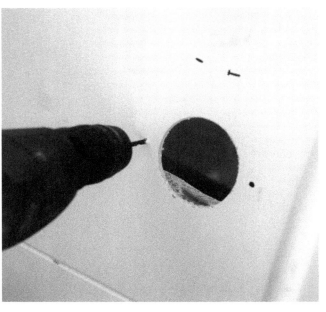

Left: The taillight attaches to the body with two mounting studs on the taillight housing. The gasket for the taillight already has holes in it for these mounting studs, making it a suitable template. Center the gasket on the 2 1/2-inch hole and then mark the holes for the mounting studs. ***Right:*** Remove the gasket and drill a 1/8-inch hole at the two locations just marked. I chose to drill the holes for the mounting studs so that they were level, but since they are never seen, except from beneath the car, their orientation doesn't really matter.

With the two taillights mounted, all that's left before they are operable is wiring.

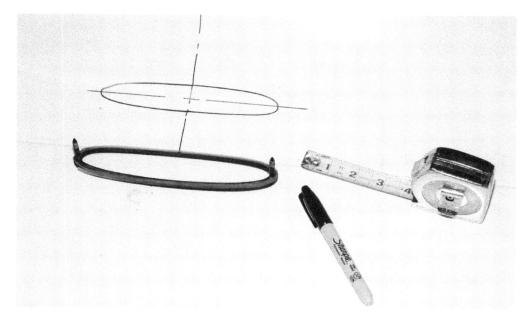

The Dodge Neon third brake light is installed much the same way as the taillights from the 1950 Pontiac, but with subtle differences. Once the location of the light is determined, mark the vertical and horizontal axis, since this light is elliptical. Use the inside of the bezel as a template for marking the area to be cut.

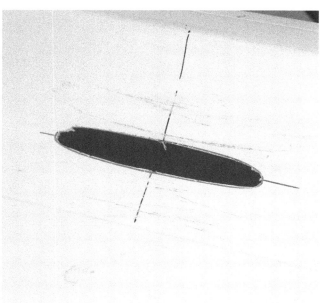

Left: A bezel (that has two mounting studs) will be located outside of the body. The light housing itself will be placed inside the car and sandwiched between the body and nuts on each of the two mounting studs. Using a saber saw, cut out the area that will be covered by the lamp lens. It will need some filing and sanding to fit correctly. **Right:** After cutting the hole in the body to the correct size and shape, slip the bezel into place. Then put light housing into position from the inside of the body and secure it in place by threading a nut on each of the mounting studs.

the pedal. Keeping that inattentive teenager at the wheel of a massive SUV from plowing into my new creation is more significant to me than a little divergence from classic hot rod styling. Besides, most rodders fit them, so my car will not be unusual for having one.

For ease of installation and superior looks, I originally planned to install an LED third brake light from Watson's StreetWorks. This unit is installed from behind and can be sanded smooth with the body. Instead, a friend of a friend suggested that I should install a third brake light from a Dodge Neon. He had just purchased a couple of these for less than 10 bucks from the local salvage yard, so they certainly were affordable. He offered to give me one, which saved me a trip. In return, I gave him a copy

I'm hoping that with the two relatively large taillights and a third brake light, the Track T can avoid any collisions from errant drivers approaching from behind. I did not run a bumper, but this chassis does include a piece of steel tubing that forms a horizontal hoop around the rear portion of the car. This won't protect the body in a collision, but perhaps it will minimize chassis damage and injuries to occupants.

of *How to Build a Hot Rod Model A Ford*, which happens to show how to install the Watson's unit.

How effective the third brake light will be depends somewhat on how close to vertical it is mounted. The logical area to mount this light is between the front of the deck lid and the back edge of the passenger compartment, even though the area is closer to horizontal than vertical. It does become more vertical as it moves forward, but an undetermined amount of the upholstery will lap over the edge, so the brake light should not be pushed too far forward.

This particular light fit behind the sheet metal (or fiberglass), with the visible portion of the light protruding through a hole in the body material. Two screws that were part of the outer bezel passed through the body and the light housing, and then were secured by two nuts.

The first step in mounting the third brake light is measuring to find the center of the car from side to side. Intersect this line with a level line, which will be the horizontal axis of the light. Remove the outer bezel from the brake light assembly, and then lay it face down on the body and centered on the horizontal and vertical axis. Using a marking pen, draw around the inside of the bezel. The body

material inside of this oval now needs to be removed. Drilling a hole and then using a saber saw works well. Just be sure that you don't make the hole too big. With the hole cut out, check the light for proper fit by sliding it in place from behind. If the hole needs some modification, a file or wood rasp will suffice, although it may take a couple of trial fits before you get it just as you want it. If you inadvertently make the hole too big, you can fill in some small areas with plastic body filler later on when doing bodywork.

FITTING THE NOSE AND HOOD SIDES

On most any vehicle, the grille shell (or nose) needs to be installed before the hood. Unlike a production vehicle, where the sheet metal is already cut to fit around any obstructions, a fiberglass nose needs to be cut to fit. During the initial mock-up stages, cut a notch out of the bottom of the nose for the front spring. To determine the location of the spring in relation to the nose, set the hood top into position at the cowl and match the nose to it. At the same time, also keep the lip of the nose parallel with the cowl so that the hood sides are square. To determine the depth of the notch, make sure that the nose is lower than the cowl,

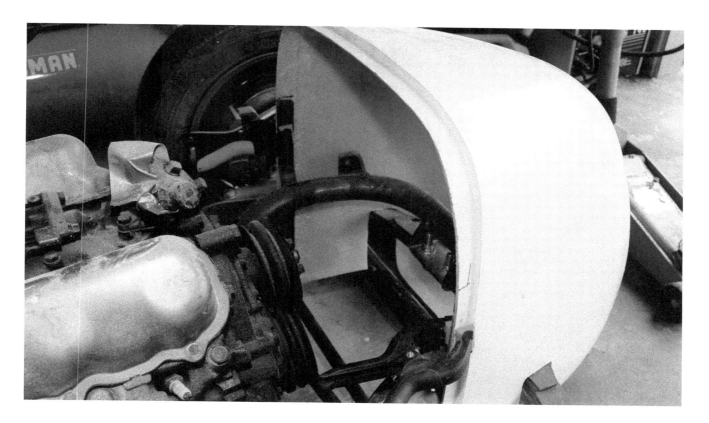

After notching the nose to allow for the front spring, you can determine the location for the two steel support straps. You can shape the latter to fit the contour of the nose and can weld them to the tubular portion of the front of the chassis.

and cut the notch deep enough to clear the spring. Cut the very minimum at first, and then trim later to allow for wheel alignment (the spring may move slightly due to caster adjustment) and engine/transmission weight.

To secure the nose to the car, Speedway Motors provides two strap steel supports that are to be welded to the outside of the front portion of the chassis. You should mount them to correspond with the vertical portion of the grille. Although the top of the nose should be lower than the top of the cowl, do not push the nose down too low or there will not be enough room for the radiator. You can clamp the nose to the afore-mentioned strap steel supports, span the vacant area between the cowl and the nose with a few pieces of masking tape, and then step back to see if the hood line looks about right.

With the nose located vertically, it needs to be located front to back before the supports are attached. The nose must also be positioned so that it is not farther away from the cowl than what the hood sides will cover. On this Track T, the nose was mounted so that the bottom of the hood sides were square with the cowl and nose, but were slanted at the top (in other words, the sides were taller in the back than at the front). With the nose clamped in this position,

mark a line on the inside of the nose around the edge and top of the supports. Remove the nose, and mark and center punch the location for two holes in each support. Drill the holes to accept a 1/4-inch flathead bolt. With the holes drilled in the support straps, clamp the nose into place again, check proper location, and then drill the mounting holes in the nose, using the holes in the support straps as a guide.

Use a countersink bit on the nose to allow the flathead bolts to fit close to flush with the surface of the fiberglass nose. Drilling the holes farther apart will help to keep the nose aligned properly. You may wish to use more bolts, but two 1/4-20 bolts on each side should secure the nose at this time. When the car becomes drivable, you many want to monitor the security of the nose to see if the four bolts are sufficient.

A peculiarity of the Track T is that the mounting point for the upper front shock mount/headlight mounting bracket is on the chassis, inside the nose. This requires another hole to be cut out of the nose on each side. With the nose in place, mark around this mounting point on the inside of the nose. Now remove the nose and square up the lines indicating what needs to be cut from the side of the nose. Drill a hole somewhere in the area that is to be cut

Above: A hole for a 1/4-20 bolt should be drilled near the top and bottom of each of the steel support straps.

Right: The nose is now put back into position. It must be located close enough to the firewall that the hood sides are long enough to cover the side opening. It also makes sense to position the nose so that the front and rear edges of the hood side are parallel. With the nose situated as desired, use the holes in the steel support straps as a template for marking the corresponding holes in the nose. Now, drill the holes in the nose and secure the nose to the support straps with 1/4-20 bolts, a lock washer, and a nut.

To measure the correct dimensions for the hood sides, the hood top needs to be in place. Additionally, a line representing the lower edge of the hood side must be transferred to the nose, since the body aprons have been trimmed to allow for suspension and steering travel. Photo by Sandy Parks

Measure and record the distance between the cowl and the nose along the lower side of the hood top. Disregard the flange, as you are just interested in the dimension of the hood side at this time. Photo by Sandy Parks

Measure and record the distance between the cowl and the nose along the top of the body apron. This dimension will vary slightly from the previous one because of the slope of the hood top. Photo by Sandy Parks

Now measure and record the distance between the top of the body apron and the hood top along the cowl. Also, measure this same distance at the nose, which should be shorter than the other one. Compare the dimensions from the passenger side to the corresponding dimensions on the driver side. They should be the same. If not, adjust the nose until they are. Photo by Sandy Parks

out so that you can insert a saber saw blade. Cut along the line, check for proper fit, trim and file as necessary, and then repeat for the opposite side.

The shock mount/headlight bracket can now be secured to the chassis with two 3/8-inch fine thread bolts. Then you can secure the front shocks to the axle and the upper shock mount.

INSTALLING THE GRILLE

Compared to the nose, installing the grille is very easy . . . once I decided how to do it. On the Track T belonging to the guy from whom I purchased my engine and transmission, the grille is secured with miniscule Dzus fasteners. This was a very slick way to attach this piece, as it allowed him to remove the grille without taking anything else apart. Not that it's something that needs to be done on a regular basis, but you shouldn't have to disassemble the entire vehicle just to remove the grille. After an extensive and unsuccessful search for these small fasteners, I decided to use countersunk stainless steel 1/4-20 bolts with a washer and locknut on the inside of each one. This required the

The bracket welded to the tubular portion of the chassis (to the right of the photo) is where the combination upper shock mount/headlight mounting bracket attaches. Both holes are threaded for a 3/8-inch fine thread bolt. A hole large enough for the mounting surface of the shock/headlight mounting bracket to pass through must be cut out of the nose. It also has to be cut in the correct location.

BODY

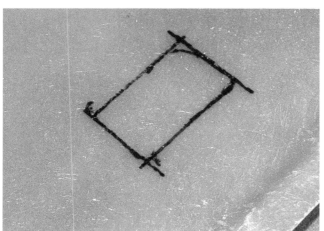 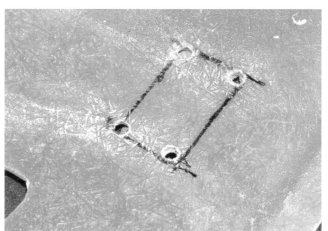

Left: Before removing the nose from its location, trace around the bracket onto the inside of the nose with a marker. Remove the nose and use a carpenter's square to square up the lines. Apply masking tape to the backside of where you will be cutting to avoid splintering the fiberglass. **Right:** It is necessary to drill at least one hole in the nose in order to insert a saber saw blade. To make the corners rounded and uniform, you can drill a hole at each corner and then simply use the saber saw to cut the straight part. This will also work if you have broken your last saber saw blade and need to use a die grinder instead.

grille to be secured to the nose before installing the radiator or the nose.

FASTENING THE HOOD PANELS

Each hood side panel has had its necessary dimensions marked, along with which side of the car the panel goes on and which side faces front. Keeping track of the front edge is particularly important when you need to punch louvers; you need to face them the correct direction and punch them from the correct side. The hood sides will sit flush with the top of the body apron, and will cover the flange of the cowl at the body, the lower edge of the hood top, and the flange of the nose. Spring-loaded 1/4-turn fasteners (commonly known as Dzus fasteners) will be used to hold the three hood panels in place.

After the hood sides are trimmed to the proper size, place 1/4-turn fasteners at all four corners. They will secure the hood sides and top to the cowl at the back and the nose in front. Most likely, you will have to install another fastener in the center of the top edge of the hood sides, to

103

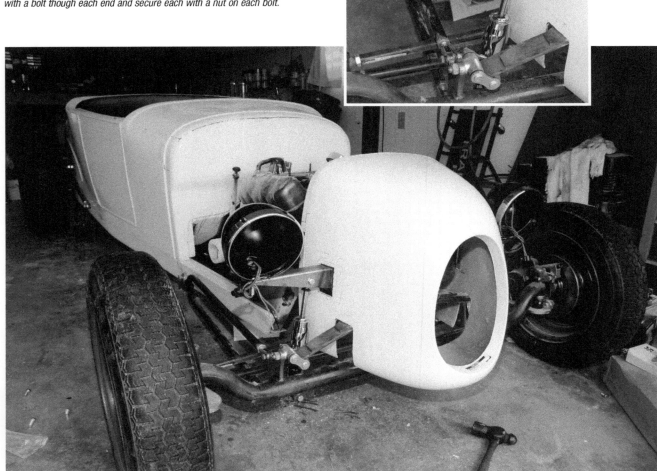

Right: If you have the headlights that you intend to use, drill the headlight mount to the correct size before securing the headlight mount to its mounting bracket. After cutting the holes for the shock/headlight mount on both sides of the nose, reinstall the nose and secure it in place with the four bolts. Mount the shocks with a bolt though each end and secure each with a nut on each bolt.

Even though the bulbs are not yet installed in the light buckets, and the buckets are not tight, this gives you an idea as to what the front of the car will look like with the headlights in place. The headlight mounting brackets will most likely also serve as a mounting location for the front turn signals.

secure the hood sides to the hood top. More than two fasteners should not be required on each side of the cowl, but they can be installed later if necessary. Likewise, a third fastener can be installed along the bottom of the hood sides, but this will require welding a tab to the frame rail to provide an attachment point.

Included with the Speedway Motors Track T kit is a fiberglass hood top and two pieces of aluminum sheet that are the approximate size necessary for the hood sides. Both sides and the hood top need to be trimmed to fit properly—that is, square with each other with uniform gaps. After having used the hood top to determine the mounting location for the nose, it was my intention to

use that same top for the actual construction of the car. However, I wasn't exactly impressed with the actual fit of the hood top with the cowl and the nose. Both the front and back edges were somewhat wavy. Cutting the hood to make it straight could have been done easily enough, however, it would have required adjusting the nose. Since the upper shock mounts extended through the nose, I didn't really want to go that route.

Someone more experienced with fiberglass than me (okay, that is almost anyone) could have probably saved the hood, but I chose a different method. It added to the cost of the vehicle's construction, but I thought it would add to the value as well. I was taking the hood sides to

continued on page 108

104

BODY

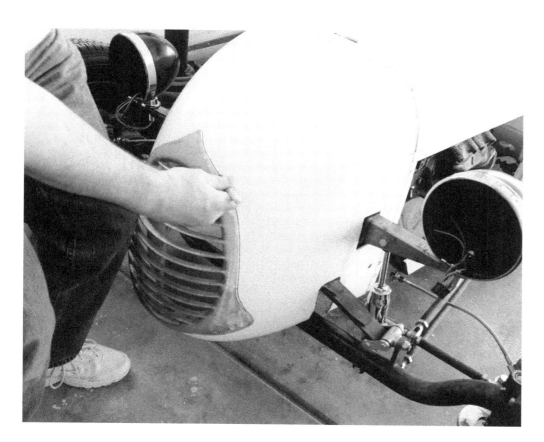

Just to make sure that the grille fits the opening correctly, I set it in place and then traced around the outline of the grille with a permanent marker.

Although the cast-aluminum grille is somewhat rough (typical of many cast-aluminum parts), it does seem to have about the same amount of gap around the grille opening.

Right: After locating and drilling three pilot holes in the grille, I placed it in position on the car's nose and drilled the proper size holes to mount it. I then installed a bolt through the top center hole and secured it with a fender washer and lock nut. This process was repeated for each of the other two remaining holes.

Below: At this point, I still hadn't decided whether the aluminum grille should be painted, polished, or chromed, but at least it was now securely in place.

The hood top was set in place and a line marked on the cowl and the nose showing the bottom edge. After doing this for both sides, I checked the aluminum hood side for proper fit. The cowl, the body apron, and the nose were all square with each other, with the lower edge of the hood having a slope to it. Since the hood sides from Speedway Motors are square, the top edge of the side will need to be trimmed. A line connecting the reference marks on the cowl and nose is where the hood side needs to be trimmed (top edge of the masking tape).

Of course, they will be punched full of louvers eventually, but this provides a glimpse of what the hood sides will look like. When completed, the hood and hood sides will cover the engine completely, so no extensive chrome plating is necessary to dress up the engine compartment to impress anyone.

Although this shot doesn't show the hood in place, it did seem like a good time to provide an in-progress profile. As indicated by masking tape between the cowl and the nose, the hood top will be sloping downhill and the hood will also clear the air cleaner, both good things. Although they are merely mocked up on a block, the side pipes are very close to their final position.

continued from page 104

KBS Fabricators to have them louvered anyway, so I asked the shop to fabricate a new aluminum hood top while the car was there. Depending on the make and model of vehicle you are building, this can be an expensive proposition. Therefore, it is prudent to ask for an approximate cost before you make your decision. A good thing about the fabricated aluminum hood was that I knew it would be built to fit my car and, like the hood sides, it could be louvered. Even though it added to the bottom line, I felt that it gave the Track T more credibility as a real hot rod.

Although I was not able to witness Vince Baker at KBS Fabricators as he built a custom hood top for me, I can tell you that typically the process involves careful measuring. It also requires a method for rolling the aluminum sheet to match the curve of the cowl and the nose, as well as a method for rolling a flange into the lower edge of the hood top.

With a final hood top in hand, it's time to determine the location and method of attaching the Dzus fasteners. These quarter-turn fasteners consist of a spring attached to the inside of the panel(s), and a mounting plate and a spring-loaded "button" that go on the outside of the panel(s). The button is free to rotate within the mounting plate. A slot in the shaft of the button allows it to fit over the spring and then pull the panels together as the fastener is rotated clockwise. When the button is rotated a full quarter turn, the panels are locked together. Releasing the button simply requires rotating the button counterclockwise a quarter turn.

With the hood top and sides secured to the body, the desired layout for the louvers can be determined and transferred to the aluminum. For this project, I used a drawing by Steve Gilmore at Stilmore Designs as a guide for the number of louvers to have, as well as their placement. Each side had two rows of louvers, with four rows on the hood top. The end of each row on the sides was placed so that none of the louvers would require being masked for two colors of paint when the scallops were applied. This same pattern was repeated on the top.

BUILDING AND MOUNTING THE DASH

Many of the dashboards that I have seen in various Track Ts and other budget hot rods have left something to be desired in my admittedly biased opinion. Several examples have been made from wood, a straight piece of metal, or aluminum or stainless steel that has been polished to a high luster. Wood is easy to work with and can become a work

Left: With minimal working room on the inside, Vince Baker at KBS Fabricators attached a mounting tab to the outside of the firewall at the base. This made it easier to install the Dzus fastener, while still securing the hood near the base of the cowl. *Right:* Vince had to trim the vertical support that mounts the nose in order to place the Dzus fastener in an appropriate spot. Two pop rivets through the front of the nose flange secured the spring for the fastener, which was located on the back side. The spring spanned the hole through which the Dzus button was inserted. A slot in the Dzus button slid over the spring and then held the panels secure when the button was turned.

Left: Interchangeable heads can be inserted in this louver press to create louvers of different shapes and sizes. An index mark on the center of the head indicates where the louver will be located. The operator aligns a centerline marked on the piece being louvered with this index mark. *Right:* Vince Baker positions a hood side so that the next louver is in line with the centerline mark, and then presses a foot pedal to activate the louver press.

The louvered hood top and sides sure improved the Track T's looks. Since the engine compartment was hidden, money that would have ordinarily been spent on dress up items could now be spent on performance or safety equipment.

of art in the hands of a craftsman, but was impractical for my open car. Metal is a better choice but, in too many examples, is simply sheared across the bottom. I suppose this is okay, but it reminds me of a guillotine. On many attempts to make the dash more attractive, the owners have polished their dash to such a high luster, that it might be unsafe from glare in an open car.

My thought is to have an oval dash similar to those found in Model A Fords, which can be made through a couple different methods. One way is to make a wooden buck and then hammer-form a rounded edge on the bottom of a piece of sheet metal to avoid having a sharp edge just above your kneecaps. A second method is to roll your own fiberglass dash panel. Depending on success or failure, you can resort to the other plan, as the first portions of both procedures are the same.

Either method requires making a pattern. I first determined the center of the body (side to side) at the location of the dash panel and marked a vertical line. Available poster board was not large enough to cover the entire dash,

so I made a half pattern. To duplicate the shape of the cowl for the top of the dash panel, I held a piece of poster board against the edge of the body and traced a line against that body edge onto the poster board. Knowing the size of the gauges I had planned to use (you have to make the dash large enough for the gauges), I flipped the poster board pattern over and traced the outline of the cowl again, being careful to get the two arcs the desired distance apart. To connect the two arcs of the pattern, I traced around a spray paint can to provide a smooth edge.

You can now cut out the pattern with a pair of scissors and then transfer it to a piece of wood. For making a one-time-use plug for a fiberglass mold, a piece of pine shelving material will work fine. If you are going to be hammer-forming a metal dash, you should use a piece of hardwood such as oak or maple. You can now cut out the wood, apply a rounded edge using a router or hand file, and then sand. If hammer-forming metal, you will have to cut out another piece of wood that is the same shape and size. Then clamp a piece of metal in place between the two wooden bucks.

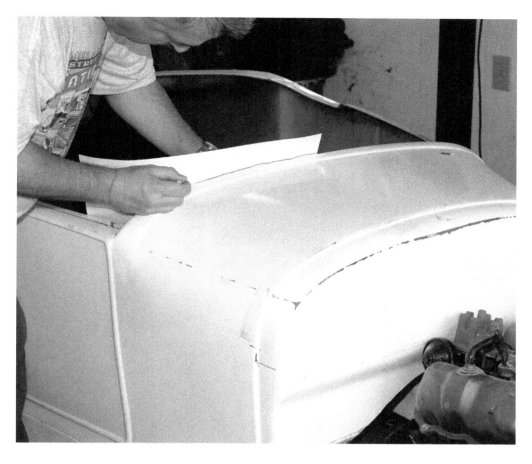

To get the curve of the dash top, I aligned a piece of poster board against the centerline of the dash. Then I drew a line along the top edge of the dash. I flipped over the poster board to achieve a mirror image for the lower side of the dash. Photo by Sandy Parks

Using a forming hammer, hammer the lower edge of the dash panel downward so that the finished dash will have a lip on it, rather than a knife edge.

After verifying that the wooden pattern fits as desired, wrap the front side of the plug with waxed paper so that the fiberglass will not stick to the wood. The waxed paper can be secured to the back of the wood with masking tape. With the wooden plug sitting atop a 2x4, cut two strips of fiberglass matte large enough to cover the plug. Then mix fiberglass resin with hardener, position the first layer of matte on the wooden plug, and brush the resin onto the fiberglass matte so that all of the matte is soaked with resin. After the fiberglass begins to get tacky, put the second piece of matte into place and apply more resin, making sure that all of the matte is thoroughly saturated. Allow to cure, and at this time the wooden plug should be easily removed. Do not discard the wooden plug, as you can use it again to make a new mold if necessary, or in my case, use it to hammer-form a steel dash. More about that a little later . . .

With the wooden plug removed from the mold, you can coat the latter with mold release or a layer of wax paper pressed into place and secured to the back of the mold with masking tape. Then cut out two strips of fiberglass cloth,

each one large enough to cover the mold. Mix fiberglass resin with hardener, position the first layer of cloth in the mold, and brush the resin onto the fiberglass cloth so that all of the cloth is soaked with resin. After the fiberglass begins to get tacky, place the second piece of cloth into place and apply more resin, making sure that all of the cloth is thoroughly saturated. After the resin has begun to cure, but while it is still tacky, add two layers of matte using the same basic procedure. Then allow the dash to fully cure, at which time the mold can be removed from the finished part.

When working with fiberglass and a mold, you need to remember whether you are working from the inside or the outside of the part being reproduced. With this dash, I made a male pattern of wood, and then created a female mold. To make the actual dash, I applied fiberglass cloth and resin to the inside (smooth) side of the mold, with the first layer of cloth ultimately being the outside face of the dash. I used cloth for the first two layers to provide a smoother surface, and then a couple of layers of matte to provide strength.

Not being overly impressed with my fiberglass dash, I decided to try my hand at hammer-forming. The fiberglass dash was strong enough and would work, but I just wasn't happy with the appearance. A person more experienced in

111

With the poster board pattern drawn and cut out, I placed it on a piece of wood and traced around it, indicating where the wood needed to be cut. I used a scrap piece of pine shelving because it was available, but for repeated use, oak or some other hardwood would have been more suitable.

After being cut out, check the wooden buck for proper fit. You should realize that the fit will be different depending on the fiberglass body being used and the thickness of the dash material. In other words, the relatively thin sheet metal will fit deeper into the gap than the 3/4-inch wood. Photo by Sandy Parks

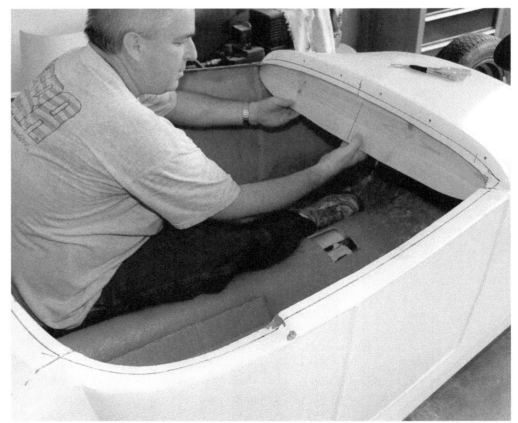

The wooden buck can now be used as a plug for a fiberglass mold. After curing, the fiberglass mold is then used to make a fiberglass dash.

working with fiberglass could have produced a nicer piece. Oh well, you never know until you give it a try.

Plan B was to hammer-form a steel dash. Although the original buck was made of soft pine, I was hoping that for a one time use, it would suffice. I purchased a piece of sheet steel from one of the local home repair centers, so it wasn't exactly what I was looking for, but now that it is finished, I can say that it worked. Aluminum would have been easier to work than steel, but no pieces in stock were big enough. The next choice was a piece of sheet steel that was a little thinner than what I wanted, but at least it was big enough to fit the pattern when diagonal. With the lip along the bottom and a steering column support brace that would be connected to the inside of the firewall and the inside of the dash, it was adequate.

The paper pattern originally used to make the wooden buck was used again to trace the pattern of the face of the dash onto the sheet steel. To allow for the lip, I made several marks approximately 3/4 inch beyond the line representing the lower edge of the face. These "dots" were connected and blended in to the line representing the lower edge of the face near each edge. To make the material more manageable, I cut away the excess sheet metal with a pair of aviation snips, although a plasma cutter would have made the job much easier.

After the fiberglass mold is made, line it with waxed paper (to act as a release agent) and then use fiberglass cloth, matte, and resin to construct the new dash. The extra fiberglass matte and cloth will be trimmed and removed later.

113

This sheet metal is what was available at the local home improvement center and was a little thin for my use. However, with the relatively small size of the dash and a rolled edge, it sufficed. Any thicker pieces available were too small for my needs. Hindsight being 20/20, I should have searched for a piece of aluminum. Photo by Sandy Parks

Using as many clamps as I had access to, I sandwiched the sheet metal between the wooden buck on the bottom (face up) and a second buck with the same curve on the top, making sure there wasn't any movement between the sheet metal and the wooden buck. Now, using a forming hammer, I began in the middle and started tapping the lip downward over the rounded edge of the wooden buck. I didn't hit it with a big swing, just used taps hard enough to bend the sheet metal slightly. Working my way back and forth until the edge as hammered flat against the wooden buck, this method provided a smooth lip.

I had already drilled holes for six 1/4-20 bolts somewhat evenly spaced across the edge of the body above the dash when making the pattern for the dash. The sheet metal dash was held in place behind the edge of the body,

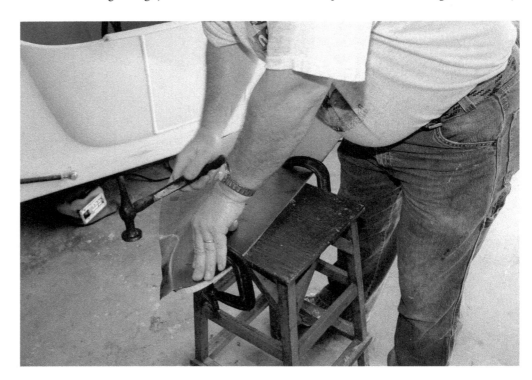

Ron Covell certainly doesn't have to worry about me taking away any of his metal working business. Still, using a wooden buck, as many clamps as I could find, and a body hammer, I was able to fabricate my own metal dash. A key here is to take your time and avoid overworking the metal. It may not be pretty, but it wasn't expensive. Photo by Sandy Parks

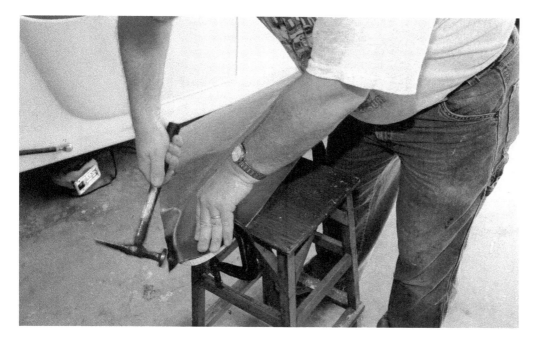

Contrary to what is shown in the photos (oops), you should start in the middle when hammering the edge over the buck and work toward the edges. Whenever you are finished working the metal to the desired shape, be sure to deburr any and all edges. Photo by Sandy Parks

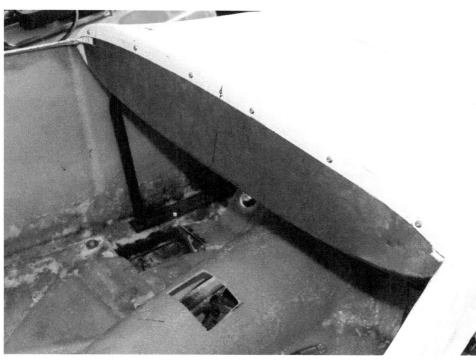

For this Track T, this dash worked just fine. It was soon full of gauges, which is its main purpose. In all actuality, it received at least a skim coat of plastic body filler before it was painted, but it doesn't look too awful as it is. At least it was inexpensive and I can say I did it myself. Photo by Sandy Parks

and I used the holes as a template to mark the holes I needed to drill into the dash. Some additional trimming was necessary at the ends of the dash, but with that completed, the dash fit properly. At this time, your dash may not perfect, but with a little bit of time with a long board sander and a wee bit of body filler, it will be fine. By the time it is filled with gauges, many of the imperfections will be gone.

MOUNTING THE WINDSHIELD FRAME

Installing a windshield in a stock configuration closed vehicle is easy because its location is predetermined. Even on a roadster with a one-piece, flat glass windshield, installing the posts is fairly easy. The main objective in that case is to install the posts square with the body and at the same height. Then it is simply a matter of cutting the glass to the right size and installing it properly.

With the centerline already marked atop the cowl, the front edge of each side of the windshield frame needs to be marked on the cowl as well. As seen in the photo, several locations will work. The key is determining which location fits the best. Having an extra set of hands to hold the frame while someone else marks the cowl will be of great benefit, as it is difficult to consistently hold the frame steady while marking a line against it. Photo by Sandy Parks

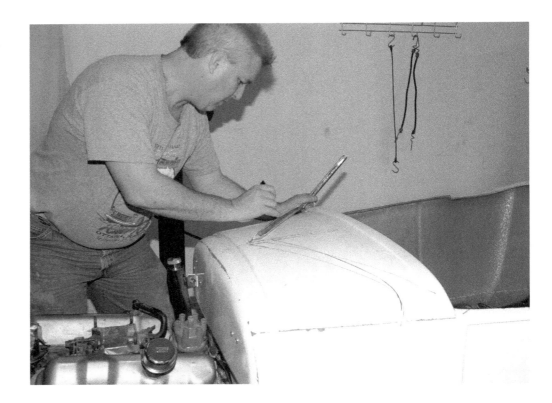

Mounting holes for the center post must also be marked. With a mark on the side of the center post's base for each mounting hole, you can mark the hole locations after centering the base along the centerline marked on the cowl. It is critical that the grooves in the side of the center post are aligned with the grooves in each side of the windshield frame. Photo by Sandy Parks

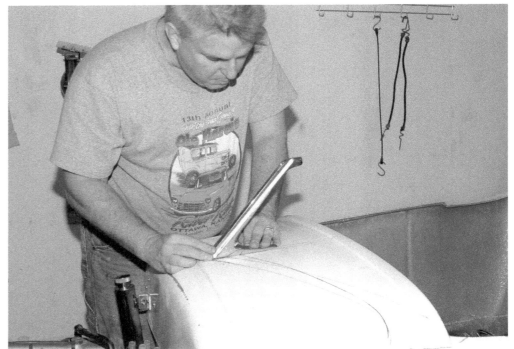

Fitting any type of multi-piece vee'd windshield frame on the cowl of a custom built body, however, may have you reconsidering a straight windshield. The cowl has a distinct curve from side to side, which is compounded due to the slope of the cowl from front to back. The bottom of each side of the windshield frame also has a distinct curve as well. The problem lies in determining where the cowl and the windshield frame most closely align with each other. You shouldn't have to remove any material from the cowl, but you may be required to fill some areas to achieve the best fit.

116

REPAIR

Whether you are searching for a vehicle for your just-turned-driving-age son or daughter, or are looking for a hot rod project, the word "budget" often works its way into the formula. Anytime this happens, words like "pristine," "like new condition," and various other implications of perfection quickly fade from the vehicle's description.

Even though a hot rod project is quite often cut, chopped, sliced, and otherwise disassembled and then reassembled during construction, there is often some actual repair work that must be done before the actual hot rod building can begin. Two of the most frequent repairs when dealing with a "budget" vehicle are collision damage and rust repair.

Collision Damage

Ranging from a broken headlight in a dented fender to a badly twisted frame, collision damage is probably the most difficult to repair for the average hot rodder working in his or her own garage. Experienced body people know how to "read" damaged panels and repair them by undoing the various dents and ripples in the opposite order in which the damage occurred. By simply hammering out the deepest dent first and then moving on to the next deepest, you would be stretching and contorting the metal beyond its capabilities, making a suitable repair very difficult.

Unless collision damage is very minor or you are experienced in collision repair, you may be time and money ahead to have repairs made by professionals who are experienced in this type of work. Although paying someone to smooth out a wrinkled fender will cost you some money up front, it may still be less expensive than buying a new repop fender after you have hammered the daylights out of the original one yourself. It may take some searching, but if you can find a shop that understands that you are building a hot rod, it may be willing to straighten the fender for you for a lower cost, if you can do the final sanding, priming, and painting (which you would probably do anyway).

Rust Repair

An aggressive automotive aftermarket is making rust repair easier most everyday. Whether the rust that you need to deal with is minor surface rust or a complete panel that has lost the battle, there are many ways to fight back. Localized surface rust can be sanded away by hand or with an orbital sander. If several larger areas are covered with rust, or if the rust is more severe than surface rust, the disassembled panels and chassis components can be media blasted or chemically dipped to remove the rust. Once the rust is removed, however, the remaining surface should be coated with an epoxy primer prior to being painted.

Depending on the vehicle that you are working on and the specific area of it, replacement patch panels may be available for the metal that has rusted away. Installing patch panels will vary from one panel to another, but basically the old rusty metal is cut out using a reciprocating saw, a die grinder, a plasma cutter, or if necessary, a pair of aviation snips. The new patch panel is aligned, clamped into place, and then MIG or TIG welded. Follow up with a skim coat or two of plastic body filler, some epoxy primer (for corrosion resistance), and then paint. The actual procedure may be a little more involved depending on the panel being replaced, but for some panels, that's about it.

Begin by finding the centerline of the cowl and marking a reference line front to back. Then measure the width of the center windshield post, and mark a reference line half of this distance on each side of the centerline. With this outer edge of the center post marked, you will have a more clear indication of where you will need to position the side pieces. You can trim each of the side pieces to abut this center post, but stretching them to meet it is impossible, or at least highly impractical. Having someone to hold the frame in place while you mark a line on the cowl will make this task easier, as the bottom side of the windshield frame is tapered to automatically rake the posts back. Before drilling any holes in the cowl, you should first mark along the front of the windshield frame on both sides of the car. There are potentially multiple locations where the frame will fit the body, so choosing one that looks the best is up to you. Don't hesitate to go back to the magazines or other photos that originally inspired your design to see where those builders placed the windshield.

After determining a suitable location for the windshield frame and marking the front edge of the frame on the cowl, you can now determine the mounting hole locations and transfer them to the cowl. By measuring

With all of the reference lines marked, the first side of the windshield frame can be installed. Right or wrong, I began by drilling holes in the cowl for the centermost mounting hole and then for the hole located second from the outside end. Since the hole for the outside end of the frame was located in the most curved portion of the cowl, I felt that its location might be better ascertained after the windshield frame was more accurately located, even if it meant slotting the hole somewhat. I was able to keep the center hole pretty tight (not slotted), which made reinstalling the frame in the same location more accurate.

from the center of the frame inward to the tapped hole, it should be easy enough to transfer the hole locations to the cowl. Realize that there are no straight lines on the frame or the cowl, so measuring is approximate at best, meaning that some of the holes may need to be elongated somewhat. Placing fender washers between the bolt head and the underside of the cowl should alleviate any problems that might arise due to the elongated holes.

With both of the side pieces bolted into position, you can determine how much they need to be trimmed to allow the center post to be installed. When installing the center post,

After mounting the first side of the frame, the second side went much easier. It helped to mark the mounting hole locations on the cowl along the line representing the front edge of the windshield frame. Some of the holes still needed to be elongated slightly, but not by much.

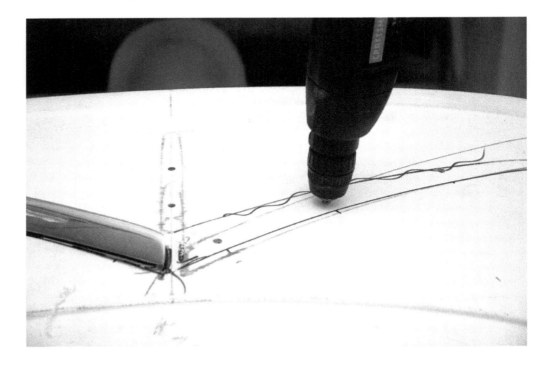

Held by appropriate size bolts and large fender washers, the windshield frame is very secure, even though it is not finished quite yet. From this shot, you can see that the windshield will have a distinct "V" shape, using two pieces of flat glass. Flat glass is always going to be less expensive than curved glass. Additionally, the V-shaped windshield, with its slant, will look much more stylish than a straight windshield. It does come with a price, however; the brass windshield frame (which, at this point, still needed to be chromed) was the single most expensive item on the car, other than the frame and body package.

You will need to trim each side of the windshield frame sufficiently. This will allow the center post to be moved forward, so that the grooves for the windshield glass are all aligned. Thin lines marked on the windshield frame indicate where it needs to be trimmed. Be sure to cut it carefully, leaving it slightly long, and then file it to the precise length. Any gaps will prove to be unsightly when it is finished.

MODIFICATIONS

Having the ability to cut metal and rejoin it with a weld that can be made to look nice (more correctly, appear to disappear), yet remain strong, will allow you to make almost any kind of modification that you can think of. A MIG welder is reasonably inexpensive, it is easy to learn how to use one properly, and the tool is quite suitable for most sheet metal fabrication for a hot rod. A TIG welder is more expensive and it is slightly more difficult to learn how to use one, but this tool does make a nice looking weld that can usually be used "as-is" on chassis work.

Top Chop

If you own a MIG welder and have enough experience with it to feel comfortable cutting up a hot rod project, chopping the top is a quick way to modify the looks of your ride. Just because you can weld, however, does not mean that you can chop the top on just anything. You need to go into this modification with a lot of forethought if you are cutting anything other than a Ford Model A or T. The door and window pillars of these Ford vehicles go straight up, so the top can virtually come straight down. It is slightly more involved than that, but not much.

On the other hand, almost all other vehicles have door and window pillars that taper in toward the top, whether it is front to back, side to side, or a combination thereof. With the roof being smaller in its stock location than the space between the pillars in the lowered location, one of two things has to happen. The roof can be enlarged to fill the gap, or the gap can be reduced by leaning the window posts inward. Which process works best depends largely on the vehicle being chopped and the desired effect.

When chopping a top, remember to cut the top off first, and then cut the "chop" out of the window and door pillars while they are still on the car. This is easier than trying to cut the chop out of a roof panel that is sliding around on the shop floor. Also, don't be afraid to weld some temporary support bracing (electrical conduit works well and is cheap) to help the body retain its shape while it is undergoing surgery. Rather than simply welding spindly door and window pillars atop each other, insert portions of the chopped material into the inside of the pillars. This will back up the weld and make a much stronger, reinforced joint. It will be necessary to slice the material to get it to fit inside, but this extra effort will make for a better job. It is also best to weld the body back together first, and then weld the doors back together to make them match the body.

Channeling

Another quick way to modify the looks of your ride is to channel the body down over the frame rails. Although I personally really like the looks of a 1932 Ford highboy sitting atop the frame rails in its stock position, one of the slickest hot rods I have seen is a Deuce coupe that has been channeled down over the rails. Perhaps Henry and the boys realized this way back when, as the 1933 Ford bodies are channeled over the frame in their stock configuration.

At the risk of over-simplifying it, a body is channeled by removing the floor, dropping the body lower than its stock location, and then reinstalling the floor in this new raised location. It should be obvious that to actually perform this modification is more involved than that, but it should give you a clear idea of what needs to be done.

Much like chopping a top, the correct amount is up for interpretation and will vary from rod to rod and rodder to rodder. What will be an appropriate amount on one vehicle will be too much on another. Before you whack the floor out of your hot rod, you should realize that channeling any vehicle is going to reduce the legroom.

Additionally, channeling may require you to modify the doors to match, which is something that detracts from some channeling jobs. On some vehicles that have a deeper channel, the doors are shortened in height, with the lower portion of the door merged into the body. If this is the style that you desire, that is okay, but it doesn't look as natural as a subtle channel. No matter what kind of modification you make to a hot rod, it should be done to improve the overall looks, rather than modification for the sake of modification.

the grooves in it must align with the groves of the two side pieces. When the windshield frame fits as desired, you can remove from the car and paint, polish, or plate in the finish of your choice. My choice was to have the windshield frame and the grille chrome plated. I took these two items to Fat Catz Plating for polishing and a dip or two in the chrome plating tank. You can read more about the chrome plating process in my book, *How to Plate, Polish and Chrome*.

CHAPTER 5
DRIVETRAIN

We discussed engine considerations in the first chapter, and you have no doubt narrowed your selection down to a few options. Here are some final thoughts on the subject. For hot rods used to haul the entire family to distant rod runs, or for any large bodied hot rod, many builders choose a V-8 with an automatic transmission. Larger vehicles are going to be heavier, you may be pulling a trailer, plus running air conditioning won't pull the rpm down as much on a V-8 when you are in hilly terrain. An overdrive transmission will help mitigate the lower gas mileage. A column shift frees up a little more legroom between the front seats.

On the other hand, if you are building a lighter vehicle, or anything that will be driven just around town, a smaller engine may be appropriate. Many six-cylinder engines have impressive torque ratings and can squeeze a gallon of gas as well. And the Offenhauser, though wildly beyond the cost limits of this project, has proven that even four cylinders can provide formidable performance in the right tune. After accurately determining your needs, you can begin searching for the best deal for your money.

SALVAGE YARD OR PARTS VEHICLE

For a budget hot rod, your local salvage yard is probably the best place to find your engine. Some cars that find their way to the bone yard are there because the engine is just about dead. Since most yards give you a warranty of 30 days or so, they have no incentive to sell you that one.

Many salvage yards with space limitations remove the engines and transmissions soon after they take possession of the vehicle; other yards leave the drivetrain in the vehicle. In either case, you should be able to find out the year, make, and model of the engine and the number of miles on the odometer. The odometer reading may not be the actual miles on the engine, but there isn't much you can do about that.

Not exactly the prettiest engine ever built, but certainly not the most expensive one either, is this Ford 2.8 liter V-6. Coupled with a Ford C4 automatic, this engine should provide more than enough power to motivate the Track T.

You should try to find out as much as you can about why the vehicle ended up in the salvage yard before you buy. Was the vehicle involved in a front-end collision that may have caused the engine to run for a length of time without coolant or without oil? If so, this may have caused internal damage to the engine that cannot be readily identified while the engine is sitting on a storage stand. If the vehicle was involved in a rear-end collision without any apparent damage to the front-end, the engine is probably okay if it passes other engine buying criteria. Is there apparent damage to the block or the heads? Is there an inordinate amount of fluid (oil, antifreeze, etc.) seeping from the engine? Are all of the necessary brackets, pulleys, and accessories intact? If not, can they be found or replaced and still be within your budget?

Another option is to buy a complete (or reasonably so) vehicle that includes the drivetrain that you desire. If the vehicle is drivable, you can actually take it on a test-drive to determine how well the engine runs and whether it is suitable for your needs. The benefit of a parts vehicle is that it may have several more usable parts than what you anticipate needing. Engine, transmission, rear axle housing, wheels, tires, brakes, seats, shifter, starter, alternator, gauges, master cylinder, and radio are all possible parts vehicle items. Whenever you have salvaged everything of possible use off the vehicle, you may be able to recoup some bucks by selling the remaining carcass. On the other hand, you may have to pay to have it towed away.

REBUILT

If salvage yards are not common in your area (admittedly, they are getting more difficult to find) or if your local bone-yard doesn't have what you are looking for, a rebuilder is another source for an engine. Whether it is from one of the large, commercial rebuilders that advertise nationwide or sell through the big auto parts stores, a local shop that rebuilds engines to your specification, or simply a guy who enjoys rebuilding engines, a rebuilt engine is a viable solution to your engine needs.

Commercial rebuilders typically build to stock specifications or with a cleanup overbore. Engines for virtually all makes and models are available, giving you the largest variety of choices for motive power. Engines are usually offered in short block or long block configurations. For the short blocks, the rebuilder will have completed all of the necessary internal machining and assembled the internal engine components. Depending on the rebuilder, the cylinder heads may or may not be included in the price, so you should be sure the rebuilder specifies what is included in the deal. External components—such as an intake manifold and carburetor, exhaust manifolds or headers, distributor, starter, alternator, and fan—are usually not included, allowing for a lower price.

During installation, the original external components from the vehicle are usually used when you purchase a short-block engine from a rebuilder. The ones that are not included on a short block are usually included when you purchase a long block engine. Since commercial engine rebuilders build to stock specs and operate in larger volume, they are typically able to do more testing, have tighter controls on their procedures, offer more in terms of warranty, and may be able to ship a rebuilt engine to your garage in less time.

Local engine builders may be your best choice if you want something other than a stock rebuild and don't have the time or ability to do the work yourself. If you don't already have an engine, they can often provide one and then build it to your specifications, using your choice from their selection of components. Depending on the size of the operation, they may allow you to do some, if not all, of the component disassembly and cleaning, which will save you some money. As this type of rebuild is custom by nature, the warranty may not be as long or complete as a stock rebuild.

Hobbyists are those guys who really like the work of rebuilding engines and use it as a method of relaxation and additional income. I believe every auto parts store that I have ever been inside of has a bulletin board where someone has a rebuilt engine for sale. These engines can be a great deal if the engine is built for the purposes that you have in mind. If the advertised engine is built for the purpose of a pulling tractor or a sprint car, it most likely isn't what you need for a hot rod.

No matter if the engine is coming from a large commercial rebuilder or a local hobbyist, proper communication between all parties is necessary to prevent unwelcome surprises. Inquire as to which components are new, which ones are rebuilt, and which ones will need to be purchased/supplied separately. Additionally, some engine builders will require a core charge, while others won't.

There is always the possibility of doing it yourself, even though it may take longer than you anticipate. If you have good manual dexterity, can read and understand an overhaul manual, and have the necessary tools and the time to see it through, rebuilding an engine can be an accomplishment of which you can be proud. You may need to contract out some of the work, such as having the block and cylinder heads resurfaced, Magnafluxed to check for hairline cracks, or bored for oversize pistons. If you do the work yourself, you can choose the components you use, whether your selection is based upon their performance or price.

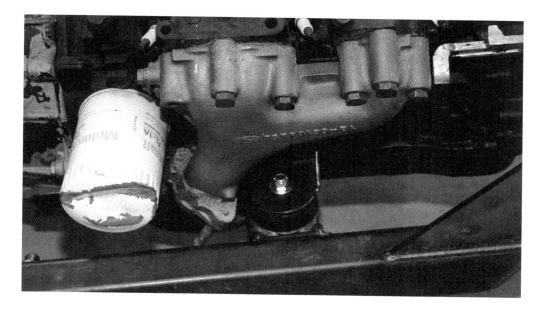

Whether you like them or not, Chevy small blocks are a hot rod standard for several reasons. First, they fit easily. However, there simply isn't enough room between the frame rails of this chassis for a Chevy V-8. The V-6 Ford's large oil filter, exhaust manifolds, and motor mounts are all competing for space in this application. Apart from limited space to bolt the exhaust onto the manifolds, it does all fit but this is the easy side.

Add starter and steering box to the mix, then locating the motor mount gets a little tricky. Donnie Karg was able to make it all work by welding folded metal motor mount plates to the frame. Basically, this is a flat metal plate that is folded down on each side to serve as a gusset. A biscuit style motor mount cushion fits between the frame mount and a folded metal plate that bolts to the engine. Both the frame and the engine brackets are gusseted. Though shown merely tack welded to the frame, rest assured that the frame bracket is fully welded to the frame now.

CRATE ENGINE

Even though the initial cost may seem high, a new engine with warranty is very often a sound investment. Compared to starting with a block that may need machining, purchasing additional components, and assembly time/labor, a crate motor may actually be less expensive altogether. Shopping around for the best deal for the most suitable engine package will be time well spent.

Although this may seem trivial, a new crate motor also has some time saving advantages. Obviously, you don't have to assemble it, depending on which crate engine you buy, but that's not the only time savings. As it comes off the delivery truck, you can go ahead and install the engine into your vehicle as it is. Even if you choose to paint the engine in a complementary or contrasting color, paint preparation is going to be minimal on a new engine.

Crate engines come in many stages of tune, from stock to race ready. A quick internet search on "crate engine" will introduce you to the wide range of options available.

INSTALLING MOTOR MOUNTS

Each and every engine and chassis combination presents a unique set of challenges. Any external component that attaches to the engine is a possible source of frustration. Probably the most common culprits are the exhaust, the starter, and the oil pan. These are typically the lowest

123

items on the engine and are the most likely to interfere with a wheelwell, a crossmember, the firewall, or, in the case of the starter and exhaust, one another. Of course, the engine must also be placed so that none of these items strikes the ground. The engine is limited the other way by air cleaner clearance, if you plan to have a closed hood, and how high you want the transmission to rise up into the passenger compartment.

The best way to determine the ideal engine location is to have the chassis and suspension assembled and supported on the wheels and tires that you plan to run on the finished vehicle. Any possible obstructions, such as a steering box or radiator, should be in position or at least accounted for. With the engine hanging from an engine hoist, lower the engine between the frame rails. If necessary, use some wooden blocks or a floor jack to support the engine from below when it is close to the proper location. Center the engine as close as practical from side to side between the frame rails. If possible, place the engine so that you have good oil filter access, but don't worry if that's not feasible. There are many remote oil filter kits and adapters to overcome any interference. Make sure that there is adequate room in front of the engine for a radiator and a fan. Also ensure that the engine and transmission will clear the firewall, or verify that the firewall can be modified. Try to make the bottom of the oil pan no lower than the adjacent crossmembers. Different oil pan and sump arrangements may allow you to relocate the low reservoir portion of the pan if it hits a crossmember. When the location of the engine satisfies all of these requirements, position it so that the intake manifold is sitting as close to level as possible.

At this time, you can install the engine mounts, which span the distance between the engine and the frame rails. Engine mounts for the most popular engines are readily available from almost any shop that sells hot rod parts. For some engine and chassis combinations, you will need to fabricate your own mounts. Luckily, all engines have some sort of motor mount, so it may be as easy as fabricating an intermediate bracket that fits between the existing engine bracket and a bracket on the frame. If you have the ability to weld chassis quality components and have some metal shaping capabilities, you should be able to fabricate suitable motor mounts yourself. Just be sure to employ some method of vibration isolation in the mount.

PAINTING THE ENGINE

Sometime after creating, buying, or modifying the motor mounts so that you can install your engine, the engine needs to be cleaned and painted. I suppose that if the engine is old and coated in grease, it won't rust, but it sure won't look too great either. Whether you choose to coat your engine, old or new, with color from a spray can or with automotive paint dispensed through a spray gun, it needs to be cleaned first. Before doing any cleaning, verify that any openings to the carburetor, distributor, or cylinder heads are blocked off. You don't want to get any liquid or cleaner where it shouldn't be.

If you are fitting a used engine, a good place to start the cleanup process is at your local car wash. Most of these facilities have a setting for applying engine degreaser, or have a separate degreasing mechanism altogether. If the grease, dirt, oil, and grime are really caked on, you can use a wire brush or a putty knife to scrape away, or at least penetrate, the surface beforehand. This will make it much easier for the degreaser to get beneath the layers of grease, making the cleanup much better.

After an initial cleaning at the car wash, or if the engine does not have lots of dust and dirt embedded in the oil and grease, you can use an aerosol oven cleaner to break loose the baked-on oil and grease from the engine's exterior. This method works best if the engine is sitting in the sun and is somewhat warm, and if possible, this portion of the cleaning should be performed outside, or at least where there is adequate fresh air, as some oven cleaning sprays can be toxic. Allow the oven cleaner to foam up and then let it sit for awhile to penetrate the grease and oil. You should be able to rinse the cleaner and the grime off with a garden hose. Again, be sure to protect any components that should not get wet. Any grease and grime that is left after this step can probably be removed with a handheld wire brush or a putty knife.

The engine that I used for this buildup was relatively clean, and it didn't have any signs of grease or oil on the exterior. However, it did have some very mild surface rust on a few spots, along with a dirt (mud) dobber nest behind one of the engine mounts. Knowing that the dirt dobber nest could have been inhabited, I removed it by smacking it lightly, but firmly, with a hammer, rather than by hand. My trusty Makita grinder with a wire cup brush removed the surface rust, along with the remaining mud from the aforementioned housing development.

To remove any residual oil and grease, I wiped the engine down with wax and grease remover on a paper towel, and then wiped it off again with a clean, dry paper towel. I then used an air nozzle on an air hose to blow away any loose dust and dirt, and to evaporate any remaining wax and grease remover. With some masking tape, I covered any areas that were not going to be painted. This included the carburetor mounting surface and mounting studs, the hole for the distributor, and the valve covers. The complete treatment for the valve covers will follow shortly . . .

As purchased, the engine is not very pretty, but at least it isn't caked in grease, oil, and dirt—a fact that will make it much easier to prep it for paint than some used engines I have seen.

I would have preferred to mount the engine on my engine stand for primer and paint, but with the torque converter still in place, it would not fit. Not being familiar with this particular combination, I chose to leave it hanging from a hoist, rather than potentially damaging it by trying to remove the torque converter.

Since I didn't remove the torque converter, I masked it off from primer and paint. An old-fashioned grocery bag fit right over the torque converter and was held in place with masking tape. Although I would be painting the valve covers differently from the block, I left them in place to help mask the valvetrain. Plastic sheeting from an auto body paint and supply store was a very good way to prevent overspray from getting all over the borrowed engine hoist.

Many stock engine colors are available in spray cans or in bulk to be applied by brush. Follow the manufacturer's instructions for applying these products, including primer. An economic approach is to purchase a couple of spray cans, which will most likely be plenty for coating an engine.

It looks glossy simply because it is still wet, but this is actually just the epoxy primer. I applied two coats of black PPG DPLF per the instructions, allowing the proper drying time between coats and also before applying the color coats.

As I had done on much of this project, though, I pushed or even gone beyond the budget in certain areas in the pursuit of what I felt would provide a better end result. This included applying two coats of PPG's DPLF epoxy primer prior to spraying the PPG DCC acrylic urethane engine color. To remain color coordinated with the wheels and scallops, I chose to paint the engine the same Toreador Red from Ford's under hood colors. The under hood color was actually a dark brown that was chosen to match the interior vinyl, while the exterior color was very red. Since I was out of clear, I decided to forego its use on the engine. Using clear would have improved the looks of the engine slightly, as well as made it somewhat easier to keep clean.

I certainly didn't want to get any paint into the valvetrain, so I masked off the stock valve covers and left them in place while I painted the engine. I could have left them unmasked and simply painted them as I painted the engine. Another option available for engines that are more popular or more common than this Ford V-6 was purchasing a set of aftermarket valve covers that would have improved the looks somewhat. I could also have had the stock valve covers chrome plated. Realistically, the stock valve covers had been damaged slightly in the past, with the repairs leaving a less than perfect surface finish. These imperfections could have potentially taken lots of my non-existent time to repair to be smooth enough to be

After allowing the proper drying time for the epoxy primer, I applied two coats of PPG DCC acrylic urethane for the color. This is the same color that was used for the wheels and most of the chassis components (some of the chassis components came from the vendor with a black powder coat, so there was no need to paint them).

The existing oil filter was left in place to mask that area, since it would be replaced by a brand new filter anyway. Some guys or gals paint their oil filter to match the engine, but that just tells me that they don't plan to drive the vehicle often enough.

Now that the engine paint has completely dried, I removed the valve covers and prepped them for their own paint. They could have been painted with the engine or polished, but they really weren't in good enough condition to receive a smooth and shiny finish. They could probably have been repaired sufficiently for paint by using some plastic body filler, but that would have taken more time than I had cared to spend on them.

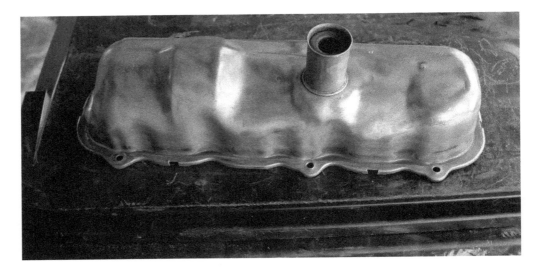

This is the worst of the two, and you can see that it has received some filler work in the past. It wasn't quite as noticeable before the paint was removed with a wire brush, but it is quite apparent now.

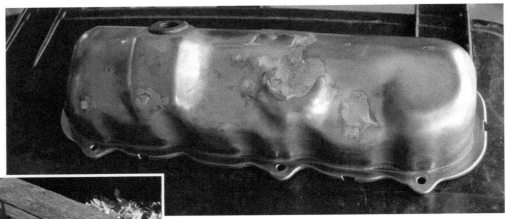

After cleaning the valve covers with wax and grease remover, I sprayed them with Eastwood's Black Wrinkle Finish aerosol paint. It goes on glossy, but dries with a wrinkle finish in a few hours. I sprayed them in the direct sunlight, which helped to speed the "aging" process. After the wrinkles set in, most of the previous imperfections in the surface were hidden. They are still there, but at least they aren't as noticeable. Now I probably need to find some Cobra badges to affix to these valve covers . . .

chrome plated or even simply painted. Anything less than a perfect repair would have been greatly magnified if the valve covers were finished using any method that required them to be smooth.

To take the inexpensive (both monetary and time wise) way out, I chose to use a black wrinkle finish similar to what is found on many of the Ford Cobra accessories. After the engine paint had dried sufficiently, I removed the valve covers from the engine and the masking tape from the covers. I used a wire cup brush in my Makita grinder to remove the previous layer of paint and to knock the bumps off some of the repaired areas. This did make the valve covers look somewhat better, but they were still not smooth enough to put on a glossy surface finish. After cleaning valve covers with wax and grease remover and masking off the vent holes, I then followed the directions for applying Eastwood's Black Wrinkle Finish aerosol paint. This product does not require primer and is easy to use. It does need to be shaken very well before use, but then it is simply a matter of applying two heavy coats. The directions do warn that it

This Ford C4 automatic transmission will be plenty strong enough to handle the power that will come out of the stock Ford V-6. Due to time constraints, I may simply prime and paint the transmission to match the engine. However, since the housing is made of aluminum, it could be polished for some labor intensive, but inexpensive sparkle, if you do it yourself.

may take up to 12 hours for the wrinkles to develop. When I had my valve covers sitting in direct sunlight, they developed in about two hours. When the valve covers were finished, the surface wasn't smooth, but it didn't look as though it had been damaged in the past either.

TRANSMISSION

The transmission is just as important to the drivetrain as the engine is. Whether it is a manual shift or an automatic, the transmission is the vital link in getting all of the engine's power to the rear wheels. Whichever engine and transmission you choose, they must be able to be mounted together. The two are usually simply bolted together with a handful of the appropriate sized bolts. For this reason, contemporary practice for hot rodders is to use a GM tranny with a GM engine, Ford with a Ford, and so on. That has not always been the case, however, as the hot ticket used to be a La Salle transmission behind a Ford flathead engine. Have we rodders gotten lazy, or are just not as creative? Adaptors for some mixing of engines and transmissions brands are still available, but they are less common nowadays. The internet is a good way to hunt down what's out there.

Salvage Yard or Parts Vehicle

If you are going to be purchasing a parts vehicle or searching the salvage yard for an engine, you might as well look for a compatible transmission at the same time. Although the purchase price of the two components might not be any less whether you buy them at the same time or not, you will more likely have everything that you need to make it all work if you buy it all as a package. Items such as a kickdown cable, vacuum modulator, pressure plate, or flywheel are all available separately at your local parts store, but will typically be included with the combined purchase of a trans-

mission and engine. The extra bucks you save now can certainly be used elsewhere during the course of the project.

Rebuilt

Some of the same businesses that rebuild engines also rebuild transmissions, yet others limit their practice to one or the other. If you have a transmission already, but feel that it is in need of repair or an overhaul, check your local telephone book for listings of several shops that regularly do this kind of work. For reasons unknown to me, it seems like there are more outlets for buying an engine than transmissions, which are simply repaired.

New

Sources for crate engines usually offer new transmissions as well. Along with at least a minimal warranty, the purchase price of a new transmission is usually within reason and worth a second thought when compared to having a transmission repaired.

Polishing the Transmission for Some Cheap Sparkle

After removing it from the engine for painting, secure the transmission to an engine stand, which makes it much easier to move around. Without the torque converter, the transmission is considerably lighter, but it is still too heavy to pick up and lug around every time that it needs to be moved. If there is a heavy buildup of grease, oil, and dirt, remove it with a putty knife or other similar device. The next step in polishing the transmission case (or any other parts you wish to polish) is to remove any wax, grease, or other substance that can be ground into the metal if not removed first. A simple way to do this is to spray or wipe on wax and grease remover, and then wipe it off with a clean

Like the engine, the transmission was not extremely dirty by any means and could easily have been used as it was. However, since it was an aluminum case, it could easily be polished to look much better. Mounting it on an engine stand was the first step toward making it easier to handle.

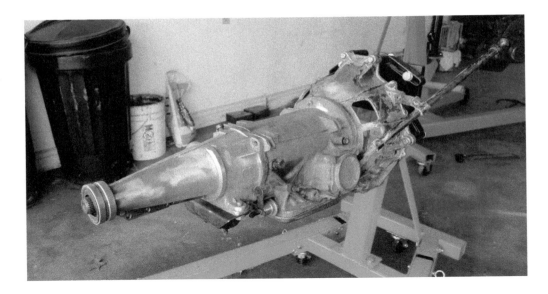

There were no heavy collections of grease, dirt, and grime to remove, but that would be the next step on a typical polishing job. Then, to avoid contaminating the aluminum case with anything, it should be cleaned with wax and grease remover. For mine, I used a wire cup brush on a grinder to remove the peeling black paint from the bell housing area and the general collection of patina from the rest of the housing. You can see in the photo that the tail shaft looks much better than the midsection, which has not yet been wire brushed.

paper towel. Then use a grinder with a wire cup brush attached to remove what is left of a coat of paint previously applied (in my case, evidently without any primer or other surface prep). With the transmission mounted on a rotating engine stand, accessibility is greatly improved.

After wire brushing to remove all of the paint, the transmission should be shiny and already looking much better, but there is still more work to do to complete the job. Nothing says that you can't stop at this point; however, the surface will still be far from smooth and will have many irregularities. These irregularities will restrict the reflectivity, causing the surface to look dull. Additionally, the rough surface will tend to collect more road rash, grease, oil, and dirt than a fully polished surface.

My transmission case still had some flashing from the casting process that could be removed. To remove the flashing (don't confuse these with structural casting ribs), a die grinder with an abrasive wheel usually works well. If you don't have access to a die grinder, a body sander will work, but may actually cause more work. The body sander typically has 6-inch or larger sanding discs, which will lap over the offending flashing quite a bit. Discs that are coarse enough to remove the flashing can leave some hefty scratches in the surface of the surrounding area, requiring additional work to remove them. Even if you don't have a die grinder, at around $30–50, they are quite affordable if you already have an air compressor.

With the flashing removed, the transmission is ready to be polished. Polishing actually consists of three different steps: rough cut, final cut/initial polish, and final polish. To remove the previously mentioned surface imperfections, you will need to cut the entire surface area with a sisal buffing wheel and Emery buffing compound. This should remove any of the scratches from the wire cup brush or any sandpaper used previously. Next, you should use a spiral-sewn cotton buffing wheel combined with Tripoli compound over the entire surface. This type of buffing wheel is more flexible than a sisal wheel, making it more suitable for the irregularities of a transmission case. All scratches and imperfections should be gone when the final cut/initial polish step is completed. To bring out the color (the bright, shiny, and clean surface), apply white rouge with a loose wheel made of cotton or flannel. Just like any painted surface should be protected with wax, polished parts should be protected with a wax type product designed for aluminum (or any other specific material).

Installing the Engine and Transmission

Whether during the mockup stage or final assembly, it's easier to keep the engine and transmission bolted together when you are determining where they need to go. Before installing the engine/transmission assembly, you will need to bolt the flywheel or flexplate to the crankshaft and install the clutch in the bell housing, if you're using a manual gearbox. You may also need to press a pilot bushing into the end of the crankshaft of appropriate internal diameter to

This photo gives a decent shot of the motor mount and how it goes together. With the frame mount already welded to the frame, you can see how it gussets on the front and back for strength. A bolt passing upward through the mount is isolated from the frame by a thick bushing. The flat washer shown serves as a bearing surface for the smaller rubber bushing and then the large rubber biscuit. The flat motor mount plate would be installed next and then secured with the flat washer, a lock washer, and a nut.

receive the transmission input shaft. Fitting these pieces will be easier with the engine and the transmission on a stand or workbench. Then you can slide the transmission shaft into the torque converter and secure the transmission housing to the engine with the appropriate bolts. Most automatic transmission housings are made of aluminum, so if there is any misalignment of the engine and tranny, you can break off mounting ears easily.

Obstacles to Overcome

For my lightweight Track T, a four-cylinder engine would have provided more than sufficient power. My preference, however, was to find a GM V-6 engine and automatic transmission from a rear-wheel-drive vehicle. The GM configuration would not have many obstructions protruding downward on the driver side front of the engine that would interfere with the Vega steering box. Perhaps the most common source of this combination would have been a Chevy/GMC S-10 or full size pickup. You would think that this combination would be easy enough to find, however, I didn't find any available that were practical to buy when I was looking. Perhaps popularity is a two-way street; there are a lot of these vehicles out there, but that means there's a good demand for them from the wrecking yards, too.

To make a long story not much longer, I wound up purchasing a Ford 2.8-liter V-6 engine, Ford C4 automatic transmission, and a like-new carburetor from the friend of a friend. This engine and transmission were believed to have been from a 1974 through 1978 Mustang, although it could have been found in Ford Ranger pickups or any of several different Ford products originally sold in Europe. It was a suitable drivetrain for this project, though it was not as convenient as the Chevy I wanted.

A minor problem that was easy enough to overcome was that a portion of the carburetor I sourced protruded down too far and hit the intake manifold before the mounting surface made complete contact. A half-inch spacer would have remedy this, but even though similar spacers for a four-barrel carburetor are readily available, I could not find any for a two-barrel. Instead, I solved the problem by whittling a piece of aluminum to the correct size and shape.

Remember me mentioning interference between engine components and the Vega steering box? I think that everything on this engine was moved down and to the left side. The thermostat housing, mechanical fuel pump, and oil pressure sender were all mounted where the steering box needed to be. The thermostat housing pretty much had to stay where it belonged, but it had to be trimmed of excess flab somewhat. A bypass hose that originally mounted on the backside of the thermostat housing was not used, thus

Aside from securing the exhaust to the manifold with two bolts, it must be secured near the back to prevent it from shaking itself apart. If it ran the full length of the vehicle, it would need more support, but for the short length of these side pipes, this will be sufficient. An L-shaped bracket bolts to a bracket that is welded to the frame with two small bolts, which are encased in a rubber bushing.

requiring a block-off plate to be made. I installed an electric fuel pump at the rear of the vehicle to replace the mechanical fuel pump, whose vacated spot likewise required a cover plate. Research indicates that the only practical place to tap in for an oil pressure reading for this particular engine is from the stock location. For this reason, I would most likely need to raise the engine slightly to allow for an angle fitting to which the oil pressure sender could be attached. Hopefully a spacer between the engine mount and the frame mount satisfied this requirement.

MOUNTING THE EXHAUST

To have an exhaust system built for the Track T, I trailered the car to the local muffler shop. I live in a small town, so there is only one. Since this is supposed to be a low dollar buildup and it is simply a stock Ford six-cylinder, almost anybody should be able to whip up an exhaust system. I had already purchased the chrome side pipes, and exhaust manifolds came with the engine, so I just needed someone to connect the two components. If I had more time to devote to the project, I would have welded up the exhaust myself. I don't have much welding experience, but I am reasonably sure that I could have done a better job than what I ended up getting. I must admit that it had been quite awhile since I had needed to have any exhaust work done, and most of what I had seen recently had been custom work done on hot rods, so maybe my expectations had been a little high. The purpose of this rant is to remind you that even though you may take a portion of your hot rod project to a professional, you may not be happy with the results.

Not that it was any fault of the guys at the muffler shop, but when they were tightening the exhaust manifolds in place on the passenger side, the exhaust flange broke off. Evidently, it had been broken before and a less than suitable job had been done to fix it. I did have to do some searching to find someone who felt capable of repairing cast iron, but I was able to get it repaired, rather than search for a replacement set of manifolds. This was but one of those situations where running a small-block Chevy engine would have been more convenient.

With the broken flange repaired, both manifolds could be bolted on to the engine block. Even though the exhaust pipe is made up of multiple pieces that allow it to change to the size required, it was a relatively short welded piece that attached to the exhaust manifold by way of two studs. The exhaust pipe extended to just outside of the body aprons. At that point, chrome side pipes with internal mufflers slipped over and clamped to the exhaust pipe. The side pipes stopped just behind the back of the non-opening door. On your hot rod, be sure that the exhaust extends beyond any door openings, especially on a closed car. You don't want to hook your ankle on it, or to discharge fumes inside if you let it idle with the door open.

Even though the exhaust system was short on my car, it still needed support near the end to avoid vibration damage from sustained vibration. To provide this support, Donnie Karg welded a small tab to the inside of each of the frame rails, and another small tab onto the inside of each side pipe (the mounting tab was welded to the outside of the casing, but on the portion of the side pipe that was closest to the body). These mounting tabs were connected with an L-shaped piece of steel plate that bolted to each tab. Two bolts on each mounting tab used rubber bushings to minimize harmonic vibration, yet hold the exhaust reasonably solid.

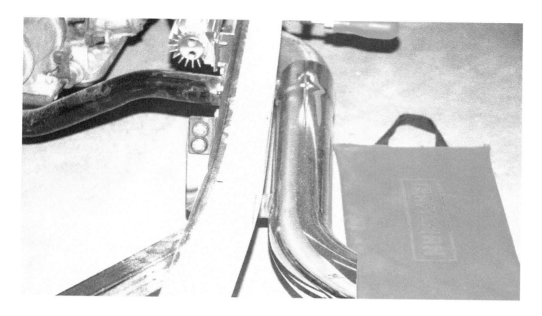

A short extension of the lower leg of the L-shaped bracket is welded to the side pipe. Then the short extension and the bracket are bolted together with two small bolts encased in a rubber bushing. This method of attachment allows the side pipes to be removed if necessary, and also helps to minimize any harmonic vibration up through the frame.

CONNECTING THE SHIFTER AND LINKAGE

Transmission shifters and linkages are a couple of items that can quite readily be found in salvage yards and swap meets, making them affordable for almost anyone who is building a hot rod. However, I chose to go the aftermarket route and ordered a new tail mount shifter from Lokar Performance Products. Buying new parts adds to the bottom line, but it also provides peace of mind to those of us who are not as adept as others at fabricating brackets or other necessary items that may not have been included with the swap meet or salvage yard parts.

A previous owner had fabricated some Rube Goldberg contraption of a shifter arm that was poorly welded to the original. The shifter arm extension was flexible enough for me to simply pull it away from the transmission, and then cut it off with a pneumatic die grinder. Its flexibility really made me wonder what it had been used for previously. With the arm cut away, I could remove the stock electrical connection by undoing two bolts.

With the unnecessary arm and electrical connections out of the way, installation of the Lokar shifter was quite straightforward. The shifter mechanism is installed by first removing the two center bolts that secure the tail of the transmission to the transmission housing. Align the shifter mounting tabs with these two holes, and then secure them with the two Allen head bolts provided. An additional feature of the Lokar shifter is that the shift lever itself can

Left: The previous owner had welded this piece of flat bar stock (diagonal in the photo) to the original shifter arm for reasons unknown. To mount the Lokar shifter, I had to amputate this extra arm and a portion of the original one. *Right:* Although in use it will not be loaded in this direction, still I could pull the extra arm out of the way quite easily. The shifter lever slides onto the round collar on the transmission shaft. Any portion of the original shifter arm that interferes with the new shifter can be cut away. It is advisable to leave at least a portion of the original arm in place to indicate what gear the transmission is in.

After literally breaking the poorly welded shifter arm away from the stock arm, I trimmed the stock piece using a die grinder. It needed to be trimmed away just enough to clear the new linkage.

The Lokar tail mount shifter is mounted to the transmission housing with two bolts and washers that are included in the kit.

be installed in one of two different mounting positions for more flexibility.

The next step is to verify that the transmission is in park, and then slip the new lever onto the shaft that protrudes from the driver side of the transmission. Be sure that both mounting surfaces of the lever are in full contact with the collar of the transmission shaft. Position the lever so that the 1/4-inch hole (where the threaded rod connects) is located at the one o'clock position in relation to the transmission shaft. Now insert a bolt through the U-shaped portion of the transmission lever, install a nut, and then tighten it to secure the lever to the shaft. Next, secure one of the rod ends provided with the kit to the transmission lever with a bolt, washer, and nut, and then use the same procedure to secure the other end to the shifter lever. Thread one end of the threaded rod into

one of the rod ends, and then extend the rod toward the opposite rod end to determine the required length of threaded rod. Using a hack saw, die grinder, or other cutting device, cut the threaded rod to the correct length, making sure that it is long enough to engage adequately into each rod end. After cutting the rod to the correct length, thread the loose end into the rod end and then tighten with a jam nut on each end. Now verify that there is no binding as the shifter moves through the gears.

CONNECTING THE EMERGENCY BRAKE LEVER AND CABLES

With the seat back and cushions temporarily set into place for reference, a suitable location for the Lokar emergency brake lever was determined within arm's length atop the transmission tunnel. The emergency brake lever does not have to be installed in the middle of the car; it can just as easily sit to the left of the driver or even sideways in front of the driver seat. The lever must be accessible, though, in case of an emergency. Also when the emergency cable adjuster bracket is installed, the cables must be pulled straight between this bracket and the clevis attaching the cables to the emergency brake lever.

After determining the location for the lever, you must cut a small hole in the floor to allow for the lever's movement during operation. Then drill four mounting holes and secure the lever to the floor with the included hardware.

To install the emergency brake cables, you will need access to underneath the car and you must remove the rear wheels. The next step is to remove the brake drums and the inner cable from the outer housing. Install the threaded end of the cable housing into the backing plate from the outside, and secure it to the inside by threading on the nut

Slip the transmission lever onto the transmission shaft, so that the small hole in the lever is at the one o'clock position when referenced to the transmission shaft. Then secure the transmission lever by inserting the supplied bolt through the U-shaped portion of the transmission arm and tighten with a washer and nut.

until it is tight against the backing plate. Outer housings are now routed toward the middle of the car and to the emergency cable adjuster bracket, which is secured to the underside of the floor with two bolts, washers, and lock nuts. Trim the excess off the outer housing, but verify that it is still long enough to slip into the adjusting ferrules.

Now feed the inner cable through the backing plate bracket, through the springs, and then into the outer cable housing. Secure a clevis to the emergency brake lever with a pin, a washer, and a cotter pin. At the back end of this clevis is an adjusting bolt, which needs to be threaded into a cable block. Then feed the inner cables into the cable

Left: *Attach a threaded rod end to the transmission arm, and thread the rod into it. Attach the remaining threaded rod to the shifter lever. Determine the required length of the threaded rod and then cut it to length.*

Below: *Verify that the rod is sufficiently threaded into each of the rod ends, but with room for additional adjustment if necessary. Tighten the jam nuts against the rod end to secure the threaded rod in place.*

block and secure the cables by tightening two setscrews against each. The excess cable can be cut off and the tension adjusted by loosening or tightening the adjustment bolt between the clevis and the cable block.

MEASURING FOR AND INSTALLING THE DRIVESHAFT

Although your hot rod won't be able to move under its own power without a driveshaft, the latter is one of the last parts that you should order. Since a driveshaft in automotive applications typically uses a slip yoke at the transmission to allow for suspension travel, the length for the driveshaft must be determined when the full weight of the vehicle is on the suspension. This may mean that you will have to enlist the aid of a skinny person to slide under your hot rod

Left: After cutting a hole in the floor to allow for operational movement of the emergency brake cable, you can bolt the lever in place. Four bolts pass through the mounting ears from the top and are secured with washers and nuts on the bottom side of the floor. Right: With the emergency (or parking) brake cable installed through the backing plate, cables from each wheel drum are routed forward toward the brake lever. Somewhere between those two locations, the mounting plate must be secured to the body of the vehicle or to a chassis crossmember. In this case, this will be bolted to the underneath side of the floor. The inner cables will then be connected to the brake lever.

to get the measurement, as using jack stands will relieve the weight from the suspension. If you have a fixed axle in the back, you can put the front tires up on ramps and use axle stands in the rear to raise the car and keep the weight on the suspension. The wheelbase must be set at the correct measurement as well. If you already have a suitable slip yoke, you should push it into the transmission until it stops, then pull the yoke out 3/4 inch. The measurement between the center of the transmission yoke (the flat mounting surface where the U-bolts thread into the yoke) to the same location on the pinion yoke of the rear axle housing is the required length of the driveshaft.

In my case, I did not have a transmission yoke for the Ford C4 transmission or a driveshaft. To obtain a drive-shaft, I contacted Driveshafts Unlimited. After discussing my hot rod project, I was told that without a transmission

yoke, I could measure from the rear seal of the transmission to the flat mounting surface where the U-bolts threaded into the pinion yoke. From that measurement, the shop could determine the correct length of the driveshaft, along with some measurements from the rear axle housing to make sure that everything fit there as well. These extra measurements were the cap diameter and the distance between the nubs on the pinion yoke. In other words, those measurements would tell the shop what size U-joint to use.

Installing the driveshaft is relatively simple. With the vehicle securely situated on jack stands or ramps, position the driveshaft above or below any chassis crossmembers as necessary. Then slide transmission yoke onto the transmission shaft. Secure the pinion end of the driveshaft to the pinion yoke with two U-bolts that are secured with nuts from the backside. Make sure that you do not over-tighten the nuts, as this will damage the bearings in the U-joint.

Each U-joint (one at each end of the driveshaft) will typically have a Zerk fitting, so that the joint can be greased. Don't forget to grease both of these grease fittings, as well as at any other locations, such as the front suspension.

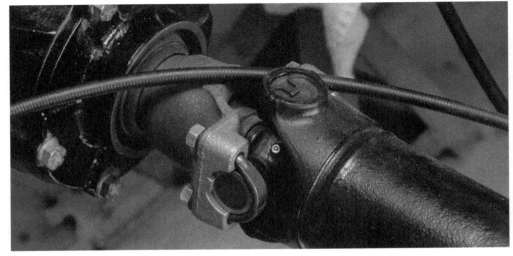

CHAPTER 6
ADDITIONAL SYSTEMS

Although the chassis, suspension, engine, and transmission make up the bulk of any hot rod, there are several subsystems that are just as important. In no particular order, these are the fuel, cooling, steering, and electrical systems. On a more refined hot rod, these subsystems can be much more complicated, but on this no-frills Track T, they are rather basic.

FUEL

Any internal combustion engine needs fuel, and therefore an onboard storage tank. Finding a fuel tank that would fit in the desired location in my Track T (rear of the axle, but within the confines of the horizontal and vertical hoops of the chassis) presented a challenge. The downward slope of the body in the rear also contributed to the dilemma. I didn't anticipate lengthy trips in this hot rod, so having a large capacity gas tank was not a huge concern, yet I wanted the tank to be bigger than something designed to run a quarter mile at a time.

I purchased a 10-gallon poly tank that seemed to have the right dimensions for my application. When I test-fitted the tank, however, and anticipated its sides bowing out some when filled, I realized that it sat too close to the rear axle housing. So now, I have a new gas tank to build another hot rod around . . .

Building the Fuel Tank

Now you really have to be careful when you mention custom fabricated fuel tanks. Due in part to liability and other insurance concerns, many people who may be perfectly capable of fabricating a gas tank simply will not consider doing so, or they will charge you a fortune for their services. What I really needed was a custom built box that fit my specific dimensions and didn't leak. A conversation with a friend whose company manufactures (among other things) stainless steel boxes yielded an answer to my gas tank problem. Not long after providing the necessary dimensions, I received of two pieces of stainless steel. One was bent into a

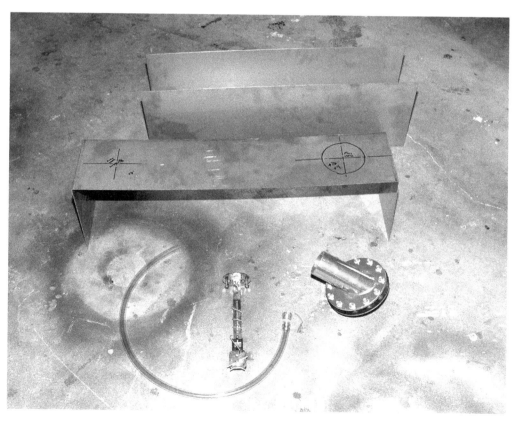

These are the major components of the gas tank: one piece of stainless steel that forms the front, bottom, and back; another piece that forms the top and both ends; the fill valve; and the fuel gauge sending unit (without the float). Instead of using the clear tube shown in the photo as a pickup tube, I decided to install a bung on the lower front of the tank that was to be connected directly to the fuel line.

To make drilling the holes for the fill valve and the fuel gauge sender easier, they were done before the tank was welded together. In this photo, two lines are marked on the inside of the top panel. The intersection of the lines will be the center of the hole for the fill valve.

"U" shape to create the front, bottom, and back of the tank. Another was bent to create the top and both ends. Three flat pieces to be used as baffles and three pieces to be used as mounting tabs were included as well. Longtime friend and former employer, Keith Moritz at Morfab Customs, offered to weld it all together for me. By using the formula of 1 gallon equals 231 ci, my custom built tank should hold 9.4 gallons of go juice.

Before the "box" could be welded together, the filler neck needed to be installed and a hole drilled for the fuel level sender. There are a couple of things that you should remember when constructing a gas tank. First of all, unless you use self-tapping screws to secure the fuel level sender to the tank, you will need to place it close enough to the fuel filler so that you can reach in with a wrench to tighten the mounting bolts and nuts. If you already have the gauges and therefore the instructions for adjusting the fuel level float, you should make the adjustment before welding the internal baffles in place. For those who may not be familiar with fuel level floats, the length of the float arm is adjusted according to the depth of the tank. I didn't adjust the length of the float rod until after the box was welded. Therefore, I didn't know until the baffle was already in place that I had centered the float ball right on the baffle. To avoid the float ball rubbing against the edge of the center baffle, I bent the float arm slightly. Whether I bent it sufficiently remains to be seen.

I had already purchased a fast fill valve for the tank, the filler neck that mounts on the body, and the hose that connects the two. Based on the required location of the filler neck, I chose to place the fast fill valve near the passenger side end of the tank's top. Since the tank was narrow (approximately 7 inches front to back), the fast fill valve needed to be centered fore and aft. I marked a line across the inside of the top portion of the tank and another line perpendicular to it at the desired distance from the end. The intersection of these two lines was the center of the filler opening. I used a center punch to further mark the hole and then drilled that location with a 1/8-inch pilot hole. Whenever you are drilling holes in stainless steel, you should use sharp bits, a slow drilling speed, and plenty of WD-40 or other lubricant to keep the bit and the material as cool as possible. Building up heat in the stainless steel material will cause it to work harden, which is not a good thing.

After drilling a pilot hole, an appropriate sized hole saw was used to cut out the hole for the gas fill. For my application, a 4 1/2-inch saw was necessary. Taking my time, using plenty of WD-40, and taking extra care to make sure that the drill was perpendicular to the surface yielded good results. Using the same procedure, but with a smaller hole saw, I made the opening for the fuel level sender. I used a grinding stone on a die grinder to deburr the edges of the new holes. Using the fast fill valve and the fuel level sender housing as templates, I marked the hole locations for mounting bolts and then drilled them with the appropriate sized drill bits. I don't know if this is true with all fuel level senders, but the mounting flange with VDO gauges does not have mounting holes that are evenly spaced. This is not a problem, but you must remain aware of which side of the surface you are marking the holes on, or they might end up backwards.

The key to drilling holes in stainless steel is using a slow drill speed and keeping the drill bit cool by lubricating it with WD-40 or other similar lubricant.

Since I was using a hole saw that had a pilot bit protruding longer than the full diameter teeth, I did the initial drilling with the sheet metal sitting on a piece of scrap wood siding. As I got closer to drilling through, I used two scrap blocks of wood as supports so that I could drill completely through the sheet metal.

The fast fill valve is made up of two basic components: a cast-aluminum fitting that accepts the fuel filler hose, and a flexible ring/gasket assembly that fits inside the tank. The gasket assembly comprises two flat semicircles of sheet metal that have six mounting studs welded to each of them. A rubber gasket holds these two pieces of metal together and allows the assembly to be folded so that it can be inserted into the tank. Since my tank was not yet welded together, the gasket assembly could be inserted from underneath, but that would not have been possible on an existing tank. With each of the 12 mounting bolts inserted through the top of the tank, the cast-aluminum part was slipped into position and then secured with 12 stop nuts. To make sure that the bolts were tightened adequately and therefore avoiding potential leaks, I used a crisscross tightening pattern to secure the nuts.

A safety feature of this type of fill valve is a round block-off plate that slides on a spring loaded shaft. This plate is attached to the aluminum housing, but located inside the tank. When gasoline or other fuel is poured in, the weight of that liquid is sufficient enough to push the plate downward, allowing you to fill the tank. If the vehicle should ever

139

After drilling both holes using the same procedure but different size hole saws, this is what the un-welded gas tank looked like. Other than the welding (which someone else did), the hard part was done.

The fill valve and the fuel level sender were used as templates to mark the necessary holes for mounting them in the top of the tank. These smaller holes could be drilled with a drill bit rather than a hole saw, which allowed them to be drilled in less time.

be upside down, the fuel in the tank will push down on the block-off plate, effectively sealing off the fuel tank and preventing it from leaking at will. There were no instructions mentioning anything about adjusting this spring, so I am hoping that plenty of testing has already been done to verify that it is correct. I will be very careful when I fill the tank for the first time and will make sure that the tank does

indeed open, filling the tank instead of flooding back all over the car.

The tank, the baffle plates, and the tank mounting flanges were taken to Keith Moritz at Morfab Customs to be welded together. Two baffles (3x5 inches) were welded to the bottom of the tank at even spacing across the back and another was welded to the bottom and centered on the front

Mounting studs welded to the flexible ring/gasket assembly secure the fill valve. The mounting studs extend up through the top of the gas tank, and the fill valve is then secured with stop nuts on each stud.

Other than the welding, the tank is essentially complete at this point, showing that this is an easy project to complete if you are in need of a gas tank. Since the gas tank must not leak, it must be constructed by a competent welder. As long as you have not yet put gasoline in it, you should be able to find someone capable of performing the welding tasks if you are not comfortable doing it yourself.

of the tank. When designing baffles, be sure to take the size of the tank and the location of the fuel level float rod into consideration. A bung was welded to the driver side bottom front of the tank for the fuel pickup, and another was located on the top near the filler hole for use as a vent. A barbed hose fitting was threaded onto the vent bung, and then a short length of rubber hose was slid over the barbed fitting. The hose was routed downward and then secured to the horizontal hoop of the chassis with a wire tie. Stainless steel mounting brackets were welded on each end of the tank and another was mounted across the back. As you will see later in this chapter, the gas tank was bolted into place without any straps.

Testing the Fuel Tank for Leaks

Not that I had any concerns about Keith's welding, but I wanted to make sure that there were not any leaks in the tank before I put gasoline in it. If there were any leaks beforehand, fixing them would not be a problem, while it would be difficult to get anyone to weld on a tank that has had gasoline in it.

To test for leaks, I placed the tank on some wooden blocks so that I could see under it, slipped a rubber hose over the fuel pickup bung, and clamped it closed. After squirting in a bit of dish washing liquid, I filled the tank with water and observed it for leaks. After waiting about 15 minutes and not seeing any leaks, I shot compressed air through the

Right: After being welded together, this is what the stainless-steel gas tank looks like. Being stainless, it can be polished to a mirror-like finish if desired. The nipple at the right side of the photo is for the fuel line connection, while at the opposite corner is a vent.

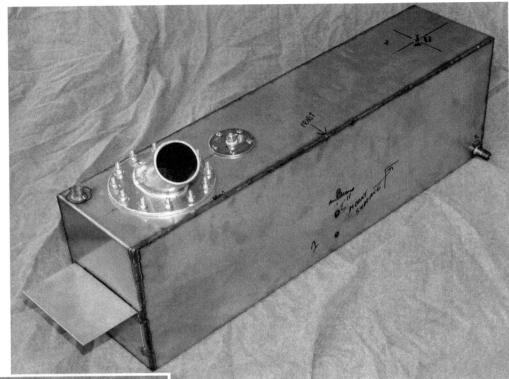

Below: This is the fuel level sender and float assembly, a component that is usually included with aftermarket gauges when they are purchased in kits. These senders usually have instructions on how to adjust the float, depending on the height of the tank.

vent hole. Still with no apparent water leaks or soap bubbles, I was thinking that the tank was leak free.

Mounting the Fuel Tank and Filler Neck

Rather than build chassis mounting tabs for the gas tank and then making the gas tank fit that, I welded the mounting tabs to the chassis after the gas tank was built. With the weight of the chassis on the suspension, the gas tank was positioned within the horizontal hoop of the chassis. I welded mounting tabs made of 3/8-inch thick steel bar stock to the frame, beneath the end and back tank mounting flanges. Since the tank was cantilevered on the end tabs

somewhat due to the radius at the back of the horizontal hoop, positioning the chassis mounting tabs inboard and flush with the top of the horizontal hoop was the most supportive setup. After centering the tank in the available space, I made alignment marks on the tank mounting flanges and on the horizontal hoop.

To facilitate mounting and securing the gas tank to the chassis, the chassis mounting tabs were drilled and tapped to accept 3/8-inch bolts before being welded in place. A chassis mounting tab was positioned beneath the tank mounting flange on each end. After being centered front to back, the mounting tabs were clamped to the tank's mounting flange so that they were adjacent to the horizontal hoop of the chassis, and then they were tack welded to the chassis. In similar fashion, the chassis mounting tab for the back of the tank was drilled and tapped for two mounting bolts, centered beneath the tank mounting flange, and then tack welded to the inside of the horizontal hoop. The tank was then removed and the welding was completed.

The gas tank's filler neck flange was flat, which pretty much dictated that it needed to be somewhere near the forward edge of the simulated deck lid opening to avoid lots of extra work or expense. I would have liked to have had an opening deck lid with a louvered skin, but due to this placement issue, I chose to forego that. After making that purely

Left: Prior to putting any fuel in the tank, you should test it for leaks. You should mount the tank on some blocks so that you can see the bottom side of the tank, as well as any of the welds. *Right:* I capped off the fuel line nipple with a piece of rubber hose, and then filled the tank with water and a bit of dish soap to make leaks more noticeable. After seeing no leaks, I used an air hose to increase the inside pressure, making any leaks more apparent. Have no fear, none of the water on the driveway came from inside of the tank.

Left: After positioning the gas tank in the chassis, I marked the mounting flanges and horizontal hoop for alignment purposes. Although the gas tank is mounted at the rear of the body, the horizontal chassis hoop should provide ample protection in the case of a collision. *Right:* During measurement for the proper size chassis mounting tabs, the tank was temporarily supported with a wooden 2x4 and a bottle jack.

ADDITIONAL SYSTEMS

143

Left: After a piece of 3/8-inch-thick strap steel was cut to the proper size for use as a chassis mounting tab, it was drilled to the appropriate size to accept a tap for a 3/8-inch bolt. *Right:* The hole was then tapped to allow a 3/8-inch bolt to thread into it. This eliminated the need for a nut and washer, making for simple installation.

Donnie Karg clamped the chassis mounting tab to the tank's mounting flange, and then clamped the mounting flange to the horizontal hoop. He then measured to double check that the tab was centered front to back. This was done on both sides.

arbitrary decision of filling the tank from the left or right, I turned the filler neck upside down to use it as a template for mounting holes. Locations for the twelve mounting holes were marked, along with the outer diameter of the flange (although it isn't necessary to mark the outer diameter). To find the center for drilling the large hole for the filler neck, I simply marked lines between two sets of opposite side holes, the intersection of which was the center. The center hole was

drilled with a 4 1/2-inch hole saw to allow for the recess of the filler neck. Then I drilled mounting holes for 1/4-20 bolts.

Chrome button head Allen bolts would have looked best, but they weren't available at my local hardware store, so I settled for stainless socket head bolts. Several different types and finishes of bolts will look decent and work sufficiently; it just depends on what you prefer and how much you care to spend.

ADDITIONAL SYSTEMS

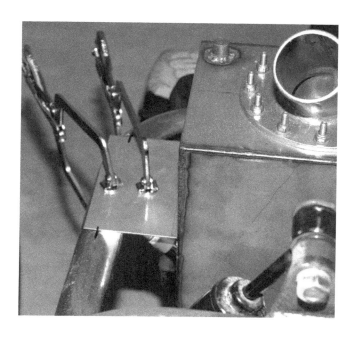

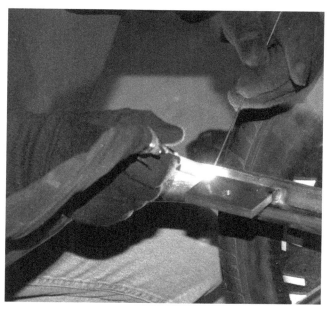

Left: *The chassis mounting tabs were then tack welded in place on the horizontal hoop on both sides of the tank. Having the tank resting on the horizontal hoop while the tabs are tacked in place ensures that the tank will be resting on the horizontal hoop and the mounting tabs when it is completed.* **Right:** *With the tank removed and out of the way, the chassis mounting tabs could be completely welded to the chassis.*

Rather than simply relying on the two side-mounting tabs for support, another mounting tab was installed in the back. Being wider, it allowed for two mounting bolts with a bit of distance between them. Otherwise, it was created and installed using the same methods as the two side mounts.

A length of heavy-duty, clear tubing sized to fit the filler neck is included with the tank fill kit. You will need to cut it to the appropriate length and then slip over the filler neck and the fast fill valve. Since this tubing will only bend a limited amount before kinking, it will most likely need to have an elbow located somewhere between the filler neck and the tank. A muffler shop or other source of exhaust tubing should be able to provide a piece of curved tubing that will be the correct diameter.

Routing the Fuel Line

Compared to finding a gas tank that would actually fit within the limited confines of the Track T, routing the fuel line to the carburetor was fairly easy. To provide ample fuel to the engine, a 3/8-inch line is typically used. For the most part, I used a

Left: With the tank out of the way, we can see the three chassis mounting tabs and also just how little space there is between the horizontal hoop and the rear axle housing. Still, the tank will hold a little over 9 gallons, which should be sufficient for a night of cruisin' Main. **Right:** The gas tank filler neck requires a relatively flat surface, so based on the location of the gas tank, this means the filler needs to be in the deck lid area. Using the filler neck as a template, the locations of the mounting holes are marked.

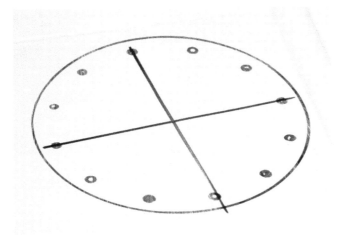

Left: By connecting two pair of opposite mounting holes, you can determine the center point for drilling the 4 1/2-inch hole for the recessed portion of the filler neck. **Right:** With this hole drilled, you can now install the filler neck with the mounting flange flush with the body. For some extra detailing points, the mounting surface can be recessed enough for the flange to be even with the fiberglass body surface around it, but I didn't do that.

3/8-inch hard line and some 3/8-inch rubber hose for some of the connections. Aside from being slightly more difficult to bend initially, 3/8-inch line is similar to working with 3/16-inch brake line and requires the same tools.

Since the supply outlet coming out of the fuel tank was somewhat close to the rear axle housing, I installed a barbed hose fitting, over which I slid a piece of rubber hose. The connection was secured with a hose clamp. This rubber hose ran up to the fuel filter, which was mounted at the top of the vertical hoop portion of the chassis. I used another piece of rubber hose to traverse along the radius of the vertical hoop, and then onto hard line, where another hose clamp was installed. I then bent the hard line to conform to the profile of the inside of the passenger side frame rail as it ran

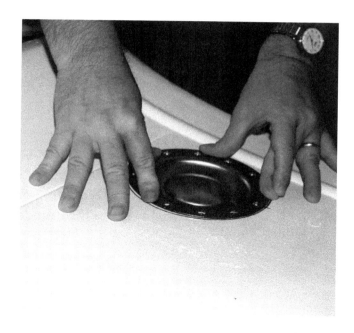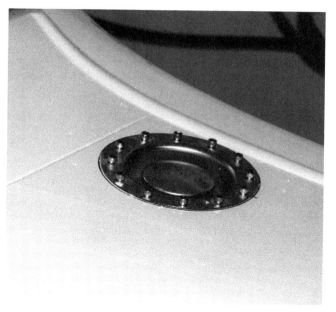

Left: I chose to secure the filler neck by installing a dozen socket head bolts and nuts that required drilling holes. The filler neck, however, can be secured with some Phillips head screws that are simply driven into the fiberglass. *Right:* At this point in the project, I hadn't made a definite decision on how to finish the filler neck. It could be painted to match the body or it could be chrome plated. Being a cheap hot rod project, I could have just left it the way it was.

Instead of installing a tube down from the top of the tank, Keith Moritz installed a pipe thread bung at the bottom front corner of the gas tank to which the fuel line will be connected. This will make for easy draining of the tank if that ever becomes necessary. Keith threaded a coupling onto the bung, and although not shown in this photo, he installed a barbed fitting and then a length of rubber fuel line hose.

forward toward the engine. Just like on the brake line, rubber coated line clamps were used to secure the fuel line to the frame.

When routing fuel lines, you must be careful to avoid pinching the line, allowing it to rub against anything that may cause a hole, or allowing it to touch exhaust pipes. If connecting two pieces of hard line, both lines should be double flared, just like brake line. When connecting a piece of rubber hose to a piece of hard line, the latter should be flared, the rubber hose slid over the hard line by at least an inch, and then a hose clamp used to ensure that the hose does not slide off. Be sure that the hose clamp is tight against the hard line inside of the hose and not just against the hose.

147

The vertical hoop of the chassis seems to be a logical location for the electric fuel pump. Fuel comes from the driver side of the tank through a rubber fuel line that is secured to the vertical hoop. After passing through the fuel pump, the gasoline follows along the vertical hoop in rubber fuel line and then connects to hard line at the base of the vertical hoop. The tan wire on the fuel pump connects to the appropriate circuit of the fuse panel, while the black wire connects to a ground.

COOLING

Anyone who has attended many large rod runs has probably been witness to a hot rod overheating, often belching coolant out of the radiator. This isn't quite the way the drivers intended to catch everyone's attention, I'm sure. Whether your hot rod overheats amongst a bunch of other rodders (where help is nearby) or out on a lonely stretch of highway, it is no fun. With some minimal routine maintenance, a properly sized radiator will typically perform its job adequately for a long time. However, if the radiator is damaged, neglected, or just plain overworked, it may fail at an inopportune moment.

Not to scare you, but a radiator is a fairly fragile piece of equipment. Being made up of soft materials such as aluminum, copper, or brass, and having several brazed connections, it is easily damaged by impact. Cooling fins that become bent can lead to inefficient heat transfer. Additionally, road debris has been known to damage radiators, causing them to leak. If the coolant level decreases because of a leak, the coolant pressure will increase because the engine makes the reduced amount of coolant hotter, eventually turning it to steam. This process can often cause additional leaks in radiator hoses in marginal condition. So, if you encounter road debris and then notice a significant increase in the reading on the water temperature gauge, stop and rectify any damage before you overheat. Letting an engine overheat is never good. It can lead to, among other things, a warped head and then a blown head gasket. Get coolant down the cylinders and you might be looking at a rebuild due to damaged crankshaft bearings.

If a radiator is neglected (i.e., not flushed and filled on a regular basis), it will begin to develop rust and corrosion, making it much less efficient. Quite often, frugal rodders will attempt to use an original radiator that was included with their budget hot rod. This can be done, however, some precautions should be taken. If you are going to use an OEM radiator that was built way back when, you should take it to a radiator shop to have it boiled out and pressure tested before you use it. This relatively inexpensive (compared to the price of a new radiator) process will remove any rust and corrosion from inside the radiator, as well as identify any leaks. Depending on the size and location of a leak, it may not be subject to repair, but it is better to find this out before you go for that first drive. Whenever the radiator passes muster, most radiator shops apply a new coat of radiator black paint, which makes them look brand new. Using a vintage radiator can save you some money, but you should spend a little bit of money beforehand to ensure that this is a practical way to go. What may not work is using a radiator that originally came with an antique car—say, if you bought a nice, running Model T. Heat transfer adequate to cool a low-compression four-cylinder engine is unlikely to be adequate for a late-model V-8.

Perhaps a more common reason for radiator related problems is expecting your radiator to be a miracle worker. If there is not enough airflow through the radiator and around

Since the nose and the chassis in the radiator area had no straight or square surfaces, determining just how much room was available for a radiator was unsure at best. Using my measurements, I constructed a mockup to verify what would fit.

After verifying that my dimensions would work, I made a sketch for Geary Portell at Portell's Radiator. A few days later, I was able to pick up my new aluminum radiator, along with a new radiator cap.

and away from the engine, it is very difficult for the radiator to perform effectively. Just because air is flowing through the grille doesn't mean that it is flowing through the radiator. The front sheet metal on some vehicles lets fresh air to bypass the radiator, leaving the engine coolant warmer than it needs to be. To prevent this, it is sometimes necessary to add some sheet metal between the inside of the grille and the front top or sides of the radiator. When using a mechanical fan, adding a shroud around the fan and the backside of the radiator will increase airflow. If this is not enough, an electric fan may be necessary. Inability for hot engine compartment air to escape also causes the radiator to overwork. Although hood louvers serve as a decoration, they are also functional for allowing engine heat to escape from the engine compartment.

When purchasing a radiator, you should know which engine, transmission, and engine accessories you are going to be running, so that the radiator can be sized accordingly. A bored out engine running a lumpy camshaft and air conditioning is going to be more difficult to cool than a stock engine with similar variables.

In addition to verifying that the radiator will sufficiently cool your hot rod, you must also confirm that it will actually fit into the rod's sometimes limited confines. The chassis for the Track T has a round tube section in the frontal area. It is kicked up (to allow the front of the car to sit lower) and it is tapered, decreasing in width as you move forward. The actual nose fiberglass also comprises several compound curves, both downward and inward. When you combine all of these three-dimensional angles and curves, obtaining a two-dimensional size for the radiator is a challenge.

Knowing that I, for sure, didn't want to pay for a radiator that would not fit within the nose area of the Track T, I built a mockup first. Using my preliminary measurements, I cut and nailed together some scrap 2x4s, forming a rectangle that would fit in the designated area. The fact that a hot rod radiator and the side dimension of a wooden 2x4 are about the same played a major part in my decision for this mockup material. With the wooden "core" nailed together, I could move it up and down to establish a suitable location for mounting brackets, which would sit atop the mounting pads previously welded to the chassis. Armed with the verified dimensions of this mockup, I was able to provide a sketch and dimensions to Geary Portell at Portell's Radiator Shop. A short time later, he was able to provide me with a new aluminum radiator, built especially for my Track T. As the radiator for the Track T is so small, if I am ever at a rod run where there is an award for cutest radiator, I think I'll have it wrapped up. . . . Many factors contribute to a given radiator's ability to meet your engine's

Portell's Radiator placed the mounting flanges exactly where I requested, as well as the inlet and outlet necks appropriate for my engine.

cooling needs. To be sure your radiator is adequate for your project, it's best to speak to a professional in this area.

Mounting the Radiator

Radiators should be mounted securely, as you don't want it moving into the path of the fan. At the same time, they require a measure of shock absorption to avoid vibration damage.

Mounting brackets on both sides of the radiator are designed to align with and sit atop mounting pads that have previously been welded to the chassis. After marking the limits of the mounting pads on top of the mounting brackets, drill a hole in each of the mounting brackets and then also drill one into the mounting pad at the same location. Tap each of the holes in the mounting pads to accept a threaded stud. After installing the threaded stud, slide a thin piece of rubber material with a hole in the middle over the threaded stud. The radiator is now installed, with a small coil spring secured by a nut holding the radiator in place. With the rubber cushion beneath the radiator, you can tighten the spring sufficiently to keep the radiator in place, yet still provide shock absorption.

Fan

If the engine is a stock V-6, the hood is louvered, and the radiator is new, a mechanical fan should provide ample air movement to keep the engine cool. If this proves to not be the case, an electric fan can be installed later. Since I don't have a stock fan for this engine and knew that there was limited

This shot gives an idea as to just how small the radiator for the Track T really is. Even though it is small, with help from a mechanical fan and louvered hood, it should be more than sufficient to keep the mild mannered V-6 running cool.

A straightedge was used to mark the location of the mounting pad onto the top of the radiator's mounting flange. Now, the hole for the mounting stud could be drilled close to the center of both surfaces. An "X" marks the spot for the stud.

available room, I purchased the smallest fan that I could find. The 12-inch fan that I chose had blades with a substantial curve to them, making a 2-inch spacer a mandatory item.

Mounting the Transmission Cooler

Quite simply, the function of the transmission cooler is to provide a remote area for the transmission fluid to flow through and be cooled. Since excess heat is the worst enemy of your transmission, keeping the fluid cool is important. Typically, automatic transmissions have two fittings on the outside of the case for connecting transmission fluid lines. Transmission coolers have two fittings as well, and since it doesn't matter which way the fluid flows, hookup is simple.

151

The radiator was clamped into place, and then pilot holes drilled in both the radiator flange and the pad below to make sure that the two are aligned correctly.

Left: After drilling the pilot hole, I removed the radiator and then drilled the mounting pad so that I could tap it to accept a threaded mounting stud. **Right:** This is a view of the radiator from behind, after it has been mounted in the painted chassis. A rubber cushion and spring-loaded bolts should minimize vibration that can cause damage in a radiator.

As long as the transmission cooler is mounted in a place with circulating air, it can be installed just about anywhere and still work properly. Sometimes, the problem is just finding a place to put it. Because I chose a small round tranny cooler instead of a flat, box style, finding a suitable mounting location was not as much of a problem as it could have been. This was partly due to the fact that the exhaust exited through side pipes along the outside of the frame rails, rather than running beneath the entire vehicle and exiting out the back.

The transmission cooler that I chose was made of aluminum and had several external fins, which allowed it to disperse heat quite efficiently. It also had mounting brackets built in to the design, so it would be easy to mount; I simply

This is the transmission cooler that I purchased from Portell's Radiator. At around 12 inches long, it will fit into small vehicles such as the Track T. Transmission coolers are available in different lengths and can have both inlet and outlet on the same end or on opposite ends.

Mounting brackets were already attached to the transmission cooler so that it could be bolted directly to a frame rail. To maximize efficiency, however, Donnie Karg bolted the cooler to a couple of pieces of angle stock, and then welded those pieces to the frame rail.

had to drill and tap four holes in the frame rails, and then bolt it in place. However, this close proximity to the frame rail would reduce the space for air circulation. To expose it more to open air, I made two angle brackets and drilled them to match the holes in the mounting brackets, then welded them to the frame rails. This additional spacing was not so great that it would interfere with mounting anything else; it was just enough to provide better cooling.

Hard brake line was bent to connect the transmission and the cooler. Since the tranny cooler was secured to the chassis and the transmission was connected to the engine (causing some potential for movement), it was necessary to use flexible lines between the two components. Since this was going to be a mild mannered, stock engine vehicle, I didn't foresee hard lines being a problem.

STEERING

Depending on the make, model, and year of your vehicle and the engine that you are using, installing the steering can be easy, or it can be . . . shall we say an enlightening experience. The amount of available room, the type of steering box, the location of the brake pedal, and the layout of the

With the mounting brackets bolted to the mounting tabs and the entire assembly clamped in place, tack welding the mounting tabs the correct distance apart was easy.

After the mounting tabs were tack welded in place, the transmission cooler was removed and the welding completed.

exhaust are all very critical issues when it comes to connecting the steering wheel and the front wheels.

The most common steering arrangements used today are rack and pinion systems, which are common with independent front suspensions; cross steering that typically uses a Vega-style steering box; or a third style that usually uses a Mustang-style steering box. On hot rods, the rack and pinion system generally mounts the steering gear just in front, or just behind, an imaginary line that would take the place of the front axle. This is usually low and forward enough so that there is not much interference from engine accessories. Cross steering usually places the steering box a few inches behind the front axle, making it prone to interference with engines that have protrusions on their lower left

Right: The transmission cooler bolted into place on the painted chassis before any lines were run to it. Be careful when handling the transmission cooler, as the fins are sharp.

Left: Two brass fittings on the right side of the transmission are the inlet and outlet fittings of the transmission. On this transmission, one is located near the front and comes straight out, while the other is located slightly above the vacuum modulator and uses a 90-degree fitting. Different fittings (straight, 45 degrees, or 90 degrees) can be used as required.

By connecting the transmission to a remote cooler, the fluid is able to circulate through the cooler to shed unwanted heat and then back into the transmission. There is no direction of flow, so either fitting on the cooler can be connected to either fitting on the transmission. As shown, these lines were bent so that stock lengths could be used, and I didn't have to flare any lines.

front portion. Mustang-style steering boxes are usually located very near the lower end of the steering column, making them easy to connect. Their drawback, however, is a longer drag link is necessary to connect to the left front spindle. With rack and pinion or Vega steering, steering shafts and U-joints are used to connect the lower end of the steering column to the steering box. By using U-joints, the steering shaft does not have to be in a straight line between the column and box. The draglink on a Mustang steering box must be straight, though.

Steering U-joints (like all U-joints) are limited in the amount of deflection they can make before they are no longer functional. So, if you have lots of room, you can route the steering shafts away from any obstructions, and everything is fine. On hot rods based on older, smaller vehicles, the options for routing the steering shafts are limited. You must plan the layout so that no U-joints are required to make more than a 35-degree deflection.

One U-joint will be required to connect the steering box to the steering shaft. If there are no obstructions to go around and if the angle is within tolerance, you can connect the opposite end of the steering shaft to the lower end of the steering column for a simple installation. If necessary, you can alter the vertical angle of the steering column to achieve sufficient movement in the U-joints to make this work. If you cannot achieve a straight line between the steering box and the steering column, you can use a third U-joint to segment the steering shaft around obstructions. If a third U-joint is necessary, a shaft support (a.k.a. pillow block) must be installed on one of the shafts to prevent the steering shaft from looping. More U-joints can be used if necessary, however, an additional shaft support must be used for each additional U-joint.

Installing the Steering Column and Wheel

The intended location of the steering column must be determined before you can establish how long it must be. You must decide, at least approximately, where the column will pass through the floor or firewall, and where its end needs to be. With the driver seat (or a reasonable facsimile) in place, and a length of wooden dowel rod with an aluminum pie pan tacked on the end, this can be closely approximated. The length must allow for the portion of the column where the U-joint attaches to be on the outside of the firewall. While you are measuring this, it will be a good time to determine the necessary column drop. This is the measurement between the centerline of the steering column and the surface to which the column drop will be mounted. The steering column drop is commonly secured to the lower edge of the dash or a support bar is mounted behind the dash for this expressed purpose.

With the desired length steering column in hand, use an appropriate sized hole saw to cut a hole in the firewall at the desired location. The hole must be large enough for the steering column to pass through, but it shouldn't be any bigger than necessary.

To provide both support for the dash and a location to mount the column drop, cut a piece of sheet metal to the correct length to fit between the inside of the firewall and the back of the dash. Bending all edges up 90 degrees gives it some additional strength. Then secure it to the firewall with two bolts and lock nuts. Use another two bolts and lock nuts to secure it to the lower edge of the dash. Drill two holes in the column drop support, so that

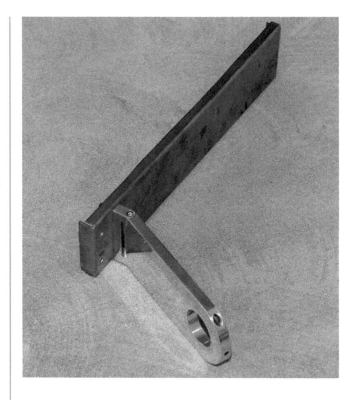

This sheet metal is merely a rectangular piece that has been turned up on all four sides. It serves two distinct purposes: one as a mounting point for the column drop bolted to it, and also as a support between the firewall and the dash.

the column drop mounting studs can pass through and then be secured on the top side with lock nuts. The swivel mount column drop allows for perfect alignment with the column. Mounting this column drop support in line with the steering column—so that the column drop hangs in line with the steering column—helps eliminate binding. However, as long as the material has sufficient strength in the required directions, the column drop or support does not necessarily have to be mounted directly above the column.

For my project, I used a swivel floor mount, consisting of a swivel mount and a two piece collar, to mount the lower end of the steering column and cover any extra opening around the column. These are available in different styles and range from pretty cheap to expensive. I originally purchased one of the cheap ones, as this was a low budget buildup. However, the minimal amount of floor space being in one single plane on the Track T didn't allow for sufficient mounting. Therefore, I ended up spending good money after bad to buy the more expensive style after all. This style included an aluminum swivel mount, which fit around the column, and a two-piece collar, which fit around the swivel to mount it flush to the firewall.

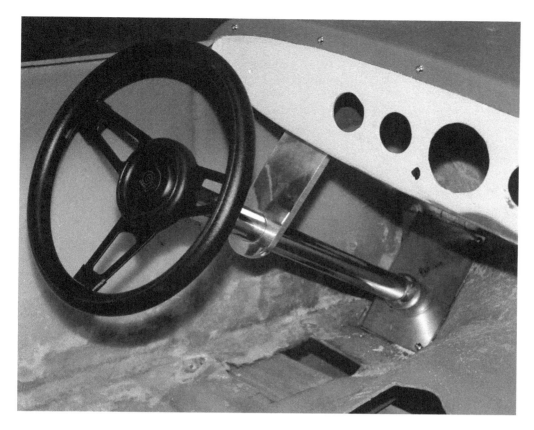

This steering column from Speedway Motors seemed appropriate for my project, as it is smooth, thin, stylish, and also uses a quick release mount for the steering wheel. Being able to remove the steering wheel will make ingress and egress much easier.

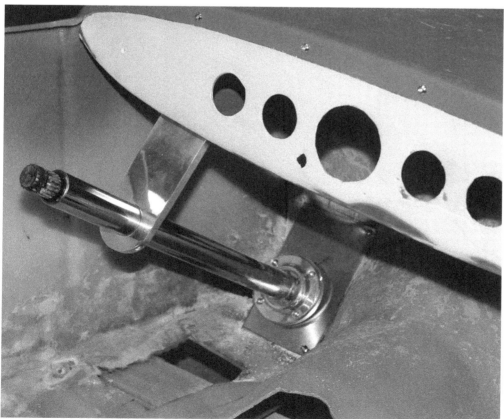

The column drop is hinged at the top to allow for the correct angle of the steering column. A two-piece flange at the lower column mount swivels around a spherical collar, sealing off the opening in the floor/firewall.

By using extensions and U-joints from my socket set, I was able to approximate what I would need to connect the steering column to the steering box. Perhaps the main point of this was to determine the best location for the shaft support.

After determining where the shaft support should be located, I drilled a hole just slightly larger than the stud of the shaft support in the top of the frame rail. I drilled another slightly larger hole on the inboard side of the frame rail. This second hole is to allow access to the nut that threads onto the stud, securing the shaft support to the frame rail. One can easily machine an aluminum plug or a simple cover plate to cover this inner hole, if desired.

Steering Shafts, Universal Joints, and Shaft Supports

Before finalizing the mounting of the steering column, it is a good idea to verify that steering shafts can be routed where they need to go. One way to check this is by using extensions from your socket set(s). Don't try to use socket extensions in place of steering shafts, but you can approximate the setup, so that you buy the right pieces the first time around. By doing this, I was able to determine that I would need three U-joints, and therefore a shaft support. Most shaft supports are an over-grown rod end—that is, a swivel enclosed in a metal ring with a shaft mounted to the outer ring. The mounting shaft is secured to the frame rail by two nuts: one on the inside, and one on the outside. The shaft support requires two holes to be drilled in the frame rails, so you should do this before the frame is painted. The locations of the holes will vary depending on your particular situation. One hole is for the mounting stud of the shaft support, while the other is an access hole to tighten the inside nut. This second hole is only required for boxed frame rails, as open frame rails do not limit the access.

With the dash mounted in the car, the next step in laying out the gauges is marking a vertical centerline and a horizontal baseline. The intersection of these two lines will be the center of the speedometer, with two smaller gauges on either side.

ELECTRICAL

Except for the power to turn on the starter, which fires up the engine, and power for the lights required in a street legal vehicle, there is no need for electrical power in a hot rod. We have become so accustomed to the many creature comforts in our daily drivers, however, that we feel the need to have them in our hot rods as well. Electrical gauges have quickly become more commonplace than mechanical ones; still electrical gauges could be classified as a necessity. Stereos and air conditioning are perhaps the most common of the electronic luxuries, but they are merely the tip of the iceberg when it comes to electronic automotive accessories. Contemporary street rods typically include wipers motors, power windows, power door locks, air ride control systems, and countless other wired gadgets. Incorporating these creature comforts and conveniences is not all bad, though, and with the support from the automotive aftermarket, wiring is no longer the dreaded task that it was once perceived to be.

Battery

Automotive batteries have been in use for quite some time and have not evolved much in recent years. The biggest problem concerning batteries is where to mount one so that it is out of the way, yet accessible. Typically, automotive batteries must be mounted in an upright orientation. The recent advent of sealed batteries that can be mounted in almost any orientation is one evolutionary development that has been beneficial to rodders. The price of these batteries is currently their biggest drawback.

Mounting the Battery

Since there is no "stock" mounting location for the battery on the Track T, I chose to mount it behind the driver seat. There simply was no room beneath the hood, and this vehicle didn't have a trunk. There was a small area between the seat back and the bulkhead separating the passenger compartment from the rear axle housing and the gas tank. This location would keep the battery low in the car and would be easy to access whenever the battery needed to be replaced. To aid in actually securing the battery, I mounted it in a plastic marine box, which would keep it secured, contained should it leak, and accessible should it need a jump.

ADDITIONAL SYSTEMS

159

I used a circle template to draw in the gauges. Once the spacing looked correct on one side, it was duplicated on the other side. Although the layout looks fine (at least to me), I should have raised the entire layout between 1/2 and 3/4 inch to allow for some additional room for the ignition switch. Remember, even though the layout may look fine, there needs to be sufficient room on the backside for the wiring.

MOUNTING GAUGES

The bigger the vehicle, the more opportunity there is for being creative with gauges and their placement. The Track T is certainly not spacious, though, and the dash is no exception. Also, if this was indeed a "track" bound vehicle, simple, easy-to–read, well-placed gauges would be the main consideration. For this reason, I chose a set of VDO Series 1 gauges. They are easy to read, easy to install, and are competitively priced—all good reasons to purchase them whether you are on a budget or not.

With the relatively small size of the flat dash, the logical choices for gauge placement would be to position the larger speedometer close to the steering wheel and the four smaller gauges to the right (either linear or stacked two above the other two), or to install the speedo in the middle with two small gauges on each side. I chose the latter layout for a couple of reasons. I was afraid that if I pushed all the smaller gauges to the right, the last one or two might have been a little too far away to read with my aging eyes. With the speedometer in the middle, it would be easy enough to monitor frequently to avoid getting any tickets. The other gauges would be easy enough to see when checking engine performance and avoiding any problems.

Once I made the decision on the gauge layout, it was time to get after it. When the dash was installed previously, the lateral centerline had been established and marked on the body's dash lip. Extending a vertical line onto the steel dash indicated the center of the dash from side to side. Next, I established a horizontal baseline by measuring down the same distance from corresponding dash mounting bolts. Hindsight being 20/20, I should have probably raised this line up about 1/2 inch, but it's done and looks fine. The mounting holes for the gauges were 3 3/8 inches for the speedometer and 2 1/16 inches for the four others, but the bezels were slightly larger (a fact that made installation somewhat forgiving).

Using a circle template, I drew a circle at the intersection of the vertical and horizontal lines as close as possible to the size of the speedometer's bezel. From this center, I measured the distance horizontally to the left and the right for the center of the middle gauges, and then drew an appropriate sized circle indicating their placement. The outermost gauges were placed in similar fashion with the distance

Good, bad, or indifferent, the first hole was drilled, so I was off and running. At least this type of dash was easier to reproduce than say, a dash for a 1940 Ford. As I improve my metal working skills, this dash will be easy enough to remove and replace.

Since everything went okay when drilling the large hole for the speedometer, I changed to a smaller hole saw and drilled the four holes for the smaller gauges. In the limited confines of the Track T, all of the gauges will be readable by both the driver and passenger.

With the holes drilled, a grinding stone on a pneumatic die grinder was used to open the holes slightly to fit the gauges and to smooth the edges. The gauges were then installed and secured from the backside.

between centers adjusted to make the spaces between gauges match. On the left side of the dash, having the same distance between centers placed the outer gauge too far away due to the larger radius of the speedometer.

The hole saws with the closest size to what I needed that I could find at the hardware store were 3 1/2 and 2 inches. I didn't figure that I'd be able to find a 3 3/8–inch hole saw and I knew that I was not going to find a 2 1/16-inch one, so I also bought a cylindrical grinding wheel for the die grinder. The hole saws would get close to the correct diameter, and the grinding stone would smooth the cut while getting the exact fit. After drilling five holes, I enlarged/smoothed each hole until the gauge fit properly. Then I slid all of the gauges into place from the outside with the bezel keeping them from sliding through. The speedometer had a plastic housing with external threads and was secured in place with a plastic collar that threaded onto the housing, sandwiching the dash between the bezel and the collar. The smaller gauges were metal with two long screws extending out the back. A metal bracket with two legs fit over these two screws. As nuts were tightened onto the screws, the gauges were secured in place.

After installing the gauges, I realized that I had not considered placement of the headlight switch and the ignition switch. The holes for these two switches are not big, but the switches do take up considerable room on the backside of the dash. Fortunately, there was plenty of room to the left of the dash for the headlight switch, and enough room to the left and down slightly from the speedometer for the ignition switch.

FUSE PANEL

Years ago, wiring your hot rod meant that you would upgrade the system from 6 volts to 12 volts, often starting with nothing more than a spool of wire and some terminal blocks. Thanks to companies, such as Affordable Street Rods, that manufacture an assortment of compact, easy to use, and—yes—affordable fuse panels, wiring your hot rod is now very easy and safe. Affordable Street Rods' Wiremaster kit allows you to complete as much wiring as necessary to get the vehicle operating to the point you desire, and then wire in other accessories later as they are installed. After mounting the panel, color-coded and numbered wires are connected to the like numbered terminals, and then

After remembering that I had forgotten to include the ignition switch into the layout, I determined that there was adequate room between the speedometer and the gauge to its left. The closest size drill bit was used to drill a hole, and then the hole was opened slightly by using a cone shaped stone on a pneumatic die grinder.

Progress on getting the hole size correct was checked from the outside. When the size was correct, the ignition switch was installed from behind and then secured with a bezel nut that threaded onto the switch from the outside.

The headlight switch, all five gauges, and ignition switch all fit nicely into the dash. The dash will look better after a skim coat of filler is applied to smooth up some of my novice hammer work. Three tiny lights (turn signal and high beam indicators) will be installed in the dash behind the steering wheel or centered over the speedometer. When finished, the dash will be painted the same color as the body.

routed and connected to the appropriate accessory, making for easy installation.

Determining What You Need

Most automotive wiring companies offer a couple of wiring panels, one designed for a bare bones hot rod, while others include more circuits for creature comforts. No matter which wiring panel you choose, you should determine as accurately as possible which electrical circuits you will need and then purchase accordingly. Wiring is not difficult, but you don't want to realize half-way through that you don't have an appropriate circuit and will have to retro fit a different panel, although it is possible. If you know that you are going to be running air conditioning, power seats, electric fuel pump, or other similar electrical components, go ahead and start with a bigger electrical panel.

Installing the Fuse Panel

Placement of the fuse panel is quite often not a question of where is the best location, but rather where is there space left over that hasn't or won't be allotted to something else. Many hot rods are relatively small when compared to stock daily

drivers, and the Track T is certainly no exception. For factory-built stock production vehicles, it is common practice for the fuse panel to be located under the dash on the driver side. This may be practical during assembly, as many of the wires run to the steering column or the dash, so the under dash location's close proximity saves a few feet of wire per vehicle. Saving a few feet per vehicle at so many vehicles produced per hour . . . well, you get the picture. Anyone who has ever had to attempt to wrap his or her body around the steering column—in addition to contorting sufficiently to access one of these fuse panels—doesn't appreciate having the steering column in the way.

The fuse panel should be situated so that it can get some air around it, but also be protected from the elements, which is especially important for an open vehicle. Occasionally, a fuse or a flasher may need to be replaced, so you should keep that in mind and make the fuse panel accessible. The fuse panel in a hot rod will get the most attention when the vehicle is being built, so you should look for alternate locations that will make wiring the vehicle as easy as practical. Typical locations for the fuse panel are under the dash, under the seat (as long as the seat can be removed for access to the panel), behind the seat,

For ease of access and protection from the elements, the fuse panel was installed on the firewall on the passenger side. It could have been installed on the driver side, but lack of access would have made changing a fuse, or any other service, somewhat difficult. Since the seat back will be removable, a possible location would have been behind the seat, but that would have taken away storage room, which was already at a premium.

or in the trunk area. If located behind the seat or in the trunk, a vented enclosure to protect the fuse panel from passengers or anything in the trunk would be a good idea.

For the Track T, the most suitable location seemed to be under the dash, on the inside of the firewall, but on the passenger side. Inside the cowl would be the least susceptible to weather and as convenient as possible for wiring or replacing fuses. Before drilling holes in the firewall, I located the panel so that the upper mounting bolt for the radiator overflow tank (mounted on the outside of the firewall) could pass through an open area of the fuse panel. I secured the fuse panel to the inside of the firewall by running a 1/4-20 machine screw through the firewall, and then through the three mounting holes previously drilled in the mounting surface of the fuse panel.

Circuits

With most of the commercially available wiring kits today, the hot rodder doesn't really have to be concerned with circuits and their loads like in the past. We no longer have to worry about the correct gauge wire, the appropriate relays, or using the correct sized fuse. The electrical engineers at the companies that make the fuse panels have done all of the engineering for us, so we just have to follow their directions to wire our hot rods successfully. Making a living as a technical writer, I know that directions for commercial products can range from excellent to the other side of useless. All too often, directions become way too complicated for the

intended audience. Rich Fox at Affordable Street Rods (makers of the Wiremaster Power Panel) has made wiring a hot rod easy enough that even I can do it. That should tell you that it is easy.

The instructions included with the Wiremaster kit are on one side of a piece of 8.5x11 paper, with some detailed schematics and company information on the other side. When the directions are this compact, you can be sure that installation is simple. Of course, Rich is available on the other end of the telephone at just about any time, should you have a question. Two panels are available for street driven hot rods (there is another panel that is intended primarily for race or off-road applications). The Wiremaster Power Panel II includes circuits for all of the basic wiring in a hot rod; while the Wiremaster Power Panel has additional circuits for air conditioning, electric fan, power seats, power windows, electric fuel pump, plus additional accessory circuits. Had it not been for the need to run an electric fuel pump, the basic Wiremaster Power Panel II would have been more than sufficient for the Track T.

A great benefit of the wiring panels from Affordable Street Rods is that you can run the circuits as your needs and time permit. Each terminal is numbered and identified. The wire that connects to the terminal comes with the terminal connector already crimped on, and a tag with the corresponding number and identification. Simply loosen the screw at the terminal, slide the appropriate wire connector beneath it, tighten the screw, then route the wire to the particular compo-

Since the radiator overflow tank needed to be mounted in a vertical orientation, lack of other available space dictated that it had to go on the firewall. I had not thought that far ahead, so finding a suitable location meant relocating the fuse panel slightly to allow one of the overflow tank mounting bolts to pass through it— hence the body filler on the firewall.

nent. After routing the wire, you can cut it to the suitable length and crimp on the appropriate connector.

If you are planning to do all the wiring for your hot rod at one time, you can start at terminal one and work your way around the panel. Or, if you desire, you can install just the wiring necessary to get the engine running, and then go back later and wire the lights, stereo, or other accessories.

ENGINE COMPARTMENT

Whether you use a wiring kit or do the wiring yourself, you will be running the wires to specific areas of the vehicle. The engine compartment typically has wires that go to the alternator, the starter, and the battery. On engines that do not have a high energy ignition (HEI) distributor, there is also a 12-gauge wire to the coil. Depending on the type of alternator, it will be the destination for two or three wires. If the alternator uses an internal voltage regulator (commonly known as a GM alternator), a 10-gauge wire

from the fuse panel will connect to the stud on the outside of the alternator. A 16-gauge wire comes from the fuse panel, passes through a diode, and then plugs into the alternator. A 12-gauge wire from the same plug also connects to the stud to which the 10-gauge power wire is connected. For externally regulated alternators, the wiring is the same, except that the 16-gauge wire from the fuse panel connects to a terminal on the external voltage regulator. Another pair of wires connects the voltage regulator to the alternator.

Wiring to the starter consists of the positive, or "hot," wire from the battery, a 10-gauge wire that runs from the fuse panel, and a 12-gauge wire from the neutral safety switch. The latter has a second wire that runs from it to the fuse panel. The neutral safety switch is activated by the shifter and, when installed and adjusted correctly, allows the vehicles with automatic transmissions to start only when they are in park or neutral. This feature is not used on vehicles with a standard transmission. For a poor man's theft deterrent, a toggle switch can easily be installed between the neutral safety switch and the starter. If used, it should be installed where only the authorized driver(s) knows the location. It should be easy to reach from the driver seat, but not necessarily out in the open. A word of caution: this security device should not be installed until after the vehicle has been thoroughly road-tested and all possible wiring problems have been diagnosed. After the wiring has been proven to work correctly, the toggle switch is easy enough to install. You just have to remember to turn it to the "on" position prior to attempting to start the vehicle, and then to turn it "off" when you park it.

There are also wires to the temperature sender, the oil pressure sender (for electric gauges), possibly an electric fan, and probably a horn. A 12-gauge wire is common for providing power to the electric fan (if used) and the horn. Both the electric fan and the horn circuits need to have a relay installed, which is sometimes included in the fuse panel. A water temperature sender can be threaded into a port in either the cylinder head or the intake manifold. A 16-gauge wire connects to the water temperature sender and runs to the temperature gauge or warning light. Oil pressure is captured by an oil pressure sender that is threaded into a pressurized oil galley. Similar to the water temperature sender, a 16-gauge wire runs to the oil pressure gauge. For mechanical gauges, the senders are similar, and tubing connects to the gauges.

You will need to decide the best route for running the wires, taking into consideration such obstacles as the exhaust system, the fan, and—to a somewhat lesser extent—the overall neatness of the layout. Common practice is to run all of the wires to any one area together (using several wire ties to keep them neatly bundled) and have them branch off as required. For wires that run to the front of the vehicle, they can be routed along one of the frame rails. This will allow you to use clamps similar to those used for the brake and fuel lines. Although it is not a functional necessity, running engine compartment wires inside of appropriately sized convoluted tubing, or other covering, seems to look better than having a rainbow of colors spanning all around the engine compartment.

RUNNING LIGHTS AND SIGNAL LIGHTS

Wiring the headlights and taillights isn't difficult, but it does require a little more concentration. Headlights and taillights receive power through the headlight switch, which received its power supply from a 12-gauge wire from the fuse panel. Courtesy lights (if used) are typically wired to be controlled by a door switch, but can be wired to be controlled by the headlight switch as well.

From the headlight switch, a wire runs to the dimmer switch, which is usually mounted on the floor or on the steering column. From the dimmer switch, a 12-gauge wire runs to each of the high beam terminals on the headlight pigtail. You can install this setup by running the wire directly to one of the headlights and then jumping over to the other light. If it is more convenient, you can instead run the high beam wire to a point and then have it branch off in opposite directions toward each light. As long as your connections are secure, either method will work well. In this high beam circuit, you need to run a smaller wire to connect to the high beam indicator on the dash panel. For the low beam headlights, run another wire at the dimmer switch and route it to the headlights in similar fashion as the high beam wires, but connect it to the low beam terminal on the headlight pigtail. A ground wire to each headlight and to a suitable ground completes the wiring of the headlights.

If parking lights are used, they each receive power from the headlight switch through a 16-gauge wire. If these lights are used as front turn signals, they receive their power from two separate terminals on the fuse panel. Either way, they must be grounded, either through the mounting of the light socket or with a ground wire.

Taillights are wired using the same basic methods as the headlights, but different connections are made. A 16-gauge wire runs from the headlight switch to each of the taillights. Just like the front turn signals, a 16-gauge wire runs from one terminal on the fuse panel to the left rear turn-signal light, and another 16-gauge wire runs from another terminal on the fuse panel to the right rear turn-signal light. The taillights and the signal lights may be combined in one housing or may be in separate ones. Each housing will need to be grounded, either through the mounting of the light housing or with a separate ground wire. If the taillights and rear signal lights are in separate housings, incorrectly routed wires should be checked first when diagnosing taillight/signal light problems.

Most late model steering columns include an integrated turn-signal lever to which wires from the fuse panel are connected. The column that I chose for this project had no provisions for turn signals or a horn button. For the turn signals, an aftermarket turn-signal mechanism from Affordable Street Rods that clamped onto the column was used. This aftermarket accessory includes turn-signal indicator lights along with a hazard flasher, and can be wired just as if it was integral to the column. A push button for activating the horn can be placed on the dash or almost anywhere within arm's length of the driver.

BRAKE LIGHTS

The brake lights are activated by a brake light switch. Typically, the brake light switch is connected electronically to the fuse panel, which automatically sends power to the brake light portion of the taillight through the taillight wire. However, it is conceivable that some lighting setups may require separate brake light wiring. Since third brake lights must only function when the brakes are used, they require their own wiring, both power and ground. Although it is possible to include the third brake light in the taillight wiring, this light being illuminated when the running lights are on would defeat the purpose of the third *brake* light.

Brake light switches used in hot rods are typically either a mechanical lever type or a pressure type. Both are connected to the fuse panel by two wires, with the switch being open in normal operation or closed when the brakes are applied, thereby illuminating the brake lights. The lever type switch is installed after installation of the brake pedal arm and is situated so that movement of the pedal arm pushes the lever on the switch. Space between the brake pedal arm and the lever dictates how long it will take before the brake light will come on. This may require some adjustment and fine tuning, but when it is adjusted, it can be forgotten. A pressure switch is plumbed into a "T" fitting in the brake line, so it can be installed as the brake lines are run, whether the brake pedal arm is installed or not. The pressure switch does not require adjustment, however, it is prone to failure and gives no indication of malfunctioning. You don't want to find out that your brake light switch failed by having another vehicle in your trunk or rumble seat.

ACCESSORIES

Electrical accessories for hot rods seem to have no limits, as more new products are available every year. Some of these accessories are safety related, while others are creature comforts. A windshield wiper and horn are beneficial safety items, whether they are legally required in your state or not. Other electrical accessories are air conditioning, stereo, power seats, power doors, air ride suspensions, and other items that are too numerous to mention. These systems all contain a fair amount of wiring of their own and therefore usually contain specific wiring instructions.

WIRING THE VEHICLE

Since the electric fuel pump is the only electrical "accessory" on the Track T, wiring was relatively simple when compared to contemporary street rods full of creature comforts. The most difficult part was lying between the interior side of the body and the transmission hump to connect the wires to the fuse panel. Since there were no opening doors on this vehicle, I wasn't able

to cantilever my body through the door opening. Oh well, so much for getting old, needing to lose weight, and building a small hot rod. Words of advice are to buy a good pair of wire crimpers, a good pair of diagonal wire cutters, and plenty of solderless electrical connectors in the necessary sizes and types before you start. Nothing is more aggravating than to be making good progress on the wiring, only to have to stop to make a parts run for the correct terminal connection. No matter what wiring kit that you use, take the time to read the included instructions thoroughly before you begin wiring, and don't hesitate to call for technical support should you have any questions.

To help keep myself organized while wiring the Track T, I began wiring at terminal one and worked my way around the fuse panel, one terminal at a time. Since I was not running a clock, interior lights, or a radio, my first terminal that required wiring was terminal three, which ran from the fuse panel to the positive side of the coil. This required drilling a hole in the firewall. Drilling the hole is not a problem, but you should give some thought to the size of the hole and its location before drilling. Whenever wires pass through sheet metal, you should install a rubber grommet to keep the wires from chafing on the edges of the sheet metal. Grommets should also be used on fiberglass, which will require thicker grommets in most instances. With the coil securely mounted, cut the wire to length, crimp on an appropriate terminal, and then secure it to the coil.

If you use heat shrink tubing to protect the connection, be sure to slide it onto the wire prior to crimping on the terminal. Also, be sure that you do not overheat or burn the wire when shrinking the protective tubing. If you burn the wire, you have defeated the purpose of using the heat shrink tubing in the first place.

As more wires are run along a similar route, you can place wire ties about a foot apart to keep the wires together and neat, adding more wire ties as more wires are added to the bundle. When running wires beneath carpeting or other upholstery, try to keep the wire bundle size small and flat, if possible, to prevent having "snakes" in the carpeting. Wires that run along the floor can be covered with duct tape to secure them in place. Wires (including stereo speaker wires) that run behind upholstered panels should be routed behind any structural supports or roof ribs to avoid interfering with the proper fit of the upholstered panel.

Electrical Ground

A simple principle of electronics is that the electrical component must be grounded to operate properly. Some components won't work at all if not grounded, while others will work sporadically. If an electrical component is not operating properly, a faulty or no ground may quite possibly be the problem.

Finding a location for the two horns (one high note, one low note) was difficult, as the engine bay was filling up fast. Because they need to be in a location where they are protected from wet weather, inside the nose on either side of the radiator seemed appropriate.

The ground cable of the battery should be connected to something substantial, such as one of the bolts that secure the transmission to the engine. A braided stainless steel ground cable should connect the engine to the chassis, with another cable connecting the steel body to the chassis or the engine. Since fiberglass is not a good conductor, there is no need to connect a fiberglass body to a chassis or engine ground. However, components inside of the body, such as gauges, stereo, and lights need to be grounded to some steel portion of the vehicle. When connecting ground wires, be sure to scrape away paint or anything else that would prevent good conductivity and use a serrated washer on the bolt.

Extra effort is required to achieve proper grounding when using a fiberglass body. Rather than lights or accessories grounding through their mounting to a steel body, a separate ground wire must be used. This ground wire must be connected to the ground terminal on the electrical component and then connected to a grounded mounting bolt, such as on the chassis, engine, or transmission. Several ground wires can be connected to a common bolt.

Wiring the Gauges

If the dash or gauge insert is built so that it can be easily removed from the vehicle (this is easier in some cars than others), wiring the gauges can be made easy. Since I built my own dash, I made sure that it would be removable for this very reason. By using quick disconnects (such as those used for trailer connections) you can wire the gauges while sitting in your living room recliner if you wish, and then reinstall the dash when you are finished.

For electrical gauges, there are three basic types of wires, which connect the senders to the gauges, a power wire, and a ground wire.

Sender (or Signal Power)

Although there are many additional gauges available, the typical (and plenty sufficient for most vehicles) gauge package includes a speedometer, an oil pressure gauge, a water temperature gauge, a fuel level gauge, and a voltmeter gauge. The speedometer is usually driven by a cable that runs from the transmission, and can be mechanical or electrical. For a mechanical speedometer, the cable contains a flexible shaft that is limited to broad, sweeping curves in its placement. Depending on the available room behind the speedometer, you may need a 90 degree adaptor in order to keep from kinking the cable where it connects to the back of the speedometer. The cable for an electric speedometer contains a group of wires rather than a flexible shaft, which can make the cable easier to route.

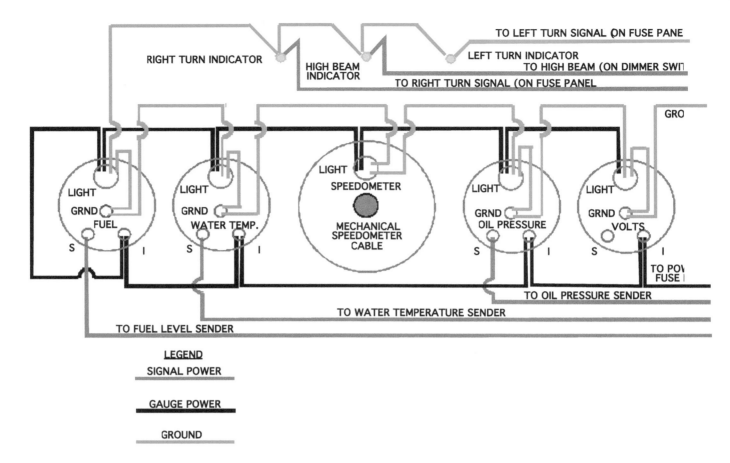

LEGEND

SIGNAL POWER

GAUGE POWER

GROUND

For electric gauges, juice can be run in series from one gauge to the next. In similar fashion, the ground wire for the gauges and lights can be run in series. The sender (or signal power) is routed directly to the appropriate terminal on the gauge.

The sender wire for the other gauges is typically a single 16-gauge wire that runs from the sender to the gauge. The oil pressure sender is located on the engine block and is threaded into an oil galley. A water temperature sender is usually located on one of the cylinder heads or on the intake manifold. The fuel level sender is part of the float assembly. Note that the fuel level sender typically has its own ground stud and therefore requires a ground wire to be connected to it. Turn-signal indicator lights receive their signal from the fuse panel, while the high beam indicator receives its signal from the dimmer switch.

Power Wire

For the voltmeter, the sender is actually a wire from a specified terminal on the fuse panel and is connected to the gauge or instrument power terminal on the gauge, rather than a signal terminal. Electrical power is indeed the signal for the voltmeter, but all of the gauges need electric power in addition to their signal feed to operate. This electrical source can be wired in series from the voltmeter to the oil pressure gauge,

the speedometer, the water temperature gauge, and the fuel level, as well as to any other gauges. It can also be continued to serve as power for the gauge lights, which is something that we all know serves as illumination in paradise.

Ground Wire

Like all other electrically operated items, the gauges and their lights need a ground to operate correctly. Just like the power wire, but connected to the ground terminal instead, the ground wire can be run in series from one gauge to the next. Since the gauges are your monitoring system and therefore are your warning if trouble is brewing, you should take extra care to ensure that the gauges are grounded properly. If they are not properly grounded, you may mistake their faulty operation for a more serious problem that doesn't really exist. Of course, you should not assume that an abnormal reading of a gauge is actually a gauge problem either. In other words, make a mental note of what the typical readings are on your gauges, and then you will have a better idea of when something is wrong.

CHAPTER 7
PAINT, UPHOLSTERY, AND GLASS

Wow, if we're talking about painting, we must be getting close to finishing this project, at least in the big scheme of things. Although it is certainly a good idea to think these things out beforehand, paint, upholstery, and glass installation are typically the last three things completed on a hot rod before it is actually "finished." I have seen more than a few hot rods that were completely painted before the chassis was even completed. That's jumping the gun, because as soon as you paint the body, you have to give it the care of a finished automobile. You don't carry wrenches, screwdrivers, big metal crossmembers, welding equipment, and axle stands back and forth past your brand-new car. Why put a finish coat of paint on your hot rod when you still have a lot of work to do with objects that can put a big gouge in it? Even if you avoid damage for the rest of the build, what commonly happens when you take the hot rod out for its first drive is that you quickly realize the hood, doors, deck lid, and anything else that can be misadjusted is, in fact, misadjusted and has now done considerable damage to your fresh paint. Not that damaged paint can't be repaired, but primer is much easier (and less expensive) to touch up.

If you are going to drive the vehicle before it is painted (this is highly recommended), you will need to install at least the windshield, if for no other reason than to be legal and keep bugs out of your teeth. Saving the rest of the glass and all of the upholstery until after the painting is completed will save considerable time and potentially money, as masking doesn't have to be as precise.

FINAL BODYWORK AND SURFACE PREPARATION

One of the most common comments from visitors to my garage was that the Speedway Motors body looked pretty decent for a budget priced piece. That was certainly a valid observation, as the body was perhaps as straight as any other fiberglass body on the market. However, it was certainly not ready for paint right out of the factory.

There are several seams that need attention. For the most part, they can be ground down flush, but this will take some time and a grinding disc or two. Additionally, the lip around the edge of the cockpit is far from uniform, and it will require a saber saw and several coarse blades to remove the extra fiberglass material. This is all relatively minor,

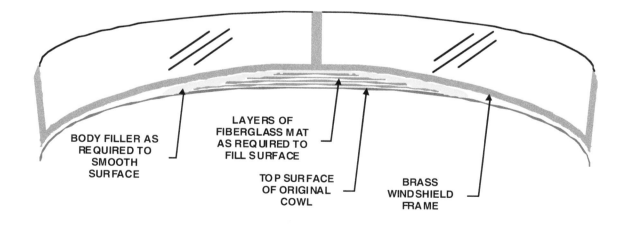

BODY FILLER AS REQUIRED TO SMOOTH SURFACE

LAYERS OF FIBERGLASS MAT AS REQUIRED TO FILL SURFACE

TOP SURFACE OF ORIGINAL COWL

BRASS WINDSHIELD FRAME

This sketch illustrates what needs to be done to the body to get the windshield frame to fit correctly. The windshield frame can't be modified to fit the body, so the body must be filled to meet the frame. Filling low areas in fiberglass bodies, whether they need to match anything or not, can be done this way if the area is too deep to fill with body filler alone.

171

however, and should be expected on a body in this price range; it is even common on the more expensive bodies.

This car's budget price shows up more when you go to fit the windshield; the cowl is in no way concentric with the curve of the lower edge of the Speedster windshield frame. Although the frame fits nicely at the outer edges of the cowl, there is a gap of approximately 1/2 inch at the center, so that must be filled. If the gap was a 1/4 inch or less, you could fill it with plastic body filler, but the gap on my project's body was beyond that. To fill a gap of this thickness and over this large of an area, you need to use layers of fiberglass matte, and then cover them with a skim coat of filler.

The area of the cowl where fiberglass will be used should be roughed up with a grinder using a 36-grit disc to make sure that the new 'glass will adhere properly. Then position the windshield frame one more time, make some notes on the thickness of the gap, and remove the frame. Make some reference marks on the cowl to indicate where one layer will be sufficient, where two will be required, and so on.

You don't want to build the area up higher than necessary, just to be required to grind it back down. Since the gap is mostly uniform from side to side, but larger in the middle, the layers of fiberglass matte can help maintain that uniformity. As shown in the related drawing, the layers of fiberglass matte can be added in a pyramid fashion. For the first piece, cut a large enough piece to cover the entire area that will be filled, and then glass it in place. Using the reference lines, add the second and succeeding layers until the gap is within a quarter inch or less of meeting the contour of the windshield frame. When the gap is thin enough to be finished with a coat of body filler, allow the fiberglass to thoroughly cure. After that, you can apply a skim coat of body filler and then sand it down to achieve a perfect fit with the windshield frame.

Another bodywork concern that I needed to resolve had nothing to do with the quality of the fiberglass body. This issue was where to place the rear license plate so that it could be illuminated. A relatively easy modification that is both inexpensive and somewhat cool, can be made by cutting out an appropriate sized piece of fiberglass from the back of the body, near the line that represents the lower edge of the deck lid. Then lean this cut out piece inward at the top, fabricate a wedge shape on both sides, lay a flat piece across the top, and glass the whole deal back into place. A small license plate light can then be installed in the top of the recess. You can have the recess deeper at the bottom, but that will require a small drain, otherwise the recess can fill with water during a rainstorm. However, the horizontal hoop of the chassis is located just inside of the body and

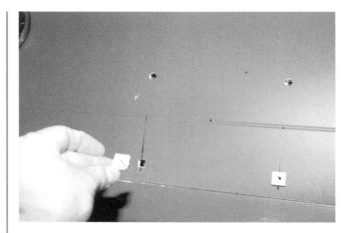

After drilling the license plate mounting hole and then filing it square, the plastic mounting tab can be pushed into place. If it doesn't go with a slight amount of pressure, file a little more and then check it again.

crosses approximately—as you may have guessed—right at the lower edge of the deck lid.

One option is to move the license plate downward, but this involves modification to the body and the rolled pan. The option that I chose was to surface mount the license plate in the desired location and to illuminate it with a lighted license plate frame. The license plate was mounted using the same method, but it was not recessed.

With my "chromium plated, fully illuminated, genuine accessory" license plate holder from the vendor in hand, along with four tag mounting tabs from the local auto parts store, it was time to get to work. I measured to find the

After the mounting tabs are pressed into the body, installing the license plate is just as simple as on a late model car. Insert the four bolts through the illuminated frame and the license plate, and then thread them into the plastic mounting tabs. Just don't forget to wire the license plate frame in the circuit with the taillights and provide a ground.

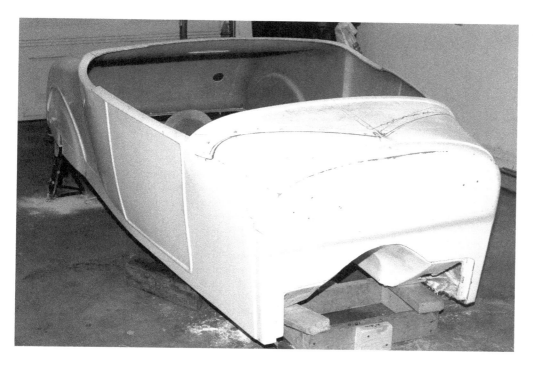

Because the body is fiberglass and won't rust, I could have waited until I was ready to paint to apply primer, but quite honestly, I was tired of looking at the white fiberglass. Still, surface prep as the same. I scuffed the entire body with 240-grit sandpaper and then cleaned it with an application of wax and grease remover.

The steel chassis was also scuffed with 240-grit sandpaper and cleaned with wax and grease remover. Having a chassis rotisserie would have been nice, so that priming (and later painting) the chassis could have been done at same time. Not having that luxury, I sprayed two coats of epoxy primer on the bottom of the chassis. When the epoxy primer had dried sufficiently, I turned the chassis over manually and then epoxy primed the top.

horizontal center of the deck lid, and then used the license plate frame as a template to mark the location of the four mounting tabs. Using a drill bit just slightly smaller than the portion of the mounting tabs that press into the body, I made four holes. Then I used a small file to square up and enlarge the holes until the mounting tabs snapped into position. I drilled another small hole in the body for the light's wiring to pass through. Installing the license plate was now just a matter of sliding each of the four bolts through the license plate frame, through the license plate, and into the plastic mounting tab.

APPLYING PRIMER

After all of the holes for brake lights, windshield mounting bolts, and other parts have been drilled, a coat of epoxy primer can be applied to the body. Likewise, you can apply epoxy primer to the chassis after completing all of the welding and other necessary modifications. Hindsight being 20/20, I recommend applying epoxy primer to the chassis components upon delivery, rather than waiting until after completing the fabrication. Although you will need to sand or grind away the primer to do any welding, that is typically easier than removing the surface rust that will

173

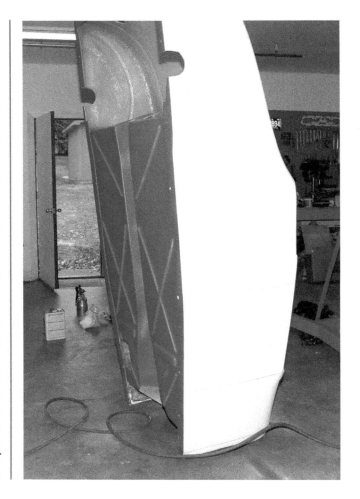

Standing the body on the firewall works for priming the underside of the floor. For final painting, place the body on sawhorses, and then move the sawhorses when painting the rest of the body so no areas are left uncovered.

accumulate during the fabrication process. Another application of epoxy primer will be required before painting no matter which way you choose to go. So, the choice is to spend some money up front for epoxy primer to keep the steel parts from rusting, or spend money and time later to get the rust removed. Epoxy primer does serve well to increase the adhesive quality of body filler, so it should be applied to any surface where body filler will be used.

With rust removed from the steel chassis components and all surfaces sanded down with 240-grit sandpaper, you can apply a final coat of epoxy primer to the chassis. First, wipe down everything to be primered with wax and grease remover, and then wipe it clean using a clean towel. Then use an air hose with an air nozzle to blow away any dust and to make sure that no wax and grease remover has pooled anywhere. Two coats of epoxy primer can now be applied and allowed to dry per the instruction sheets.

For the body and any other surfaces where body filler is used, priming is slightly more involved. Wipe down surfaces with wax and grease remover, and then wipe them clean using a clean towel. Use an air hose with an air nozzle to blow away any dust and to make sure that no wax and grease remover has pooled anywhere. A coat or two of primer surfacer or sprayable polyester filler should then be

When the body was primed, I was working by myself in the garage, so no help was around to lift the body onto sawhorses. To keep from painting the body to the floor, I placed 2x4s under the Track T's floor to lift it slightly.

After receiving two coats of epoxy primer on the bottom side, the chassis was turned over (using the arm-strong method), and then two coats of epoxy primer were applied to the top. Because this involved touching the chassis, the epoxy priming stage took an extra day.

After the epoxy primer was dry, the chassis was painted with two coats of the same single stage paint used on the wheels and the engine. As was the case with the epoxy primer, the first side had to dry and then be flipped over to paint the remaining side.

applied per the applicable instruction sheets. After the proper drying time, you should dry sand this primer with 150- to 220-grit sandpaper, and then wet sand it with 400-grit sandpaper.

APPLYING SEALER

Other than sanding out runs, blemishes, or color sanding the color coats or later applications of clear, no more sanding can be done to the body once sealer is applied. So, you should double check for imperfections in the primer or any other irregularities or blemishes that need to be addressed before applying sealer. If you are working with a surface (steel, aluminum, or fiberglass) that did not have any body filler added and had no prior application of primer or paint, you can primer and paint it without sealer. On my chassis and suspension components, no filler was added to smooth any joints, so sealer was not required. The body, however, had some filler in a few spots and had fiberglass, along with body filler in the cowl area. To serve as a barrier between these various undercoats and the color paint coats, sealer was required. Sealer keeps the hardeners and resins of these undercoats from seeping through the topcoats, plus it provides a uniform base coat for the color. If I had not used sealer, these areas where I had added additional fiberglass and body filler would have begun to show through the paint.

The same epoxy primer that was used to prime everything can be mixed (using different ratios included with the directions) for use as a sealer. This minimizes the number of paint products that are actually required. However, specific sealer products are available. The sealer is applied in similar fashion to primer, but you should consult the instructions for appropriate air pressure and drying times.

APPLYING PAINT

With the vast amount of different paint products available, you must pay particularly close attention to the instructions for the specific products you are using. Such application instructions as mixing ratios, air pressure from the spray gun, and time between coats vary with each and every product. Painting is a detailed subject that can fill a whole book. Everything I know about it, you can learn from *How to Paint Your Car*, by David H. Jacobs Jr. and yours truly.

Base Coat

Although single-stage paints are available, most aftermarket automotive painting today uses the base coat/clear coat systems. An exception to that is this Track T, where single-stage paint was used on the chassis. This was done for a couple of reasons particular to this project. For one, when the Track T is finished, most people will not see the chassis, so I chose to forego the expense of the clear. Secondly, at the time when the chassis was painted, scheduling and use of the garage made the additional time required to apply clear impractical.

Single-stage paint, or the base coat of a base coat/clear coat system, is obviously what provides the color to a painting project. Single-stage paints are somewhat less expensive than their base coat/clear coat counterparts, and they also don't require the additional expense and labor of multistage paint systems. They don't offer the protection that is afforded by a few coats of clear, yet single-stage paint is easier to touch up. Should you obtain some road rash, these blemishes can be touched up easily with a tiny brush and some of the original paint used on your hot rod. Merely dab the paint on to cover the blemish, allow it to dry, and then sand down any rough edges with some 2000 or finer grit sandpaper, if necessary.

If using a base coat/clear coat system, apply the base coat to achieve complete coverage, but do not expect any gloss from the paint. Some primer coats appear to have more gloss than a base coat, but this is to be expected. Applications of clear are what really bring out the gloss in multistage paint systems.

Clear Coat

When applying clear to a paint job, be sure to read the instructions for both the base coat beneath it and for the clear itself. Just like products that provide color, there are several types of clear, and all are designed for specific applications. Some of these clears are more suitable for use in a collision repair shop, where infrared heaters are available to speed up the process, while others are more suitable for those of us working in our garages.

Before choosing a specific product, you should discuss your situation with an expert at your favorite auto body and paint supply store and ask for a recommendation. Painters at the local body shop will surely know the products they use on a regular basis, but what they use might not be the best recommendation for your particular situation. By sanding and buffing, you can get most any paint job to look good, but some products will make that perfect finish much easier to achieve.

Laying Out Scallops

Unlike painting a hot rod, where the body is typically disassembled as completely as possible, laying out scallops should be done with the body completely assembled. Unless you are applying scallops to just one piece, all of the body and related components (fenders, hood, etc.) should be positioned and secured as if you are about to go for a drive. If a painted scallop line extends onto any part that is not latched completely or fastened securely, you can bet that once it is, your careful paint work will be misaligned. Avoid that aggravation by getting everything secured, latched, and placed exactly where you want it to be in the finished car. Get the panel gaps perfect, drive it, tweak it; let things shift and settle. Then paint it.

Layout

Having a drawing or a photo of scallops that you want, on a vehicle similar to yours, really helps when laying them out on your hot rod. The tips of the scallops usually (but not always) end in a layout where an imaginary straight line could connect all of them. A common exception has the tips end at a door edge, or other bodyline (or some predetermined distance away from those bodylines). This imaginary straight line may be vertical, but it usually isn't. In a similar fashion, the bellies of scallops are typically located along a common line, but the line for the tips and the line for the bellies do not have to be parallel to each other.

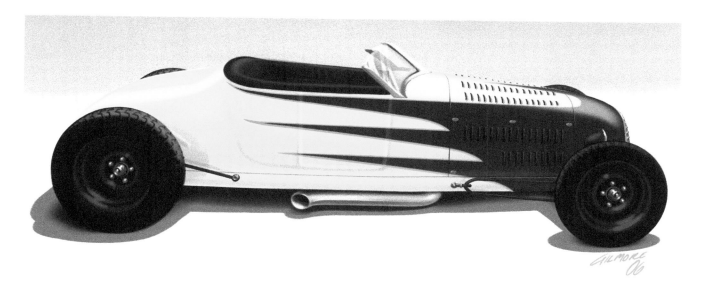

Steve Gilmore had worked on the Mattel Hot Wheels Track T as an intern (before landing a full-time gig with Ford Motor Company), so he has a soft spot in his heart for Track Ts. After stumbling across my website, he contacted me to discuss my Track T. How could I refuse when he offered to do a rendering? I knew that I wanted scallops, but Steve was the one who created the layout. Artwork courtesy of Stilmore Designs

Additionally, scallops are geometric and therefore really need to be identical on both sides of the vehicle. Using some 1/8-inch or 1/4-inch Fine Line tape, begin laying out the scallops based on your drawing or photos on one side of the vehicle. Tape is cheap, so work with the layout until you feel that it is exactly what you want, keeping in mind that it will need to be duplicated on the opposite side.

To help duplicate the layout on the opposite side, you may need a baseline from which to measure, so some reference lines in the form of 1/8-inch Fine Line tape might be advantageous. These reference lines may be from a particular suspension bracket, mounting bolt, or anything that has the same location on both sides. They may simply be vertical from a common point or be connected to two distinct points, as long as they are to similar points on both sides. Being able to measure along a straight line will help you to duplicate the pattern for the opposite side.

Scuffing the Existing Paint

Any items that are not to be painted, such as the grille, should be removed rather than masked. Small items, such as the headlights, that still need to be painted the same color as the scallops should be removed and painted separately. With the layout outlined completely with Fine Line tape, apply 1/4-inch-wide masking tape with the edges of both pieces of tape aligned at the edge of the proposed scallops. Apply an additional width of the masking tape on the area that will be masked off. For the paint that will be applied to the clear coat underneath, scuff the scalloped area using 800-grit wet or dry sandpaper and lots of water. The water helps to get rid of the loose particles, so you don't grind them into the surface. Make sure that you scuff only the clear and don't cut into the color below, or you will need to repair that paint.

Masking

When the scalloped area has been scuffed, rinsed off, and dried, the area that is not to be painted should be masked off completely. How this masking is done depends somewhat on if the vehicle is disassembled or left fully assembled. Relatively small items such as the hood and hood side panels may be easier to work with if they are removed for painting, but remember that the layout must be done with all panels in place. These panels can be masked off with masking tape and masking paper. Larger areas, such as the body of the car and the engine compartment, can be masked with plastic sheeting sold at auto body paint and supply dealers for the expressed purpose of masking large areas. This material is much like food plastic wrap used in the kitchen, but it comes in much wider rolls and folds out to even larger sizes.

Painting Scallops

To appear "finished," scallops and flames need to have a pinstripe around the edge. Nothing says that this pinstripe is required, but if you compare two similar vehicles where one has a pinstripe while the other doesn't, you will quickly notice the difference. Pinstripes can be added afterward,

177

either by brush or by using a striping tool. However, a smooth way to add this pinstripe so that it will be protected by clear is to paint it while you are painting the scallops. It does require a few more steps at this point, but it will eliminate steps later.

As a contrasting color to the light tan Harvest Moon body and the dark chocolate color of the scallops, I wanted a bright orange, such as GM's Omaha Orange or Tangier Orange. A pint of this will go a long way when used just for pinstripes. I wanted an 1/8-inch pinstripe, so with the area that was not to be painted (the Harvest Moon color) masked off, and the area to be scalloped scuffed up, I sprayed a couple of coats of orange along the edge of the masking tape defining the scallop layout and allowed them to dry completely. Then I applied masking tape to the desired width of the pinstripe so that the edge of the masking tape abutted the outline masking tape.

Applying Base Coat to Scallops

The color you have chosen for the scallops can now be applied, using two or three coats, or until coverage is complete if using lighter colors. When the scallop color has had ample time to dry, you can remove the pinstripe masking tape, revealing your pinstripe. The additional masking material can be removed as well.

Applying Clear Coat to Entire Vehicle

To provide a smooth glossy surface to the entire vehicle, three or four coats of clear can now be applied. Again, this can be done with the vehicle assembled or apart as necessary. Allow the proper amount of time between coats and afterwards for the clear to dry thoroughly. Then wet sand the clear, using a circular motion, a light touch, and plenty of water. Begin with 800-grit wet or dry sandpaper and work your way up to 3000-grit sandpaper to eliminate any blemishes. The surface should then be finished by buffing and then adding a good coat of paste wax.

UPHOLSTERY

I must say that I was pleasantly surprised with the quality of the Track T's upholstery kit from Speedway Motors. It wasn't going to rival a Ridler Award winner, but for the Track T it was more than sufficient and saved me from having to do any sewing. That in itself is a good thing.

The upholstery in the Track T is minimal, as befits a budget hot rod. The steps and photos discussing it should give you a basic idea of how to handle this stage of your hot rod project. For a more detailed look at upholstery—and some of the tricks award-winning pros use—refer to my book, *How to Restore and Customize Auto Upholstery and Interiors.*

Insulation

Steps toward noise abatement in an open hot rod are probably a futile effort, but many of those same steps can reduce heat in the passenger compartment, and that does make a difference in a warm climate. Although the exhaust on this project runs out the side rather than directly beneath the passengers, there would not be much to keep some of that heat from radiating upward. In order to minimize engine heat at the firewall, exhaust heat from the sides, and roadway heat through the floor, I contacted QuietRide Solutions for its advice on how to properly insulate the Track T. Even though this is an open car, the same process can be very successful on a closed car or truck.

Sound deadening is accomplished by damping or absorbing. Damping is the process of reducing vibration; even though it may not eliminate the roar or purr of the exhaust in a roadster, it will help to minimize resonant vibration in body panels, door panels, and floor pans. Damping material should be at least half as thick as the material to which it is being applied. It is not necessary to cover the entire surface area, as it only needs to cover one-third to one-half of it. The most effective damping material is a self-adhesive, rubberized asphalt material that is acoustically "dead." Sound absorption is done by applying dense fibrous materials with open pores, such as open cell foam. Thick materials are best at absorbing low to high frequencies, while thinner materials are more effective at minimizing medium to high frequencies.

QuietRide Solutions' Dynamat is easily cut to size and shape with scissors or utility knife. After peeling off the protective backing and pressing the Dynamat onto the surface, use a small roller to work out any air bubbles. If air bubbles remain, you can slice the Dynamat material and work out the air with a roller. To apply Dynamat onto vertical surfaces or upside down, first apply an upholstery adhesive (such as 3M Top and Trim Adhesive) to both surfaces to be joined, allow them to become tacky, and then apply the Dynamat. After applying sound deadening material, you should apply a reflective heat-barrier type insulation to maximize your efforts. Depending on the source, the reflective insulation may not be self adhesive, but it can be secured in place by using upholstery adhesive, as mentioned above. Aluminized tape should be used to cover all of the seams.

Carpet

Speedway's Track T upholstery kit consists of a piece of carpeting, two interior panels, two seat cushions, and a seat back. The carpeting will need to be trimmed to fit the firewall, floor, and back panel, as well as the transmission

Why is yours truly smiling? Most likely because the upholstery kit has arrived, the steering is installed, and the author actually fits between the seat back and the steering wheel. Photo by Sandy Parks

Although fiberglass bodies are not as susceptible to noise caused by vibration as steel bodies, efforts to minimize noise can still be taken. To address this, a layer of Quiet Ride Solutions' Dynamat sound barrier is installed. This heavy rubber-coated material can be cut to shape easily with a pair of scissors. The backing can then be peeled off and the sound barrier pressed into place.

shifter and emergency brake lever. When cutting for the shifter and brake lever, you should start with a small incision, making sure that the carpet is laid out as necessary, and then enlarge the holes to allow for operational movement for these two protrusions. With carpentry projects, you should measure twice for each cut. You can always remove more carpet, but fixing a hole that's too big, or misplaced, is a problem you will want to avoid.

When you have trimmed the carpet to fit as desired, remove it, apply automotive carpet adhesive to the back, and then reinstall it. You should be able to find automotive carpet adhesive at your favorite auto parts supply, but if not, you could use strips of hook and loop material to secure the carpeting in place. After the carpet is installed, add boots to the base of the shifter and emergency brake lever.

After all of the sound barrier insulation is installed, the foil-faced heat barrier from Quiet Ride Solutions can be cut to size (aluminum face up). When it is trimmed to the correct size and shape, spray adhesive (included with the insulation kit) is applied to the back of the heat barrier and the surface to which it is to be applied. After it becomes dry to the touch, the heat barrier is pressed into position. Any seams should be covered with aluminum faced tape.

PAINT, UPHOLSTERY, AND GLASS

The interior kit from Speedway Motors is supposed to be manufactured especially for the Track T, however, fit of the interior side panels was somewhat disappointing. At the area that would be in front of the door, the panels are too tall to pass beneath the dash rail, which prevents them from sliding forward as far as they should. To remedy this, the vinyl will need to be pulled loose from the cardboard backing board, the backing board trimmed to fit, and the vinyl reattached. Realize that you may need to rework some components, even though they may be designed for the vehicle you are working on.

Interior Panels

No part of the kit is difficult to install, but the interior panels do require the most work. After they are installed, you are all but finished. The panels are to be upholstered on one side and are marked on the back to indicate which side of the car they fit. Place the correct panel on the correct side, making sure that it is tight against the inside of the body. Now pull the upholstery flap over the top edge of the body. Starting at the center, snap, mark, drill, and then Pop-rivet each snap into place. Placing the seats into position will hold the lower edge of the interior panel in place. Instead, I opted to install some hook and loop material along the full length of the interior panel at the bottom and vertically at each end.

Surprisingly, the seats are actually quite comfy. The two seat cushions and seat back shown are included in the upholstery kit. Also included, but not shown, are two matching interior panels and carpeting. No sewing is required, so the kit is easy to install.

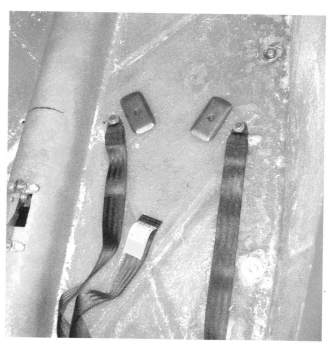

After determining the mounting locations for the seatbelts, drill appropriate sized holes. Pass the mounting bolts through a washer, the mounting tab, and then through the floor. Beneath the floor, thread the mounting bolt into a large anchor plate that has rounded corners. The larger size of the anchor plate will help to distribute forces, while the rounded edges will be less likely to slice through the floor in the case of an impact.

Seats

The seat back pretty much sits in position, but it needs to be secured somehow or it will be out of place by the time you and your passenger get to where you are going and get out of the car. You can attach a pair of hinges to the backside of the seat back so that it will fold forward. Since I have installed the battery box behind the driver seat, I will eventually need access to that area. For this reason, I installed a strip of hook and loop material between the bottom edge of the seat back where it rolls over the body and the corresponding location of the body. This adequately secures the seat back, but allows for simple removal to access the battery and fuel pump.

The seat cushions will obviously stay in place when I have my butt parked in them, but getting in and out of the vehicle will cause them to move around a little and look unkept if they are not secured. They can be secured with screws from underneath, but as with the seat back, I chose to use more hook and loop material. A strip across the front and across the back of each seat cushion should be sufficient.

Seatbelts

There is no suitable location for mounting the third point of a three-point shoulder belt, but that is no excuse for not installing lap belts. (If you are building a closed car, B-pillars and various seat options may make a three-point belt more feasible.) After installing the Track T seat back in position, I made a reference mark indicating the back of the seat cushions on the transmission tunnel. Mounting bolts for securing the seatbelts to the body would be located along this line extending to each side. Making sure that nothing was in

the way below the floor at these locations, I drilled four appropriate sized holes. Installation of the seatbelts was then as easy as passing a bolt through a washer and the mounting tab of the belt, then through the floor and into the anchor plate. Having someone tighten the bolts from the top, while someone else holds the anchor plate below will make this an easy task.

INSTALLING WINDSHIELD GLASS

Since glass is expensive and breakable and can cut you, I fully believe that its installation should be left to the professionals. Almost any professional glass shop can probably install auto glass, but if you can find one that is also owned by a hot rodder, it will be to your benefit. Such is the case with Chippewa Glass. It typically doesn't install auto glass, but its employees are hot rodders and therefore realize that our old cars are much more than just old cars. Poor fitting window glass that rattles quickly takes the fun out of driving a hot rod. Taking the time to make sure the glass fits properly, the exposed edge is sufficiently smoothed, and the glass is caulked neatly are just a few of the things that shops like Chippewa Glass do to ensure the windshield is installed correctly.

CHAPTER 8
NOW THAT IT'S BUILT . . . ENJOY

Finally, the car's done and it's time to hop in and put some miles on the odometer. As anxious as you and I may be to do that, we better cool our jets just a minute and check out a few things. I for sure don't want to wrap this project around a utility pole or blow up an engine the first time out, and I doubt if you want to either.

BEFORE THAT FIRST DRIVE

If for no other reason than keeping you out of jail should something go wrong, call your favorite insurance broker and get some insurance on your latest rolling artwork. Whether you get complete replacement coverage to rebuild your hot rod or just liability to pay for the damage you cause is up to you. But, please be prudent; obtain *and keep* liability insurance at the bare minimum. Okay, I'm off my soapbox now. It's windy up there.

Double Check Everything

Walk around the car and double check everything possible on it. Crawl under it, or put it on a lift or jack stands, and thoroughly check everything beneath and inside of it that you can't see during the walk around inspection. After you have checked everything yourself, invite one of your hot rodding buddies to come over and check everything again.

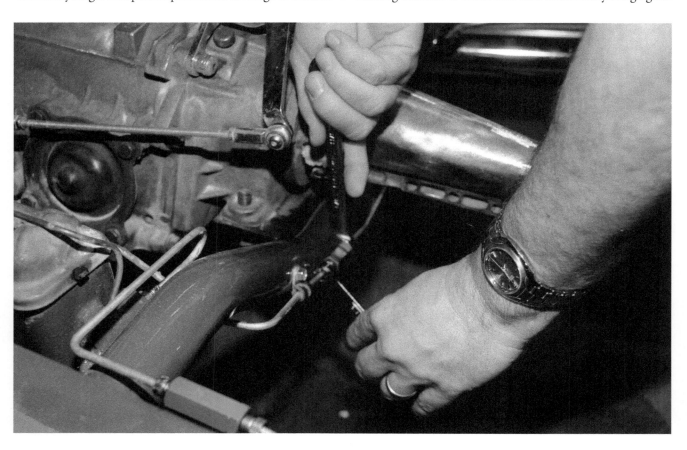

Double check all of the brake line and fuel line fittings before taking that first drive to verify that there are no leaks. It won't take long to lose all of your brake fluid if you have a leak, so that could be deadly. Depending on the size of the leak, you might not lose all of your gasoline, but you could easily start a fire with a leaking fuel line. Photo by Sandy Parks

Another good idea to keep in mind after you have had your new hot rod on the road awhile is to take advantage of National Street Rod Association (NSRA) Safety Inspection that is offered at all of its events and some other independent events. Its inspection doesn't take the place of any state required ones, but a second set of eyes that are very familiar with hot rods can often find something that you had missed. It's all about safety and keeping the fun in hot rodding.

Tighten Fasteners

Check and tighten all mechanical fasteners (nuts and bolts) to the proper specifications. Verify that appropriate flat washers are used where necessary, such as on radius rods, and that lock washers are used where they are needed. Also, check to see that cotter pins are properly installed in the various steering joints (drag link and tie rod). Double check that the lug nuts are properly tightened. On steel wheels, the tighter the better seems to be the norm, but aluminum wheels call for particular torque. This torque should also be checked on a regular basis.

Also, check for any loose electrical connections. There's no need for pulling your hair out when you try to start the engine just to find out that a wire connection is loose.

Check Fluids

You also need to verify that your hot rod has all of its vital fluids. Does the engine have engine oil? Is there transmission fluid in the transmission, coolant in the radiator, and grease in the rear end? Is there any brake fluid in the master cylinder?

HOT ROD START-UP CHECKLIST

- Verify that all fasteners are tightened, cotter pins are installed, etc.
- Verify that all electrical connections are connected and wiring is safely routed.
- Verify that properly sized fuses are installed in the fuse block. (Some wiring panels include fuses, while others don't.)
- Disconnect the battery at the starter solenoid. With a voltmeter set on the resistance scale, verify that there is no drain on the battery with the key in the "off" position. If resistance measures less than 50,000 ohms, there is a draw in the system that will drain the battery when the car is shut off. If this is the case, trace the wires until you find the problem.
- Reconnect the battery to the starter solenoid.
- Use a battery charger to check that the battery has a full charge. Charge if necessary.
- Change the engine oil and filter on a used engine, or if it's a rebuilt or crate motor, after the short number of break-in miles recommended by the builder. Be sure to

not cross thread the drain plug when you reinstall it. Make sure the drain plug and filter are tight, but not over-tightened.
- Drain and change the transmission fluid as appropriate. If you are using a salvage yard transmission, now would be a great time to replace the filter as well.
- Drain and replace the rear end fluid.
- Turn the light switch on and verify that running lights and dash panel lights are working.
- Turn the headlights on and verify that both the headlights and taillights come on. Verify that both high and low beams work, as well as the high beam indicator on the dash.
- With the help of an assistant, press the brake pedal and verify that both brake lights come on, along with the third brake light. If there is no one around when you want to do this, back up toward a somewhat reflective surface and apply the brakes. (Test the pedal to make sure you have brakes before you do this, as you only want to get near the surface, not back into it.) You most likely won't be able to see the actual brake lights, but you can usually see the brake light glow reflecting off the inside of the garage or the garage door.
- Verify that the emergency flasher works properly.
- Verify that the brakes hold and check the brake lines for leaks.
- Check for correct operation of the emergency brake.
- Disconnect the feed wire from the ignition coil.
- Turn the ignition switch to "on" and check for proper operation of the turn indicator lights (front, rear, and dash indicators).
- Turn the ignition switch to "start" to verify that the starter system is working properly.
- Reconnect the feed wire to the coil. Disconnect the coil wire from the distributor cap. While an assistant bumps the starter over by turning the key in the ignition, hold the coil wire close to the cap and check for spark. Reconnect the coil wire to the distributor cap.
- Check for proper operation of the throttle pedal. Verify that the throttle pedal never over-centers (a situation that could result in a stuck wide open throttle condition). Also, verify that throttle pedal movement is similar to throttle linkage movement. In other words, if the amount of latter from fully closed to fully open is, say, 80 degrees around its axis, the throttle pedal will need to be able to rotate 80 degrees as well.
- Verify that the shifter functions properly and that the gear selector indicator is correctly aligned.
- Verify that carburetor inlets and the air filter are clean and free of debris.

- Fill the radiator with water and check for leaks. After the radiator has been filled and the engine run for several miles, the radiator should be drained and refilled with a 50/50 mix of antifreeze and water.
- Check the fuel filter to verify that it is clean and that the fuel lines on either end are properly secured.
- Transport the vehicle to a muffler shop and have an exhaust system installed if not already done.
- Using a gas can, slowly fill the fuel tank. Watch for leaks. You may want to do this outside of the garage, just to minimize excessive gasoline odors in the garage if you do have any leaks.
- Make sure that you have a properly charged fire extinguisher within reach before you attempt to start the engine for the first time. Again, you may want to do this outside of the garage just to be on the safe side.
- With someone watching fuel lines and fittings, pump the throttle a couple of times, and turn the ignition switch to "start."
- When the engine starts, look for fuel, water, or oil leaks. Slight amounts of smoke may be from the engine paint getting hot for the first time. If there are large amounts of smoke or *any* flames, shut the ignition off immediately and take appropriate measures.
- Assuming that there is no smoke and flames, pay close attention to the oil pressure and voltage. If you have gauges, the oil pressure should indicate at least 40 psi and the volts should read approximately 14 volts. If you have warning lights instead of gauges, the lights for these functions should go out after a short time. Watch the water temperature and fuel gauges for proper readings.
- With the engine running and the transmission in neutral, check the level of the transmission fluid.
- Place a piece of cardboard in front of the radiator to minimize airflow. Allow the car to idle long enough for the engine to reach its normal operating temperature to verify that the water temperature gauge is working properly. *Remove the cardboard when this is completed.*
- Turn the ignition off. The oil pressure and voltage gauges (if used) should return to zero.
- Disconnect the cable from the positive terminal on the battery. Using a voltmeter, check that the voltage at the battery's positive terminal is between 12 and 15 volts.

HOT ROD FIRST DRIVE CHECKLIST

If everything checks out so far, you and your project vehicle are ready for a *short* test drive. Take your cell phone with you and have someone follow you in a second vehicle to help check that all systems are working properly.

- Check for leaks

- Check for loose hardware
- Check for wires that may need to be rerouted or tied in place
- Check all fluid levels
- Check the brakes and brake lights
- If you have a programmable speedometer, calibrate the speedometer; if it is not programmable, take the vehicle to a speedometer shop and have it calibrated
- Drain the water from the radiator and refill it with the proper antifreeze/water mix for your area or climate, if not done already

OBTAINING A TITLE

Undeniably, the best way to obtain a title for any vehicle is to have a clear title included in the deal when you purchase the vehicle in the first place. With the original title of your hot rod in hand, you should be able to go to your local license office, pay the applicable sales tax, and transfer the title into your name. At such time when you are ready to license the vehicle, you simply have to pay the required license fees, meet the applicable inspection requirements, and then be on your way. If your vehicle is from another state, some states require you to have a law officer verify and sign an affidavit stating the vehicle identification number (VIN) from the title matches that of your vehicle.

If you are building a hot rod from reproduction parts or you don't have a title, you have a couple of basic choices. The necessary requirements are different in each state and are constantly being revised, so check your local laws for exact

A major step closer to having a licensed vehicle is having the VIN tag attached to the vehicle. This is usually on the top of the frame rail or on the firewall on older vehicles. Just make sure that it is in an easily accessible area so that the necessary licensing personnel can see and read it. Make sure that the number on the tag matches the number on the title . . .

Make sure that you add differential fluid (grease) to the rear axle housing. A plug located somewhere on the housing must be removed, the fluid poured in, and the plug reinstalled. The short nozzle on the gear lube bottle makes it somewhat difficult to empty the contents into the differential, so a short piece of tubing inserted into the access hole makes this easier. Photo by Sandy Parks

requirements. You can often title a reproduction hot rod as a specially constructed vehicle or, in some states, as a street rod. You will need to have paid receipts for most, if not all, major components used in the vehicle's construction if you choose to go this route. Another method is to purchase a title from any of several dealers that advertise in automotive magazines. These titles are original titles for vehicles that have been destroyed or otherwise disposed of. For a fee (that varies from vendor to vendor), you can request a title for a specific year, make, and model. This original title will have the VIN on it. You will also need to obtain a vehicle identification tag to which this VIN can be inscribed. This tag can then be attached to your vehicle in a conspicuous location, such as on a door pillar, a frame rail, or on the firewall.

GETTING IT INSPECTED

Inspection requirements no doubt vary from state to state. Some states may require a visit to a state run inspection station, while others may require a visit to the highway patrol, and still others may simply require an inspection by a state certified mechanic. The rules and requirements should be the same for all passenger vehicles, but you would do well to ask some of your hot rodding buddies if there are any differences between the inspection of your daily driver and that for your hot rod. Anything you can do to avoid surprises will make the inspection and licensing portion of owning a hot rod go more smoothly.

After you have found out the requirements to pass inspection and you are reasonably sure that your hot rod will pass, drive or transport your new hot rod to the inspection station. Some states may require that an unlicensed vehicle must be transported, while others may be more forgiving, should you be pulled over on your way.

WHEEL ALIGNMENT

Before doing much driving, treat your hot rod to a four-wheel alignment. Having a vehicle that is properly aligned

Although it isn't finished at this point, many of the final exterior details can be seen in this during-construction photo. The exhaust is in place, as are the headlights and rearview mirrors. One side of the windshield is in place with the plywood template being used to verify that both windshield posts lean back the same amount.

will not only minimize tire wear, but it will also make your time behind the steering wheel safer and more enjoyable. This will also be an opportunity for another person to check out your hot rod and make you aware of any safety issues that you may have overlooked.

For a vehicle that uses a straight axle, camber is already built into the axle and cannot be adjusted without bending the axle—a situation that should be avoided. This leaves the caster and toe to be adjusted. You should adjust both of them to the specifications recommended by the manufacturer of the front suspension components on your vehicle. However, this information is not always available from the manufacturer. If this is the case for your hot rod, begin by setting caster at about 5 degrees and toe-in at 1/8 inch. After setting the wheel alignment at these specs, you should at least be in the ballpark, but can fine tune the adjustments based on drivability characteristics. For a vehicle with independent front suspension, the caster, camber, and toe can all be adjusted. The specifications for all of these angles will vary somewhat depending on the manufacturer, so you should consult with the manufacturer to obtain the correct ones. Armed with these specifications, any reputable alignment shop should be able to align your hot rod.

GETTING IT LICENSED

Once you have passed the necessary inspection requirements, proceed directly (or as soon as practical) to the local license bureau. At minimum, you will probably need proof of paid personal property taxes, your recently acquired vehicle inspection, the vehicle's title, and your checkbook. At this point in time, whatever the person behind the counter asks for is all that is keeping you from legally driving your hot rod, so try to be patient and comply with that person's requests.

ROAD TRIP

Start out with short trips, such as around the block. Listen for strange noises and look for abnormal readings on the gauges. Verify that everything is working as it should. When you get back to your garage or driveway, take the time to look under the hood and under the car to make sure that no fluids are dripping, no wires are pinched, and in general everything is okay. Any loose nuts and bolts should be tightened.

If everything went well on the first few trips, begin taking longer trips around town to confirm that the cooling system is working properly.

THE BOTTOM LINE

Okay, as promised, here it is. The following is the overall parts breakdown for the Track T as I built it. You can build it for less and you can certainly spend more, but this is what it cost me. Shipping and taxes are included in the prices shown, but I have not included the initial travel expenses for Dad and me to travel to Lincoln, Nebraska, to pick up the basic components of the Speedway Motors Track T. That time, those memories, and the lack of sleep are priceless . . .

Rolling chassis components	Retailer	Cost
Track T basic kit (includes chassis and body components)	Speedway Motors	$2,700.00
Front axle kit	Speedway Motors	$449.00
Spindle and brake kit	Speedway Motors	$250.00
Cross steering kit	Speedway Motors	$479.56
Rear axle mounting kit	Speedway Motors	$180.00
Master cylinder mount	Speedway Motors	$107.00
Chrome front shock kit	Speedway Motors	$81.00
Front hubs and brake calipers	Speedway Motors	$200.00
Ford 9-inch rear end housing and axles	Swap meet	$100.00
Ford third member, 3.70:1 gears, 28 spline axles, and drum brakes	Danny Miller's Rear Gears	$994.06
Vintique 15x5 Smoothie wheels (pr., primed)	Coker Tire	$124.08
Vintique 15 x 7 Smoothie wheels (pr., primed)	Coker Tire	$135.58
Chrome lug nuts	Morfab Customs	$30.00
Michelin 145R15 XZX tires (pr.)	Coker Tire	$179.98
BFGoodrich P255/70R15 (pr.)	Coker Tire	$177.18
Afco multi-leaf springs	Summit Racing Equipment	$229.90
Borgeson steering joint (at column, polished stainless steel)	K. C. Street Rod Parts	$94.79
Borgeson steering joint (at Vega box, polished stainless steel)	K. C. Street Rod Parts	$94.79
DD x 3/4 steering shaft (polished stainless steel)	K. C. Street Rod Parts	$53.20
Steering shaft support (polished stainless steel)	K. C. Street Rod Parts	$81.25
Borgeson DD steering joint (polished stainless steel)	K. C. Street Rod Parts	$94.79
Rolling chassis components subtotal:		***$6,836.16***

Brake system components	Retailer	Cost
Proportioning valve	Speedway Motors	$32.95
10-pound residual valve	Speedway Motors	$16.95
2-pound residual valve	Speedway Motors	$16.95
Lever type brake light switch	Speedway Motors	$6.95
3/16-inch brake line and fittings	High Ridge Auto Parts	$25.08
Master cylinder/brake line fittings and line clamps	High Ridge Auto Parts	$13.01
Brake hose, fittings, and screws for clamps	High Ridge Auto Parts	$23.88
Brake system components subtotal:		***$135.77***

Body components	Retailer	Cost
Fender fill kit	Speedway Motors	$83.76
Fill valve	Speedway Motors	$57.22
Nut ring	Speedway Motors	$14.76
Speedster windshield frame	Speedway Motors	$850.50
1950 Pontiac taillights (pr.)	Speedway Motors	$69.90
Aluminum grille	Speedway Motors	$129.95
Dietz style headlights (pr.)	Speedway Motors	$44.95
Illuminated license plate frame	Yogi's Inc.	$44.22
Body components subtotal:		***$1,295.26***

Drivetrain components	Retailer	Cost
Ford V-6 engine, Ford C4 automatic transmission	Ralph Wideman	$275.00
Transmission tail shaft support	Karg's Hot Rod Service	$12.78
Trunk mounted battery box	Summit Racing Equipment	$45.95
Starter	High Ridge Auto Parts	$55.23

Mufflers	Speedway Motors	$108.80
Edelbrock air cleaner	RJay's Speed Shop	$17.56
12-inch mechanical fan	Summit Racing Equipment	$34.14
2-inch fan spacer	High Ridge Auto Parts	$12.41
Electric fuel pump	High Ridge Auto Parts	$44.38
Radiator (12 3/4x18 inches, aluminum)	Portell's Radiator Shop	$478.02
Transmission oil cooler	Portell's Radiator Shop	$52.05
Radiator cap	Portell's Radiator Shop	$15.93
Alternator bracket	Used	$65.00
Alternator	High Ridge Auto Parts	$109.11
Spark plugs	High Ridge Auto Parts	$11.27
Sparks plug wires	High Ridge Auto Parts	$23.61
Ignition coil	High Ridge Auto Parts	$16.98
Thermostat	High Ridge Auto Parts	$5.90
Drivetrain components subtotal:		*$1,384.12*

Interior components	Retailer	Cost
Upholstery kit (brown)	Speedway Motors	$849.90
Steering column, 1 3/4 inches	Speedway Motors	$146.08
Steering column drop	Speedway Motors	$49.90
Flaming River lower steering column mount	Morfab Customs	$96.09
Steering wheel	Speedway Motors	$33.86
Wiremaster wiring panel, deluxe wiring kit, ignition switch, light switch, turn-signal kit	Affordable Street Rods	$330.00
VDO Series 1 gauges with electric speedometer	Morfab Customs	$272.09
Lokar spoon throttle pedal	RJay's Speed Shop	$46.53
Lokar emergency brake lever	RJay's Speed Shop	$80.10
Lokar emergency brake cables	RJay's Speed Shop	$90.57
Lokar automatic transmission shifter	RJay's Speed Shop	$160.96
Lokar throttle cable	RJay's Speed Shop	$30.94
Juliano's lap seatbelts (two pair)	K. C. Street Rod Parts	$61.38
Juliano's seatbelt anchor plates (two pair)	K. C. Street Rod Parts	$32.46
Interior components subtotal:		*$2,280.86*

Final assembly components	Retailer	Cost
Radiator recovery tank	Speedway Motors	$29.17
Juliano's dual horn	K. C. Street Rod Parts	$32.67
Motor oil and filter	High Ridge Auto Parts	$13.08
Upper radiator hose	High Ridge Auto Parts	$11.29
Lower radiator hose	High Ridge Auto Parts	$14.69
Fan belt	High Ridge Auto Parts	$12.20
Battery	High Ridge Auto Parts	$59.17
Fuel filter and fuel line	High Ridge Auto Parts	$13.82
Brake fluid	High Ridge Auto Parts	$4.77
Momentary switch for horn	High Ridge Auto Parts	$3.66
Lokar emergency brake boot	RJay's Speed Shop	$22.24
Lokar shifter boot	RJay's Speed Shop	$34.59
Outside rearview mirrors	Jen-E Products	$72.36
Inside rearview mirror	Jen-E Products	$40.49
Front turn signals (pair)	Jen-E Products	$37.25

Spark plug wire looms
Final assembly components subtotal:

Made For You Products	$14.87
	$416.32

Labor and materials
PPG paint and related products
Rear suspension, engine, and transmission welding
Fiberglass resin and related products
Exhaust labor
Fiberglass resin, sanding discs, and various other project supplies
Various fasteners, drill bits
Exhaust manifold repair
Suspension component painting
Fuel line, fittings, miscellaneous nuts and bolts
Valve cover and exhaust paint
Aluminum hood top and hood louvers
Body filler and related supplies
Driveshaft, pinion yoke, and U-joints
Windshield glass and installation
Chrome plating
Labor and materials subtotal:

Retailer	Cost
The Paint Store	$1,197.19
Karg's Hot Rod Service	$211.99
The Paint Store	$94.42
House Springs Discount Muffler	$259.91
High Ridge Auto Parts	$75.29
Sears	$37.14
JCM Machine and Coatings	$65.00
Tim "Mayhem" Kohl	$500.00
High Ridge Auto Parts	$66.70
Eastwood Company	$20.97
KBS Fabricators	$400.00
High Ridge Auto Parts	$34.41
Driveshafts Unlimited	$158.13
Chippewa Glass	$200.00
Fat Catz Plating	$250.00
	$3,571.15

The Bottom Line   **$15,919.64**

A few unique factors came into play that affected the bottom line for this Track T, ones which you will most likely not incur, or at least not for the same reasons. Some of these were purely unforeseen, others were in the back of my mind, and some were conscious decisions.

First of all, I did have to spend some money to have one of the exhaust manifolds repaired. When I had the exhaust installed, it became apparent that one of the cast-iron manifolds had been damaged and insufficiently repaired previously. This wasn't a large expense in the grand scheme of things, but it did add to the bottom line. The more used parts you plan to use in your hot rod, the more likely you will experience this problem.

Other expenses involved additional materials that I didn't really count on. My experience with fiberglass (or more accurately, lack thereof) required using much more fiberglass resin than I had anticipated. Combine this with the fact that they aren't giving this away, and it added to the cost. Again, not a deal breaker, but an additional expense.

Another situation that added to the expense is the fact that I was writing a book that had a deadline, while you will probably just be building your own cheap hot rod. All of this work was on top of a full-time job. I had originally planned to do all of the painting myself, but as the chassis was ready for paint around the first of

November, this was not practical. My garage isn't heated, it is not large, and there simply wasn't enough time available on the weekends and while it was still warm outside to get all of the chassis and suspension components painted. To combat that situation, I enlisted the help of Tim Kohl to paint the suspension components. His work turned out much better than mine would have been and he didn't charge me his normal rate, but still again, it added to the bottom line.

Although I admittedly exceeded my proposed budget of $15,000, I was well within 10 percent of that mark. Most any building project that is within budget by 10 percent is considered successful, so being around 6 percent over budget is certainly acceptable.

LESSONS LEARNED

Building a hot rod, like most things in life, becomes easier with experience. Now that the project is complete, a look backwards may be in order. Experience from each project is never really gained unless we make the effort to learn from it and put it into practice the next time a similar opportunity presents itself. Part of that learning comes from admitting our mistakes and realizing our shortcomings.

I should have done more research on the chassis for the Track T from Speedway Motors before I made my purchase. That chassis is severely tapered in the front

I really wanted to have a photo of the finished and painted Track T in this book, but that just wasn't possible. Although the photos won't be in the book, the Track T should be finished by the time you actually read this. With me behind the wheel in this photo, you can gain a better perspective on the size of the vehicle.

portion, while the chassis designed for a V-8 has frame rails that are closer to being parallel. Using the wider chassis would have prevented some problems and thereby saved some time and money. First, it would have allowed the use of a small-block Chevy engine, and therefore would have made finding some of the parts much easier and probably a bit cheaper. Secondly, the wider chassis would not have caused so many fitting problems between the Vega steering box and the mechanical fuel pump, thermostat housing, and oil pressure sender, which all became apparent with the Ford V-6 engine. A repop Model A chassis would have been more familiar to work with, even though it would have been more expensive.

Another fact that has become apparent is that I could have probably saved money on the overall project had I purchased a donor vehicle. To provide an engine and transmission for a hot rod (read that as rear wheel drive), the donor vehicle would have needed to be a compact pickup; a Chevrolet would have been my choice. A vehicle such as this could have provided the drivetrain, including the rear axle housing, rear springs, shifter, and various other cables, brackets, and items that have added to the bottom line. I know these vehicles are out there to be had, but I couldn't find any that met my requirements when I was looking. Perhaps I gave up too soon.

Lastly, it is good to have goals and to set milestones, but you must realize that when building a hot rod, many of these goals cannot be met on schedule. Don't let missing a self-imposed deadline deter your progress or get you discouraged. If something is worth doing at all, its worth doing right—at least as right as you can with what you have and what you know.

I hope this book has inspired you and answered at least a few questions. I, personally, have learned a lot through building the Track T and documenting its buildup in this book. Happy and safe rodding to you . . .

SOURCES

Affordable Street Rods
1220 Van Buren, Great Bend, KS 67530
www.affordablestreetrods.com
620-792-2836
Wiring panel, wiring kit, turn-signal switch

Castlemaine Rod Shop
P. O. Box 1245, Castlemaine 3450
Australia
www.rodshop.com.au/bellhousings.htm
Bell housings and transmission adapters

Coker Tire
1317 Chestnut Street, Chattanooga, TN 37402
www.cokertire.com
800-251-6336
Wheels and tires

Driveshafts Unlimited
3608 Market Place, Arnold, MO 63010
www.driveshaftsunlimited.com
800-300-2841
Driveshaft and U-joints

Fat Catz Plating
814 Olive Road, Park Hills, MO 63601-8235
573-431-5082
Chrome plating on windshield frame and grille

High Ridge Auto Parts
3032 High Ridge Boulevard, High Ridge, MO 63049
636-677-3811
Brake and fuel lines, filters, hoses, belts, starter, alternator, and miscellaneous accessories

Karg's Hot Rod Service
6505 Walnut Valley Road, High Ridge, MO 63049
www.kargshotrodservice.com
636-677-3674
Rear suspension installation, custom motor mounts, and chassis modification

KBS Fabricators
108 St. Joseph, O'Fallon, MO 63366
www.kbsfabricators.com
636-272-1008
Hood fabrication and louvers

K. C. Street Rod Parts
3709 North College, Kansas City, MO 64117
www.kcstreetrod.com
816-453-2761
Steering joints and shafts, seatbelts, horn

Morfab Customs
301 South Pine Street, Union, MO 63084
www.morfabcustoms.com
636-584-8383
Gauges, lower steering column mount

Parr Automotive
4933 N.W. 10th Street, Oklahoma City, OK 73127
www.parrautomotive.com
405-942-8677
Turn-signal indicator lights

QuietRide Solutions
6507 Pacific Avenue, Suite 334, Stockton, CA 95207
www.quietride.com
209-942-4777
Firewall insulators, AcoustiSHIELD automotive insulation, and sound dampening products

RJay's Speed Shop and Performance Center
7079 Highway ZZ, Cuba, MO 65453
www.rjays.com
866-439-7529
Transmission shifter, emergency brake lever, spoon throttle pedal, and cables

Speedway Motors
340 Victory Lane, Lincoln, NE 68528
www.speedwaymotors.com
800-979-0122
Track T kit, chassis, suspension, and body

Stilmore Designs
11458 Lucerne, Redford, MI 48239
www.stilmoredesigns.com
Concept drawing

Summit Racing Equipment
P.O. Box 909, Akron, OH 44398-6177
www.summitracing.com
800-230-3030
Rear leaf spring, battery box, and mechanical fan

The Paint Store
2800 High Ridge Boulevard, High Ridge, MO 63049
636-677-1566
PPG paint products and supplies

Tim "Mayhem" Kohl Custom Paint and Airbrush
430 MacArthur Avenue, Washington, MO 63090
636-390-8811
Custom artwork

INDEX

CPSIA information can be obtained
at www.ICGtesting.com
Printed in the USA
LVHW07s1503270318
571327LV00018B/306/P

9 780760 323489

"When you are inspired by some great purpose, some extraordinary project, all your thoughts break their bonds: Your mind transcends limitations, your consciousness expands in every direction, and you find yourself in a new, great, and wonderful world. Dormant forces, faculties and talents become alive, and you will discover yourself to be a greater person by far than you ever dreamed yourself to be."

- Patanjali

"YOUR success is not just about changing YOUR habits, it's about changing the way YOU think."

- Ben Newman

Dedicated to the three people who clearly help me realize what I am fighting for every day, and for whom I am willing to sacrifice anything: my wife, Ami, my son, J. Isaac, and my daughter, Kennedy Rose.

In Loving Memory of

Janet Fishman Newman

ABOUT BEN NEWMAN

🐦 📷 @ContinuedFight ✅
The Burn 🔥 Podcast

Meet Ben Newman. You may have seen him running up the sidelines as a Mental Performance Coach for your favorite sports team or recognize him for his bestselling book UNCOMMON Leadership.

He's an Entrepreneur, Investor, #1 Wall Street Journal and USA Today Bestselling Author, Philanthropist, **AND THE NATION'S TOP CONTINUAL PEAK PERFORMANCE COACH.**

Internationally-Renowned Speaker. Ben's authentic, powerful, and engaging storytelling has become internationally recognized and has been a featured speaker at the world's biggest business, sports, finance and motivational events. He has shared the stage with Jerry Rice, Ray Lewis, Colin Powell, Ed Mylett, Jackie Joyner-Kersee, Jon Gordon, Tim Grover, Eric Thomas, Tony Dungy, Brian Tracy, Jenna Kutcher and other legends in the world. **Ben was selected by Influencive.com as one of the TOP 10 Motivators in Sports and Real Leaders Magazine selected him as one of their TOP 50 Speakers in the World the last four years.**

Performance and Mental Conditioning Coach for some of today's greatest professional athletes and highest performing teams in the NFL, NBA, PGA, MLB, UFC and NCAA. Ben has worked with coaches and players from the last 6 Super Bowl Champion teams and currently serves as the Performance Coach for the Big 12 Champion Kansas State football team in his 9th season (3 National Championships at North Dakota State) with Head Coach Chris Klieman. Ben is also serving as the Performance Coach for Michigan State University's football and basketball program with Coach Mel Tucker and Coach Tom Izzo. Lastly, he served 5 years as the Mental Conditioning Coach for the 18-time National Champion football team Alabama Crimson Tide.

For the last two decades, Ben has been serving as the Peak Performance Coach for the top 1% of financial advisors globally and for Fortune 500 business executives. Ben's clients have included: Microsoft, United States Army, Anheuser-Busch InBev, Quicken Loans, MARS Snackfoods, AstraZeneca, Northwestern Mutual, AFA Singapore, Mass Financial Group, Frontier Companies, Wells Fargo Advisors, Great West Life Canada, Boston Medical Center, Boys & Girls Club of America,

New York Life as well as thousands of executives, entrepreneurs, athletes and sales teams from around the globe.

Millions of people and some of the top performers in the world have been empowered by Ben through his books, educational content, coaching programs, podcast, and live events.

Ben is also the host of the top podcast, The Burn, where he takes you into the minds of some of the highest performers in sports and business to tell their full story.

Ben lives in his hometown of St. Louis, Missouri with the true measure of his success, his wife, Ami, and their children, J. Isaac and Kennedy Rose.

YOUR
MENTAL
TOUGHNESS
PLAYBOOK

BEN NEWMAN'S COACHING SYSTEM

- BUILD A BULLETPROOF DAILY ROUTINE
- DEVELOP ELITE MENTAL TOUGHNESS HABITS
- REWIRE YOUR BRAIN TO THINK LIKE A CHAMPION

SELF-PACED COURSES

- NEW COACHING VIDEOS MONTHLY
- STAY ON TOP OF YOUR PERSONAL GROWTH
- NEXT LEVEL MINDSET TRAININGS
- EXTENSIVE LIBRARY OF EXCLUSIVE VIDEOS

SPECIALIZED COACHING MEMBERSHIPS

- LIVE GROUP COACHING WITH BEN NEWMAN AND SEAN O'BRIEN
- 2 LIVE CALLS EVERY MONTH
- EXCLUSIVE ACCESS TO PRIVATE FACEBOOK GROUP
- LIVE Q&A EVERY MONTH

LIVE GROUP COACHING AND NETWORKING

UNCOMMON
★ L I V E ★

- OUR HIGHEST LEVEL OF COACHING PARTNERSHIP
- THE MOST INDIVIDUALIZED PROGRAM WITHIN OUR SYSTEM
- CUSTOMIZED MONTHLY ACCOUNTABLITY AND ACCESS

PRIVATE COACHING

EXCLUSIVE
1-ON-1 COACHING

www.BenNewmanCoaching.com

THE BEN NEWMAN COMPANIES

LET THE RESULTS SPEAK FOR THEMSELVES...

OVER
$1 BILLION
PROFESSIONAL SPORTS CONTRACTS

$4.3
BILLION
BUSINESS PARTNERS REVENUE ANNUALLY

$25 MILLION
LIFE INSURANCE POLICIES ANNUALLY
OVER
$1 BILLION
ASSETTS UNDER MANAGEMENT ANNUALLY
FINANCIAL SERVICES

BEN'S WORK HAS BEEN FEATURED IN:

BEN'S PREVIOUS/CURRENT CLIENTS:

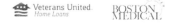

PRAISE FOR BEN NEWMAN'S
MENTAL TRAINING TOOLS...

"The qualities of those who possess mental toughness and achieve greatness in life are abnormal and uncommon. Ben Newman's fire and passion show you how to go beyond what's common to own your success."

Dr. Ellen Reed
Best-Selling Author,
Performance Coach, Speaker

"I talk about the mental side all the time and this book is something I truly believe has helped me in every area of my life. I promise it will not disappoint and I fully advise to check it out."

Will Compton
NFL Linebacker,
Co-Host Bussin' with the Boys

"Ben has worked with my teams for over eight years as a Performance Coach. The 'Pound the Stone' presentation he gave our Kansas State football team was right on the money and was timed perfectly as we begin to head into Spring football and we continue to build on our great tradition. His energy and enthusiasm was felt throughout the entire room. Our work outs now end with 'FINISH. FINISH. POUND THE STONE'."

Chris Klieman
K-State Football Head Coach
(Former 4 time National Champion Head Coach with the North Dakota State Bison)

"I learned while at Alabama that you have Prizefighter Days. When stacking Prizefighter Days, you develop the uncommon mindset. You prepare to attack the field and you take an uncommon mindset to the game. You see, high levels of success are uncommon. Sustaining them is even more uncommon. Prizefighter Days prepare you to attack the big goals that you create which allows you to reach peak performance."

Mac Jones
2x National Champion with
Alabama Football, Davey O'Brien
Award Winner & Heisman Finalist,
New England Patriots Quarterback

"Year after year I continue to work with Ben and we focus on what drives me daily. My obsession with the process and what many financial firms overlook which is the importance of Mental Training for Advisors and never being seduced by success. I can attest to the fact that this is the powerful secret of the highest performers."

Claudio Gambin
Gambin Financial Group,
Top 1% Financial Advisor,
$10M+ Career Life Insurance Production

"The most successful athletes and business leaders in the world have mental toughness and an "it" factor that allows them to achieve at the highest level. Ben Newman's tools and techniques make him one of the best in the world at helping people gain that edge."

Drew Hanlen
Top NBA Skills Trainer

TABLE OF CONTENTS

INTRODUCTION

Are you ready for the next level of YOUR success?

One of the first rules of sports psychology for an athlete to perform at their highest level is that they can't solely rely on their natural talents and abilities. Instead, they have to understand the mental toughness side of what it takes to achieve peak performance.

I believe this is the same for all of us in our lives. This does not just apply to athletes, but also to teachers, Fortune 500 executives, salespeople, professionals, and those leading others in business and life. This concept applies to all individuals fighting to achieve peak performance in their lives.

This playbook and video series is about YOUR mental toughness and embracing the fact that your success is not just about changing your habits. It's about changing the way that YOU think. The most successful people are those who exemplify the importance of combining great habits and passion for the process with their ability to embrace adversity and challenge; to remain strong in driving their goals to completion.

In this program we will explore six rounds of YOUR mental toughness. The rounds include YOUR Burn and Attaining Belief in Yourself, The Power to REFRAME, YOUR "I AM" Statements, YOUR Prizefighter Day, YOUR Legacy Statement, and Creating YOUR Environment for Greatness.

Get ready for your pre-assessment to test your current level of mental toughness. After completion of the playbook and video series, you will have a post assessment to apply what you have learned through the course. This program has seen proven results and led to championships with athletes at all levels and across many sports as well as with Fortune 500 executives and top business professionals and companies all over the world. Are you ready to embrace YOUR mental toughness?

Harvard Business Review, in July of 2008, did research which showed that all individuals that experience change will go through turmoil, even if the change is positive. Not 2 out of 10, not 6 out of 10, not 8 out of 10, but all people that go through change will experience turmoil. Change is never easy but often times necessary to drive YOUR peak performance.

This playbook will test your mental toughness and empower you to attack your fears, push your comfort zones, and drive you to achieve peak performance by identifying your passion for the process of what you do. Often times we hold on too tightly to results that we can't control rather than identifying the daily behaviors that will drive performance. YOU will learn to shift YOUR mindset to focus on the process that will drive YOUR success.

With YOUR open mind and willingness to identify these behaviors, you will create more certainty in your life. If adding additional dollars to your bottom line is important, you will see it happen. If having a greater impact on other people is important, you will see it happen. If becoming a stronger leader is important, you will see it happen. If having a more significant legacy that you leave behind is important, you will see that happen as well. This about YOUR life and YOUR legacy.

This is YOUR opportunity to drive more significant results in YOUR life by coupling the mental toughness side of what it takes to achieve peak performance with YOUR natural talents and abilities to serve others and make a difference in the world.

Go Do Great Things,

Ben

FOR OPTIMAL PERFORMANCE:

This playbook is a standalone product, but to take it to the NEXT level, Ben will walk YOU through and further explain each round in the corresponding online videos found in YOUR Mental Toughness Academy.

Get YOUR access here:
www.BenNewman.net/MTAcademy

Keep ATTACKING the PROCESS!

YOUR MENTAL TOUGHNESS
PRE-ASSESSMENT

Let's find out what YOUR starting point is. Take this pre-assessment below and rate yourself over the last year in each category using numbers 1-5. 1 means you hardly do it at all, and 5 means it is a concrete part of your life.

	No ⟶ Yes				
	1	**2**	**3**	**4**	**5**
I believe that I can accomplish anything I set my mind to.					
I have a purpose or "Burn" that I connect to daily to drive my actions.					
I have a core set of values that help me keep perspective when things get hard or I face adversity.					
I have a strong and clear vision of the person I want to be in my life.					
I have a solid and trackable routine that is activity based and not just focused on getting "results."					
I have complete clarity on what I want my LEGACY to be.					
I have cultivated an environment that fully supports my goals and values.					
Overall I feel that I have a good foundation of mental toughness.					
Totals					
Final Score					

8-15 Needs Some Work	16-23 Showing Potential	24-31 Mentally Tough	32-40 Peak Performer

ROUND 1
UNCOVERING YOUR BURN
& ATTAINING BELIEF IN YOURSELF
SETTING THE FOUNDATION

No matter what industry or discipline has brought you into this playbook, YOUR next level must begin by addressing the belief you have in yourself.

In our work with some of the top athletes and business professionals in the world, we've uncovered that building unshakeable self-belief begins by connecting to what we call the **BURN**.

In this first round we're going to set the foundation by helping you connect to your Burn and showing you the 5 key factors for attaining belief in yourself.

This is going to require you to be honest with yourself and your story. Be vulnerable, be present, be where your feet are. Your next level starts now.

To make the most out of this round, refer to the "Round 1" videos from Ben in YOUR Mental Toughness Academy: www.BenNewman.net/MTAcademy

UNCOVERING YOUR BURN

Here in Round 1 we're going to inspect and craft a belief system to build upon. Everything you do in life stems from YOUR belief system.

Now, I'm not going to tell you what to believe, but we are going to take a deeper look into your mental toughness structure.

I've found over the last 15+ years of working with some of the world's top performers in both business and sports that there is something that DRIVES them to that greatness.

And it goes deeper than just their WHY or their PURPOSE.

The Burn is what really lights them up to believe anything is possible. It's the mindset that causes them to fight on a different level.

I'm a firm believer that the same Burn lies inside each and every single one of YOU.

When you uncover it and connect to it on a consistent basis, it will light YOUR why on fire and drive YOU to take the necessary actions.

The Burn in your heart, that underlying passion will help YOU fight through anything in your life and emerge on a different plane than that of where YOU started.

My deep inner passion to constantly become the best version of myself stems from a few things. However, my biggest driving force (BURN) is to carry on the LEGACY that my mother left behind when she died of a rare muscle disease when I was only 8 years old.

She lived in a way that was so selfless and incredibly profound that I've crafted my life around the lessons she left me inside of a blue mead notebook. I have created an environment to remind myself of that every day. (We will talk about that later)

UNCOVERING YOUR BURN

My Burn will always be the same - to continue writing my mother's story. It will never change, and it will always cause me to show up differently.

This may not be the case for everyone. For some their Burn may be materialistic, but it's important to recognize a materialistic Burn is temporary.

If it's going to be a goal or something you're fighting for, once you reach it, you must redefine and reconnect to something deeper.

That being said, it's also okay if your Burn changes over time based on your different stages of life, adversities you may face, etc.

This is not rocket science. There is no equation to finding the perfect Burn, and it's not something you are glued to from here on out.

All that matters is you understand your Burn and connect to it daily. With that you will create an environment that drives accountability and causes YOU to do what it takes.

This is about attacking the next level and becoming YOUR best self. **The Burn ignites it all.**

Use this area to brainstorm ideas of what YOU think YOUR Burn might be...

Want to hear how some of the highest performers in the world connect to their Burn? Check out The Burn Podcast on all podcast platforms and YouTube!

THE BURN JOURNAL CHALLENGE

Now that you've explored your Burn, I have a challenge for YOU.

Over the next **30 days** I want you to challenge yourself to connect to your unique Burn every single day using what I call, "The Burn Journal Challenge." Now, you can use a physical journal (how I do it) or you can start a journal in your phone. Whatever works for you. Every morning for the next 30 days you're going to write your Burn in this journal and connect to it.

This will help you decide if the Burn you wrote down is powerful enough or if you need to dig a little deeper. When you've truly uncovered what your current Burn is you will be flooded with energy and passion to take the necessary action in your daily life.

Your greatest level of performance relies on your ability to connect to your true Burn.

STEP 1: YOUR ALARM

I'm not saying you have to wake up the same time I do every day, but whenever you set YOUR alarm clock, go in and rename the alarm to YOUR Burn. Mine says "Janet Fishman Newman. LEGACY." After seeing that, there's no way I'm hitting snooze. I lock in, and I'm ready to ATTACK.

STEP 2: THE JOURNAL

Grab a small journal or notebook and commit to writing down your Burn every morning for the next 30 days. This is what I mean by "connecting" to your Burn. This will help YOU build the environment that it takes to consistently connect to this inner FIRE and allow it to light up YOUR actions to a whole new level of consistency.

FIVE FACTORS TO ATTAINING BELIEF IN YOURSELF

True mental toughness starts with attaining belief in yourself. I'm not talking about the surface level belief or happy go-lucky positivity. I'm talking about honest and deeply rooted foundational belief that is based on the truth. Here are the 5 factors that contribute to attaining true belief in yourself.

1. ACCEPT THE TRUTH

Realizing and identifying with the person you are today is the key to becoming the person you want to be. Remember the lesson Pierce learned: we never actually *fail* in life. We just don't always get the results that we want. You cannot live a lie. You have to acknowledge and identify with what is most important in your life to ultimately, *"Attain Belief in Yourself."*

2. SPEAK THE TRUTH

You may be reluctant – even scared -- to talk about or acknowledge past behavior and habits that you regret. However, avoiding it only serves to amplify the pain and make us feel like victims. Get the truth out into the light by talking about your experiences with a trusted friend or a professional.

3. BREATHE THROUGH THE TRUTH

Even though every fiber of your being wants to react by believing that your actions up to this point have been correct, know that you can change. Avoid acting from a place of pain or anger. The best way to reclaim your dignity is to behave rationally and treat yourself lovingly – which will keep you from self-destructing.

4. PROCESS THE TRUTH

Give yourself time and space to find your equilibrium. Believe confidently and whole-heartedly that making these changes will prompt you to develop a stronger foundation. However, recognize that this will take time – and give yourself that time.

5. CREATE A PLAN BASED ON THE TRUTH

Don't expect things to be perfect right away; you can't simply flip a switch and have a new life. Old behaviors and mindsets often come back into the realm. Stay strong and acknowledge that you must continue to believe and actively engage in this process in order to experience concrete change for your future. With this in mind, define how do you want to live your life from now on.

YOUR MENTAL TOUGHNESS PLAYBOOK

YOUR VISION

Use this section to really think through what YOU want out of YOUR life. Open YOUR heart and mind and dump it onto this worksheet below. Don't hold yourself back. Think BIG and get extremely clear on exactly what YOU write down in each of the boxes. This is the foundation of our work together inside of this playbook.

YOUR BURN

PERSONAL GOALS

PROFESSIONAL GOALS

ROUND 2
THE POWER TO REFRAME
OVERCOMING ADVERSITY & CHALLENGE

In life we are only guaranteed a few things. One of those being that at some point in your life, you will face some type of challenge or adversity.

These hurdles come in different shapes and sizes, but regardless of their form we have a few choices to make.

We either focus on the problem and let it take over our emotions and actions, OR we acknowledge challenge and decide to REFRAME to focus on a solution.

The highest performers in the world have built this muscle to maintain the correct perspective when things go sideways.

It's time for you to build that same response. The Power to REFRAME will change your life.

To make the most out of this round, refer to the "Round 2" videos from Ben in YOUR Mental Toughness Academy: www.BenNewman.net/MTAcademy

OVERCOME ANY ADVERSITY USING THE POWER TO REFRAME

My mother Janet Fishman Newman taught me the greatest life lesson of all: "It's not how long you live. It's how you choose to live your life."

As a young boy I watched my mother battle a rare disease called Amyloidosis. However, I watched her unleash her positive mental attitude on the world through a journal that she kept. I recognized that she still had to lead my brother and I in order to show us that we could fight adversity and challenge to be the best we could be in our lives.

Oftentimes, my mother would receive phone calls from the Boston Medical Center and Dr. Martha Skinner telling her that she needed to come to Boston for painful procedures, or they needed to increase her medications. She had to wear jobst stockings around her legs to control the swelling and a mask to to go outside. As a single mom, divorced when I was 6 months old, my mother would hang up the phone and immediately pick the phone back up and call her boyfriend Alan. She was focused on a solution and recognizing she was still leading my brother and me. She knew we were watching her response to her adversity.

Her focus was to turn the medical trip to Boston into a family trip. Because her boys liked Chinese food, she planned visits to Chinatown, and because we liked bowling, we would go candlestick bowling. My mother made a conscious choice to focus on the positive solution rather than holding on too tightly to the negative results that she couldn't control for her prognosis.

I believe that this exemplifies for all of us "The Power to REFRAME." The next time you face adversity or challenge in your life, rather than holding on too tightly or spending too much time on the negativity, choose to focus on a positive response to maintain a path of success.

HOW TO REFRAME

Choosing to reframe will not be an easy skill to build. It will take work and practice to subjectively look at whatever adversity shows up in your life and make the decision to shift your perspective away from where your emotions might take you.

There is a psychology principle called "The Expectancy Theory" that states, "that in which you focus on will expand." If you focus on the positive you get more positive, and if you choose to focus on negative, you get more negative. This is a choice for you when you face challenge or adversity. What will you choose the next time YOU face adversity?

EXERCISE: Think of a time when you faced some kind of adversity or challenge. It could have been something that affected you, your family, your business, etc. Use that experience in the boxes below to analyze your emotional response and how you could have used the power to reframe in that moment.

HOW YOU REACTED

HOW YOU COULD HAVE REFRAMED

REMEMBER: When faced with adversity, reframe your initial emotional/negative response and choose the positive solution to keep you on your path to GREATNESS.

USING THE POWER TO
REFRAME

ACKNOWLEDGE

Acknowledge your initial response or emotions to encountering a challenge or obstacle. We're not trying to avoid feelings here.

CHOOSE

Understand that we have complete control in how we respond to any situation, including this one. It's now up to you to choose how you're going to respond.

REFRAME

Make the conscious decision to focus on solutions rather than dwelling on problems. It won't be easy, it will be uncomfortable, but it will be worth it.

ROUND 3
YOUR "I AM" STATEMENTS
FORGING THE NEXT VERSION OF YOURSELF

The challenging part about building the next version of yourself, is that you have to truly picture that person before you actually arrive there.

Think of Muhammed Ali and his confidence in stating that he was the "heavyweight champion of the world" even before he was. His vision was never broken.

In Round 3 we're going to help YOU look at that future version of yourself and bring that person into today using "I AM" Statements.

This is a critical part of building YOUR highest level of mental toughness.

To make the most out of this round, refer to the "Round 3" videos from Ben in YOUR Mental Toughness Academy:
www.BenNewman.net/MTAcademy

YOUR "I AM" STATEMENTS

YOUR "I AM" Statements, are the answers to the "Who are YOU?" question.

You have the ability to answer this question based upon the person that you are or based upon the person you believe you have the talents to become. Get yourself FIRED UP as you explore these videos and stories within the playbook to drive your beliefs toward thinking bigger for yourself.

Remember the key is challenging yourself to think bigger than the person that you currently are and the things that you have already achieved. Connect to the person you desire to become and grab your future to bring it into today.

Take the example of Muhammad Ali. Ali had surreal confidence in himself through his belief, "I AM the heavyweight champion of the world" before he achieved that goal. Nobody else thought that would be possible. But Muhammad Ali believed, and he surrounded himself with advocates who believed in him, supported him, loved on him, and inspired him to grow. For Ali, this was more productive than surrounding himself with adversaries who believed against him.

When you look at the story of Muhammad Ali, not only did he become the heavyweight champion of the world, but he is now recognized as one of the greatest athletes to ever walk the face of the earth.

These "I AM" Statements will feel uncomfortable to say, and they should. This is one of the most powerful tools you can use to solidify your self-belief that we talked about in Round 1.

Take the next workbook page very seriously.

YOUR "I AM" STATEMENTS

I want you to look into what you want your future to look like. Take a look back at what you wrote in the Vision section in Round 1. Now bring that future vision into today. Write these "I AM" Statements in present tense like you have already achieved them. This is critically important to build the self-belief required to truly unlock YOUR highest potential.

I AM

I AM

I AM

I AM

I AM

ROUND 4

YOUR PRIZEFIGHTER DAY
THE DAILY HABIT BUILDER OF CHAMPIONS

Daily routines are the backbone of building the type of life that YOU want. The problem is that far too many people focus on results-based activities when building a daily routine.

In Round 4 we're going to help YOU build the proven daily HABIT builder that we call, "Your Prizefighter Day."

I have used this strategy for years myself and have taught it to thousands of high performers.

We're going to break down the actual daily habits and disciplines that are going to help you attack the most important things in YOUR life.

Get ready to build YOUR Prizefighter Day routine.

To make the most out of this round, refer to the "Round 4"
videos from Ben in YOUR Mental Toughness Academy:
www.BenNewman.net/MTAcademy

BUILDING YOUR PRIZEFIGHTER DAY

THE KEY: The Prizefighter Day is not just another daily routine. It's an ACTION plan. It's been proven that to reach your highest levels of performance, you have to become obsessed with the process and not the results. The Prizefighter Day brings together the three areas of life that have been proven to have the biggest impact. Remember, these are not goals. These are ACTIONS. I've included some examples below to get you in the right mindset to build your own Prizefighter Day.

1. PERSONAL ACTIVITY EXAMPLE:

Waking up every morning and getting in your morning workout (because it releases endorphins and builds confidence)

2. BUSINESS OR ATHLETIC ACTIVITY EXAMPLE:

Setting a specific goal for the number of phone calls/ follow-ups/ reps/ workouts that you have to make every day knowing that will further your success, regardless of the results

3. SERVICE TO OTHERS EXAMPLE:

This could be lending an ear to a friend, giving compliments to a stranger, calling your parents, etc. What activity can you consistently do in the service of others?

Take your time. After watching the video, create your three focal points that are activity-driven to give you a sense of accomplishment in creating a balanced life, both personally and professionally.

Before you know it, you will imperceptibly start to pull away from old disempowering conversations, noting that even an "ordinary" day is a ***Prizefighter Day*** on your individual path to greatness.

YOUR PRIZEFIGHTER DAY

Your BEST results come from periods in your life when you're completely locked in on a process - NOT results. The sooner you uncover those daily disciplines that make the biggest difference in YOUR life, the faster your goals will manifest right in front of YOUR face. Take your time and fill in each box with what YOU feel is the most important ACTION in each area of your life.

PERSONAL

PROFESSIONAL/ATHLETIC

ACTS OF SERVICE

"I learned while at Alabama that you have Prizefighter Days. When stacking Prizefighter Days, you develop the uncommon mindset. You prepare to attack the field and you take an uncommon mindset to the game. You see, high levels of success are uncommon. Sustaining them is even more uncommon. Prizefighter Days prepare you to attack the big goals that you create which allows you to reach peak performance."

- Mac Jones
2x National Champion with Alabama Football,
Davey O'Brien Award Winner & Heisman Finalist,
New England Patriots Quarterback

Stay connected to daily motivation to drive consistency in YOUR Prizefighter Day.

#ATTACKthePROCESS

YOUR PRIZEFIGHTER DAY MORNING

Research shows that the most highly successful people wake up very early in the morning, often times well before 8 a.m., as they are preparing themselves to be victorious for the day.

What time do you currently wake up?

One of the things that many authors and speakers are talking about today is giving individuals a time that they should wake up. I don't believe in the type of coaching where someone is telling somebody what they need to do.

YOUR Prizefighter Day Morning is all about identifying behaviors that will put you in a position to be mentally prepared to take on your day. The most important aspect of this is choosing a new time to get up. The choice is yours.

Whatever time you were currently getting up, ask yourself the question, "If I get up 15 minutes earlier? 30 minutes earlier? and started building my habits to wake up more intentionally, how would it impact my performance?"

If you take the example of somebody waking up 30 minutes earlier on 5 work days in a week, that individual would have an additional two and a half hours per week of time to prepare. Over an entire month, that is 10 additional hours, more than an additional workday of time that person would have for their performance.

The individuals who are organized and focused in their mornings are prepared to take on their day, face adversity and challenge, as well as create new victories. YOUR Prizefighter Day Morning is all about identifying YOUR ideal morning to put yourself on a path to perform, regardless of any obstacles and challenges that come your way.

Enjoy the video regarding this concept and the realizations you will reach on the following worksheet. Examples are provided as to what YOUR Prizefighter Day could look like in terms of habits performed to prepare for the day. After watching the video, please note that the design of YOUR morning is YOUR choice!!!

YOUR PRIZEFIGHTER DAY MORNING

Winning the game of your mind starts with building a morning routine that serves YOU and sets the tone for YOUR day. Below I've included suggestions that have worked for me over the years, but are in no way required for a successful Prizefighter Day Morning. This needs to be filled in with **intentional** actions. Find what works best for YOU.

1. WAKE UP & CONNECT TO YOUR BURN 🔥

Intentionally create my environment and honor my commitment to myself and family. NO EXCUSES.

2. HYDRATE

8 oz. of cold water to get my body working.

3. ACT OF SERVICE & PRAYER

I like to start the day with something positive for others. I send out my daily texts and make social media posts.

4. VISUALIZATION

I read my "I AM" Statements and reflect on my LEGACY Statement. I feel it's important to see yourself in the ACTION of achieving.

5. READ

Reading is important to me. I read 10 pages per day which averages close to a book per month, drastically improving personal growth over time.

6. ORGANIZE & PREPARE

Review my to-do list and take action on immediate items.

7. WORKOUT

*Critically important for my physical and mental health, here I do my **UNREQUIRED** workout.*

8. NUTRITION

Food is fuel. It's vital for me to fuel my mind and body with the right nutrition.

Continually refine YOUR Prizefighter Day Morning!

YOUR **MENTAL TOUGHNESS** PLAYBOOK

ROUND 5
YOUR LEGACY STATEMENT
BUILDING A VISION FOR YOUR LIFE

Your Legacy Statement is the culmination of all the work we have done thus far cast into a vision of what you want your future to look like.

It is extremely important to pull together all of the tools we have gone through and bring that same energy into Round 5. (If you didn't complete them all, go back and do that now.)

At the end of this round, you're going to have a concrete visual of what the next level of YOUR life looks like.

It has been proven that consistent connection to this Legacy Statement dramatically changes the performance of athletes, entrepreneurs, people in business, and everyone else in between.

Build this Legacy Statement with full attention and focus. It is the catalyst to reaching your peak performance.

To make the most out of this round, refer to the "Round 5" videos from Ben in YOUR Mental Toughness Academy: www.BenNewman.net/MTAcademy

UNDERSTANDING HOW TO USE YOUR LEGACY STATEMENT

This is the mental training tool that connects you to YOUR LEGACY by tying together all of the tools we have been through so far: YOUR Purpose Statement (YOUR Burn), YOUR vision, YOUR "I AM" Statements, YOUR Prizefighter Day, quotes that FIRE YOU UP, the true measure of YOUR success, and once again reconnecting to YOUR "I AM" Statements.

Once you complete YOUR Legacy Statement, you will have the tool to take action which will positively feed your mind and drive YOUR performance.

At what point during the day would it make sense for you to visit YOUR Legacy Statement?

We've seen business professionals and athletes drive significant success by reading and connecting to their Legacy Statement in the morning. In addition, they choose to read it when they feel like they have been knocked down during the day or when faced with adversity or challenge. Many also find great fuel by once again revisiting it in the evening before they go to bed.

Staying deeply connected to the reasons WHY you want to continue to drive your performance is critical to achieve success on YOUR journey. YOUR Legacy Statement connects you to the reasons why you want to continue to make a difference.

Take your time on this exercise and enjoy connecting to what drives YOU. Allow this to become the action step to fuel YOUR daily behaviors and drive peak performance in YOUR life.

YOUR LEGACY STATEMENT

YOUR Burn 🔥

YOUR Vision

YOUR "I AM" Statements

YOUR Prizefighter Day

Personal

Professional/Athletic

Service

Quotes that inspire YOU

"

"

"

"

YOUR "I AM" Statements

ROUND 6

CREATING YOUR ENVIRONMENT FOR
GREATNESS
THE ACTION PLAN & WHAT TO DO NEXT

Welcome to the final round of YOUR Mental Toughness Playbook.

In this round we're going to bring it all together to help you create your personal action plan and what your next steps are.

At this point I want to make a point that the environment you create is going to be crucial for your success. Too many people lie victim to what life throws at them, instead of flipping the script to **ATTACK**.

This section is extremely important and where you will map out the exact action steps and environmental changes you are going to put into place. If you don't take the time to do this and complete it in its entirety, you might as well not have went through this playbook.

Be honest with yourself, answer the questions, write down the changes. YOUR next level is right around the corner.

To make the most out of this round, refer to the "Round 6"
videos from Ben in YOUR Mental Toughness Academy:
www.BenNewman.net/MTAcademy

YOUR PLAN OF
ACTION

"You haven't made any decisions until you've taken ACTION."
- Ed Mylett

WHAT LIMITING BELIEFS ARE YOU LEAVING BEHIND?
Doubt, laziness, vague goals, self-deprecating talk

WHAT CHANGES ARE YOU MAKING TO YOUR ENVIRONMENT?
Intentional reminders and environmental changes are the key to solidifying the changes you want to see in your life.

HOW WILL YOU HONOR THIS COMMITMENT MOVING FORWARD?
Join a coaching group, journaling, reward system, hire a coach

YOUR MENTAL TOUGHNESS
POST-ASSESSMENT

Now that you've completed all 6 rounds of YOUR Mental Toughness Playbook, take the post-assessment below and rate yourself in each category using the scale 1-5. This will connect YOU to what you have learned and prepare you for your next level of GREATNESS.

	No ⟶ Yes				
	1	**2**	**3**	**4**	**5**
I strongly believe that I can accomplish anything I set my mind to.					
I uncovered my purpose or "Burn" that I will connect to daily to drive my actions.					
I have a core set of values that help me keep perspective and REFRAME when things get hard or I face adversity.					
I have developed "I AM" Statements that will allow me to think bigger for myself.					
I have built a strong Prizefighter Day routine made up of important daily actions in alignment with my goals.					
I have crafted a LEGACY Statement for my future and have committed to reflecting on it consistently.					
I have identified and made adjustments to my environment that will support my path to success.					
I have a clear ACTION PLAN that is in alignment with the life I want to build and the person I want to become.					
Totals					
Final Score					

8-15 Needs Some Work	16-23 Showing Potential	24-31 Mentally Tough	32-40 Peak Performer

STANDARD OVER FEELINGS

When I talk to people about succeeding in the significant personal and professional goals in their lives, I always start by focusing on three things.

PURPOSE, PROCESS, AND REFRAMING.

Are you staying connected to the purpose that will cause you to take significant action in your life?

Are you staying connected to the process--not focusing on results you can't control--that will drive success in your life?

Are you reframing your goal by staying focused on solutions rather than problems?

Success means overcoming challenges, adversity, and hardship. Focusing on purpose, process, and reframing gives you the tools you need to overcome these challenges.

When I introduce these concepts to people, it invariably leads to two questions.

What makes the greatest great?

What makes the best performers the best?

FOCUS ON A STANDARD VS. FEELINGS.

To truly be the best of the best, high achievers don't allow feelings to dictate how they show up.

We all go through tough times in our lives. But the greatest of the great accept those setbacks. They embrace challenges as part of life. And if the purpose is significant enough, they continue to fight with everything they have.

But many others show up and allow feelings to dictate their performance.

That's why the most successful people in life live to a standard and not to their feelings.

THE WORKOUT EXAMPLE.

Here's a perfect example of how a standard vs. feelings can impact your life. You can apply this simple illustration to everything you do.

Let's say you decide to start a new workout program. On Day One, the alarm goes off at 6 a.m. But because that warm bed and soft sheets feel so good, you snuggle in, hit the snooze button and go back to sleep.

"Heck, it's only the first day," you tell yourself, "I can always start tomorrow."

You hit the snooze button a couple more times, and before you know it, there's not enough time to get up and start your new routine. That is a perfect example of living to your feelings.

But if you realize the benefits of getting up and out of bed, and committing to a workout is going to make you healthier, feel better and have more energy, you will recognize this standard is important enough to wipe the sleep from your eyes, gladly hop out of bed, and dig right in to your morning workout.

BELIEF. POTENTIAL. ACTION. RESULTS.

Many people think that the most successful people have found a way to skip ahead, to go around the process that is required to be successful. They're wrong. Success is simply the direct result of hard work.

To put people in the right frame of mind about what it takes to set a standard that incorporates hard work, I ask people to think about four elements -- belief, potential, actions, and results.

Having a **belief** in yourself is the first key to achieving success. Underperformers almost always don't believe in themselves enough or in their purpose in life. Assuming that you can succeed in whatever task it is in front of you is the first challenge you must meet.

If you don't have a full belief in yourself, it is impossible to access the full **potential** you have. When you create a barrier that walls off a belief that you can achieve your goal, by extension, you automatically also wall off the full amount of potential as well.

Without a strong enough belief that limits the ability to tap into our full potential, what will your **actions** look like? As you can guess, they're going to be less than what you are fully capable of executing.

This underperformance means our results will be less than we had hoped for.

And when our results are less than what we had hoped for, our feelings come into play. We begin to doubt ourselves. We undermine our own potential. This leads us back to substandard actions and poorer results yet again.

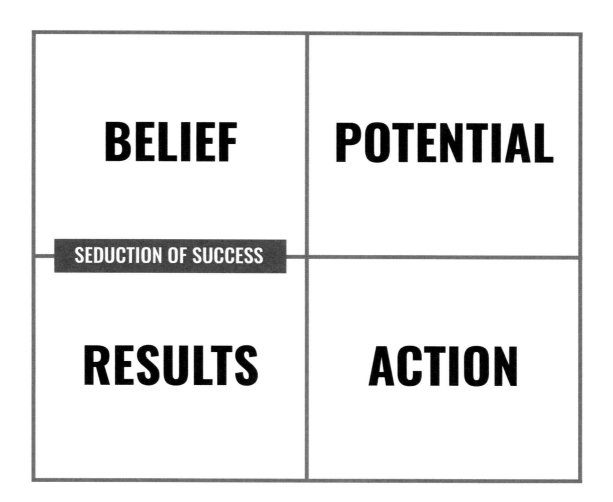

If you implement these core actions, you will enjoy greater success. But there is one landmine you need to be careful of as you go about your business. I call this the **seduction of success**.

Simply put, it means that after enjoying a certain measure of success, some people decide to ease up, take time off, and coast for a while, enjoying what success they have already achieved.

When you do this, you're fooling yourself into believing that you're living up to your full potential. But you're not. True high achievers are never seduced by success.

JERRY RICE AND THE 100% CHOICE.

If anyone knows about being a high achiever, it's wide receiver Jerry Rice. When Jerry and I shared a stage in Las Vegas a few years ago, exchanging ideas in the green room before we went on, he said to me, "You know what I've never understood? How could somebody not give 100 percent when it is 100 percent their choice?"

Simple, but profound. If ever you wanted an example of what it means to live to a standard vs. living through your feelings, that is it.

Jerry never was seduced by success. Like other high achievers, he recognized what made him feel good was his belief in himself and how it allowed him to reach his full potential, optimal actions, and superior results.

TAKING RESPONSIBILITY.

If we aren't getting the results we want, it's not because of how the world has treated us, it is because of the choices we've made. We are responsible for our own decisions and our own actions.

When we fall short, it's because *we* didn't believe enough in ourselves. *We* didn't tap into our full potential. *We* didn't take the actions to drive the results we wanted to get.

I define winning a bit differently than most people, as a result. To me, winning is the direct result of the quality of your actions. You can't always control the final score or the outcome, so I define winning as giving it your best at all times. If you can say that you gave it everything you had, in whatever it is you do, then nobody can take that away from you.

That's winning. And you can never ask any more of yourself than that.

You must be responsible for continuous focus on purpose, process, and reframing, doing the same things over and over and over again with grit and perseverance. If you do, the story you write for your life will stagger your imagination.

YOUR EMOTIONAL TRIGGER

1. Close your eyes...and connect back to the moment in your career when you were dominating at peak performance. Maximum focus and drive and nothing could stop you or get in your way.

2. Once you identify the moment...visualize the specifics of that performance in great detail. Where was it? How did you feel? What was the emotion? Capture the POWER OF YOUR INTENSE FOCUS AND DRIVE.

3. Now open your eyes...and take your right hand and touch your right thumb to your right middle finger. This is "YOUR EMOTIONAL TRIGGER".

4. Close your eyes again...with the right thumb and right middle finger touching. Once again, visualize the specifics of that performance in great detail. Where was it? How did you feel? What was the emotion? Capture the POWER OF YOUR INTENSE FOCUS AND DRIVE.

NOW FOCUS ON PUSHING ALL OF THAT FOCUS AND ENERGY IN BETWEEN THOSE TWO FINGERS. SQUEEZE THAT ENERGY IN BETWEEN THOSE TWO FINGERS. This is "YOUR EMOTIONAL TRIGGER."

5. Utilize "YOUR EMOTIONAL TRIGGER"...every time you are prepared to take the field of battle and when YOU are ready to lock in. In the tunnel, on the sidelines before you take the field. Own the emotion, lock in and DOMINATE.

EVERYTHING YOU NEED IS ALREADY IN YOU!!!

NAVY SEAL BOX BREATHING

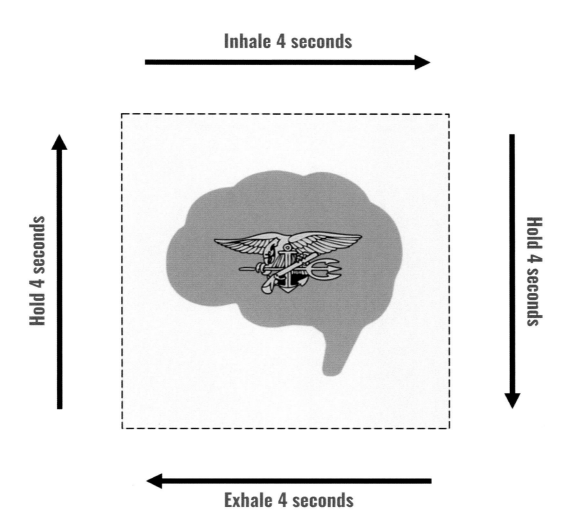

Inhale 4 seconds

Hold 4 seconds

Hold 4 seconds

Exhale 4 seconds

INTENTIONAL FOCUS

NOBODY BREAKS YOUR FOCUS. What YOU see NOW will happen IN THE FUTURE. VISUALIZE and prepare and the race will slow down for YOU. Use INTENTIONAL FOCUS in all areas of the daily PROCESS.

LOCK IN to YOUR ideal state of FOCUS. LEAD and BE YOU one day at a time. Take action with your team and EXECUTE.

Focus on ACTIONS versus the PRESSURE created by other individuals' attention to the results, the things they can't control. Pressure causes YOU to look ahead. Pressure causes YOU to feel defeated in anticipation of what may happen. That is not how winning is done.

VS. PRESSURE

OTHER BOOKS BY BEN...

THE STANDARD: WINNING Every Day at YOUR Highest Level

In *The Standard*, Ben Newman explores the philosophy, strategies, and tactics of how to create and implement standards to produce incredible results in YOUR life. YOU will learn about what it means to live a standards-based life as Ben reveals more than 20 factors YOU must consider when building effective standards. This detailed deep dive into the nature of standards also introduces Ben's 4-P process of Problem, Planning, Performance, and Payoff to put YOUR standards to work for YOU.

Tapping into more than 18 years of experience as a peak performance coach, Ben also illustrates several practical examples of standards in action by some of America's best-known businesses, sports teams, and individual athletes. YOU will learn how standards are integral to the success of legends such as 7-time Super Bowl winner Tom Brady, Alabama head football Coach Nick Saban, or Michigan State basketball coach Tom Izzo. Ben also reveals how he introduced *The Standard* to Wounded Warriors, Microsoft employees, wealth management advisors, and thousands of others to turn them into higher achievers.

The Standard is a must-read for anyone who wants the best outcomes using time-tested strategies to create challenging plans and processes that will transform YOUR life forever.

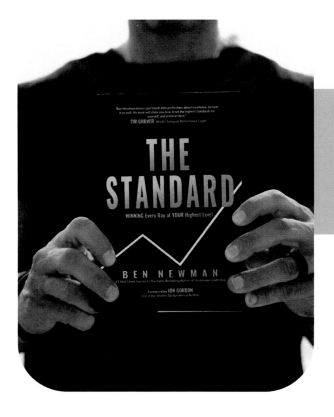

ALL HIGH PERFORMERS LIVE TO A STANDARD.
IT'S TIME TO UNCOVER YOURS.

Available on Amazon at
https://amzn.to/46UurhD

UNCOMMON LEADERSHIP: 11 Ways the Greatest Leaders Lead

If you want to unleash the champion inside of YOU, there's no better way than to study and imitate other champions who have paved the way. *Uncommon Leadership,* the #1 Wall Street Journal and USA Today Best Seller, gives YOU the inside track to becoming all that YOU can be.

Available on Amazon at
https://amzn.to/3fRP8RQ

Stories and lessons learned from the following leaders:

1 **The way YOU do one thing is the way YOU do everything.**
Nick Saban, Head Football Coach at Alabama,
6x NCAA National Champion Head Coach

2 **Leading from the HEART.**
Jon Gordon, Best-Selling Author, Keynote Speaker
& Mentor to Ben

3 **Be the UNDERDOG. STANDARD over FEELINGS.**
Will Compton, NFL Linebacker & Entrepreneur

4 **Find YOUR edge in the details.**
Chris Klieman, Head Football Coach at K-State,
4x NCAA National Champion Head Coach

5 **Reverse engineer YOUR success and work in the UNSEEN hours.**
Drew Hanlen, NBA TOP Skills Trainer
& CEO of Pure Sweat Basketball

6 **Leadership is not for everyone.**
Andy Frisella, CEO of 1st Phorm, Creator of 75 Hard
& Host of REAL AF Podcast

7 **Small circles create big damage.**
Tyron Woodley, Former UFC Welterweight Champion
of the World & Future UFC Hall of Famer

8 **Champions do EXTRA. Embrace the adversity.**
Chaunte Lowe, 4x Olympian & Breast Cancer Survivor

9 **How can somebody not give 100% when it's 100% their choice?**
Jerry Rice, NFL Hall of Famer & 4x Super Bowl Champion

10 **UNREQUIRED MINDSET.**
David Goggins, Navy SEAL & Best-Selling Author of *Can't Hurt Me*

11 **It's not how long YOU live; it's how YOU choose to live YOUR life. Leave YOUR Legacy.**
Janet Fishman Newman, Ben's Late Mother
& CHAMPION of Life

LEAVE YOUR LEGACY: The Power to Unleash YOUR Greatness

Learn to live a truly exceptional life with the help of author, speaker, and performance coach Ben Newman. In *Leave YOUR Legacy*, you will see firsthand how to drive impact by changing your perspective and connecting to your life's purpose.

Newman shows you how to be your best self with this touching story that clearly illuminates the steps needed to create major change in your life by following the ups and downs of the protagonist, Pierce. Join Pierce on his journey to greatness--from the humble beginnings of enacting change and resisting old behaviors to the reframing of his thoughts and actions and eventually understanding his legacy.

Experience for yourself the ripple effect of leaving YOUR legacy. Pierce's story will inspire you to go do great things. And, as you strive for excellence, you will inspire excellence in others. Are you ready to unleash your full potential? It's time to uncover your drive, your passion, and your purpose--leave YOUR legacy.

"Own Your Success connects you to your life's purpose. Leave YOUR Legacy will redefine your thinking to embrace change and leave an impact on others."

Will Compton
NFL Linebacker,
Co-Host Bussin' with the Boys

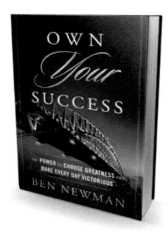

OWN YOUR SUCCESS: The Power to Choose Greatness and Make Every Day Victorious

What if you could make each and every day victorious by focusing on daily activities rather than obsessing over results that you can't control? Based on author Ben Newman's popular program, *Own YOUR Success* gives you the power to make each day a triumph. The most successful people find great success when they focus on having a passion for the process. The key: make today victorious regardless of the obstacles that come your way. Figure out what fires YOU up without exception and ignite that passion so that you can routinely create your prizefighter day.

Own YOUR Success will lead you to uncover your true potential and create a life that belongs to YOU.

"I firmly believe that we are where we are in life because of our choices. Being great is also a choice and it helps if there are resources that would help us understand the process that causes one to be great. Well now you have it! Own Your Success is one of those resources. Read it and it will help you release your potential."

Aeneas Williams
NFL Hall-of-Fame Cornerback
14 year NFL Veteran
and 8 time Pro-bowler

FIGHT THE GOOD FIGHT: A Mother's Legacy Lives On

Fight the Good Fight provides inspiration for individuals who choose to embrace adversity in order to reach success. Over twenty years ago Ben Newman suffered the loss of his mother after years of watching her health deteriorate. After her tragic passing, his grandmother gave him an unexpected gift, in the form of a journal his mother left behind... A journey that is poignant, emotional, and sometimes heartbreaking, this is a story that you will remember forever in your soul.

"Fight the Good Fight is one of those quick reads that I had trouble putting down. The heart gets involved as Ben Newman exposes his own, with the tragedies that motivated him to help others. The idea of persistence, and legacy are right on track with every successful athlete and businessman I know, and the insights in this book will hit the competitor in each of us, right between the eyes."

Mike Matheny
Former Manager
of the St. Louis Cardinals

POCKET TRUTHS FOR SUCCESS: 365 Daily Principles to Become the Most Successful Person You Know

Pocket Truths for Success is your succinct guide to establishing priorities and achieving success in life. *Pocket Truths for Success* was written to be an inspiration for anyone facing the seemingly insurmountable challenges on the road to life's great successes. Personally and professionally, success is a difficult endeavor and possibly even harder to sustain once achieved. This book was written to address the two pivotal issues of achieving and sustaining success, in the complex ever-changing world we live in today. *Pocket Truths* delivers simple and powerful quotes for those ready to inspire and lead.

"Pocket Truths will inspire you to lead yourself, to lead others, and to make positive waves of change in the future. This book will concisely enable you to define your LEGACY!"

Jon Gordon
New York Times Bestseller
of *"The Energy Bus"*

PARTNERING WITH BNC

The Ben Newman Companies, a professional speaking and consulting company, works with organizations and teams all over the world.

Our customized speaking and coaching leaves audiences inspired, educated, AND empowered! Participants are able to uncover their true potential, readying them to create the life they are meant to fight for and enjoy and emerging poised to take on THEIR relentless pursuit of GREATNESS.

WHAT WE OFFER:

1-ON-1 PERFORMANCE COACHING

GROUP & LEADERSHIP PERFORMANCE COACHING

COACHING SYSTEMS • KEYNOTES • SEMINARS • TRAININGS

PUBLISHING SERVICES • LIVE EVENTS/BOOT CAMPS

MEDIA SOLUTIONS & PACKAGES

If YOU are interested in partnering with us, please contact
The Ben Newman Companies at *info@BenNewman.net*.

CONNECT WITH BEN & OUR TEAM:

 @ContinuedFight    Ben Newman

 Ben Newman | The Burn   www.BenNewmanCoaching.com and www.BenNewman.net

Made in the USA
Middletown, DE
16 August 2023

36817374R00055